JOHN WESLEY'S MORAL THEOLOGY

John Wesley's Moral Theology

The Quest for God and Goodness

D. Stephen Long

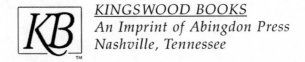

KINGSWOOD BOOKS
An Imprint of Abingdon Press
Nashville, Tennessee

JOHN WESLEY'S MORAL THEOLOGY
THE QUEST FOR GOD AND GOODNESS

Copyright © 2005 by Abingdon Press

This book is printed on acid-free paper.

Library of Congress Cataloging-in-Publication Data

Long, D. Stephen, 1960-
  John Wesley's moral theology—the quest for God and goodness / D. Stephen Long.
    p. cm.
  Includes bibliographical references and index.
  ISBN 0-687-34354-2 (binding: pbk. : alk. paper)
  1. Wesley, John, 1703-1791—Ethics. 2. Christian ethics. I. Title.
  BX8495.W5L66 2005
  241'.047'092—dc22   2004011520

All scripture quotations unless noted otherwise are taken from the King James or Authorized Version of the Bible.

The scripture quotation marked NRSV is from the *New Revised Standard Version of the Bible*, copyright 1989, Division of Christian Education of the National Council of the Churches of Christ in the United States of America. Used by permission. All rights reserved.

Excerpts from Stephen J. Pope, ed., *The Ethics of Aquinas*, copyright © 2002, reprinted with permission from Georgetown University Press.

Excerpts from David Hume, *An Enquiry concerning Human Understanding*, edited by Tom L. Beauchamp, copyright © 1999, reprinted by permission of Oxford University Press.

Excerpts from John Locke, *An Essay concerning Human Understanding*, edited by Peter H. Nidditch, copyright © 1975, reprinted by permission of Oxford University Press.

Excerpts from Nicolas Malebranche, *The Search after Truth*, translated and edited by Thomas M. Lennon and Paul J. Olscamp, copyright © 1980, reprinted by permission of Oxford University Press.

05 06 07 08 09 10 11 12 13 14—10 9 8 7 6 5 4 3 2 1

MANUFACTURED IN THE UNITED STATES OF AMERICA

FOR PHILIP MEADOWS

FRIEND AND COLLEAGUE

CONTENTS

PREFACE

I never intended to write a book on Wesley; it happened by accident. Had I not been invited to lecture at Point Loma Nazarene University on the relationship between Wesley's ethics and Niebuhr's, had I not been invited to lead a retreat on Wesley's theology by the Division of Chaplains of The United Methodist Church, had I not been a graduate student in need of money and offered a teaching assistance stipend at Duke Divinity School in Methodist theology, polity, and history this book would not have happened. All these invitations and others made me read Wesley more carefully than my own work in theological ethics otherwise would have led me to do. I was richly rewarded; Wesley is worth reading. I am thankful for these opportunities because, for better or worse, I am a Wesleyan theologian. This work is an effort to repay the many debts I incurred to the theological tradition that bears his name. It has given me more than I could ever return.

Friends, colleagues, and students greatly assisted me in this work. Randy Maddox, Richard Heitzenrater, and Ted Campbell provided some key bibliographical material on Wesley's study of ethics. I am deeply grateful for that material and for their work. We are all in their debt for their many invaluable contributions to Wesley studies. Kenneth Oakes, Elizabeth Agnew, Jacob Goodson, John Wright, and Philip Meadows read all or part of the manuscript and offered helpful criticisms. Of course, none of these persons should thereby be held accountable for failings present in this work, or presumed to stand by its thesis. Philip Meadows has been my friend and teacher on things Wesleyan during our six years as colleagues at Garrett-Evangelical. I have learned a great deal from him. I enjoyed our conversations and our many runs together on the shores of Lake Michigan. In gratitude for his loyal friendship I dedicate this book to him.

INTRODUCTION

Might the ongoing significance of John Wesley's work lie less in the work itself than in its relationship to the changes that took place in moral philosophy and theology in the seventeenth and eighteenth centuries? Those changes reordered the relationship between theology and morality, between God and goodness. Ethics became a discipline independent of theology, which no longer needed God for its intelligibility. Ethics proceeded on the basis of the human body alone, both individually and corporately. Now as we come to the end of ethics and the end of humanism, Wesley's work must appear differently than it did to those who lived in the nineteenth and twentieth centuries, when ethics was assumed to be a more universal category than was theology. Could Mr. Wesley's work have something still to teach us about how to relate God and goodness once ethics has come to an end?

The two questions in the preceding paragraph animate my inquiry into John Wesley's moral theology. I find his work compelling precisely because of its alien character to our modern sensibilities. I am attracted to those aspects of his work that seem somewhat outrageous to us, those statements of his that we no longer utter in polite company. To ask why they seem outrageous to us may say more about us than they do about him. It may help us understand our own times better and also receive Mr. Wesley's witness for the church catholic in these times.

Given the questions that motivate this inquiry into Wesley's moral theology, the following work does not take the form of a traditional historical analysis. I have not found some piece of information in the Wesleyan corpus that unlocks it and renders it more intelligible. I have not discovered Wesley's lost manuscripts on moral theology. My work assumes the historical work of many other persons, some noted and some not, but is itself not a historical study. In its classical sense, history is more of a scientific discipline than a theological one. It works by bracketing out confessional claims and seeking to find the objective causal connections between events. Such a discipline would try to discover precisely what Wesley read when, exactly what he thought about it, and how it influenced him, his work, and those who received it. This discipline is necessary to pursue truth well. Much merit is to be found in it, and I have benefited greatly from those whose lives are committed to such an activity. But it also has limitations. At its worst, it reduces the past to memorabilia to be gathered and collected as museum pieces for onlookers to observe.

Such a history is similar to Mr. Wesley's death mask that I passed regularly on my way to the reading room in Duke Divinity School's library. There in the middle of the library was a copy of his face preserved at his death. I recall passing that museum piece countless times during my graduate school days and wondering if the books I was taking off the shelves were like that death mask: dead fragments from the past that functioned like curiosities in the present. Like any scholar, I am intrigued by such curiosities. I find them interesting and can gaze on them for long periods of time, much as I spend great quantities of time reading what people now dead had to say in times past. The collection of such items is important and necessary for the life of any scholar. But as a moral theologian, I seek to know how Wesley's work can help us discover God and the good. If it cannot do that, if it is only of antiquarian interest, then I would rather use my time elsewhere. I assume that everyone who works in Wesley studies finds his work to help us in our quest for God and goodness and that this is why we preserve his work, even those death masks that function as relics in the lobbies of our seminary libraries. But the search for truth and goodness is more than a search for memorabilia, for "empirical" verification alone.

Many interpreters of Wesley appear to assume a logical-positivist framework and seek to fit his work within it. For instance, Richard Brantley finds in Wesley something similar to the "verification hypothesis" developed by the logical positivists.[1] This hypothesis, which was originally set forth by Rudolf Carnap, states that "meaning is rooted in the principle of verification, namely that a word or sentence is meaningful only if it is in principle verifiable."[2] It opposed all metaphysical questions of being and thought the problems they produced could be remedied through a careful analysis of logical and empirical reality. What verifies a principle is empirical reality. Truth is found by the correlation of words to empirical realities where the causal explanations are, like that death mask,

---

1. See Richard E. Brantley, *Locke, Wesley and the Method of English Romanticism* (Gainesville: University of Florida Press, 1984), 2.

2. See Simon Critchley, *Continental Philosophy: A Very Short Introduction* (Oxford: Oxford University Press, 2001), 100.

clearly observable. Wesley is often, perhaps nearly always, read as a prototype of this kind of logical-positivist or pragmatic thinker. That is odd, given his insistence that clergy read and study metaphysics. But it could be that this has to do as much with the method and training of those who analyze his work as it has to do with his work itself.

I am not persuaded by logical positivism and have not adopted that method in this analysis of Wesley's work. I find myself much more influenced by Ludwig Wittgenstein, whose philosophy was a therapy to overcome logical positivism. Meaning is not found simply because the truth of a word or sentence can be verified through an objective, observable procedure. It is not the words or sentences and their causal references that allow for truth to emerge; it is in the practices within which we hear, interpret, and know how to go on. It is not the relic itself that finally discloses the truth, but the journey to it. Truth is less the result of a technical method than it is something that can be shown in and through language. As Wittgenstein taught us, words do not all do the same thing anymore than all the controls on a plane have the same function. Their function depends on the narrative context within which they are intelligible.

Martin Heidegger also opposed Carnap's verification hypothesis. He found it to be "at one with will-to-power and domination of nature that defines the age of technology."[3] It reduces everything to technical thinking and loses the rich texture of language. In his ongoing debate with Carnap, Heidegger raised the question, what verified the verification principle itself? Why was it given the definitive position of mediating truth when it stood outside the very method it required of all other approaches to truth? Simon Critchley puts Heidegger's concern this way: "the verification principle is a modern version of Occam's Razor, which shaves off superfluous metaphysical entities from the realm of empirical facts. The question is: how can this razor shave itself? If a razor cannot shave itself, then we cannot a fortiori verify verification. The verification principle is a performative self-contradiction."[4] Wesley never employed Occam's or Carnap's Razor. He was no empiricist precisely because he had no desire to shave off metaphysical realities from empirical facts. When he made his often-quoted statement, "'Is thine heart right, as my heart is with thy heart?' . . . 'if it be, give me thine hand,'" the first essential he laid down for having a heart as his was metaphysical. To have a heart as his, one first had to believe in God's "being and perfections."[5]

---

3. Ibid., 103.
4. Ibid., 106.
5. See Sermon 39, "Catholic Spirit," *Works* 2:81-95, esp. 85, 89.

I find too much of Wesley Studies reads him in terms of logical positivism and the verification hypothesis, overlooking the explicit references to a Christian metaphysics in his work. This fits too nicely the replacement of metaphysics by "ethics" in the modern era. It allows for a kind of scientific, technical thinking to take hold of our ability to receive Wesley's witness. The crucial question becomes when he read what and how we can place it within his corpus. His work becomes reduced to facts, like that memorabilia, and loses any ongoing significance that could help us in our quest for God and goodness.

I have approached my study of Wesley somewhat differently than this. I want to know how his theology makes sense in light of the philosophical changes that occurred in the eighteenth century in the newly emerging discipline called "ethics." I want to see how this discipline took hold of Methodist theology in the later nineteenth and early twentieth centuries and what this meant for how we could or could not think about Wesley, how we can or cannot receive his witness or see his vision. I think it is more important to show why Wesley's work might matter in our quest for God and goodness than to detail all the causal connections between him and his sources. Rather than an "apodictic" analysis where we think in terms of these causal connections, I have tried to follow Albert Borgmann's philosophical analysis that sets forth "deictic" explanation. This is explained in the first chapter. And this is the reason I do not begin with Wesley.

I begin with the reception of Wesley's work in the nineteenth and twentieth centuries. I ask why it is that the ecclesial traditions that bear his name either neglected his work altogether or were preoccupied with it in terms of "John Wesley *for today*." Here is where I think those of us who stand in this tradition have been insufficiently critical of the technical rationality that logical positivism produces. By reading Wesley as an empiricist we fall prey to this kind of logic. But as Heidegger taught us, the more Christianity seeks relevance to the technical rationality in which modern western culture ends, the more it forsakes any orienting power in the world. For this reason I begin my analysis of Wesley's work "at the end of ethics," where we can clearly see the implications of the divorce between God and goodness that began in the eighteenth century. I seek to show that the ongoing significance of Wesley resides in the inability to fit his work within that tradition. It is precisely because Wesley's moral theology cannot be relevant for today that it has an ongoing significance. I recognize the irony in my own position. Wesley's ongoing relevance for "today" arises from his irrelevance for "today." But those two "todays" differ. The first "today" takes place at the end of ethics, which is nothing but a recognition that no universal reason can deliver us an uncontested theory of the good.[6] The second "today" assumes the quest for such a universal reason, a quest that began in Wesley's day. Wesley is not a good modern theologian. That is why he still matters.

After discussing the end of ethics in the first chapter and examining Wesleyan theology in the nineteenth and twentieth centuries, I then find us able to see more clearly what took place in the seventeenth and eighteenth centuries. We see the ripple effects of the philosophical movements that occurred in Scotland, England, and Germany in the eighteenth century, which culminated in the death of God and the reduction of ethics to values. This allows us to see in stark contrast the context of moral theology within which Wesley worked.

I will not argue that Wesley's work matters because it is so exceptional or unique. It is not. It matters because it is part of an important conversation about God and the moral life that he inherited from others and to which he made some faithful contributions. To be faithful to the Wesleyan tradition, we should read and hear the witness of those others as much as we read and hear the witness of Wesley. The second chapter traces that conversation by looking at the sources Wesley himself read and used in teaching "ethics." That conversation assumed an important debate between scholastic voluntarism and scholastic intellectualism. Wesley acknowledged that debate. He made references to it. But, I will argue, he did not always develop those references well. He did not see how his own anthropology, with its acceptance of the "liberty of indifference" to avoid Calvinist predestination, would also lead to the divorce between God and goodness that he opposed.

This liberty of indifference, with its separation of will from intellect, became central to modern political and social formations. It contributed to the policing of God out of social and political matters, such that God would have to be forced back into them through "social" creeds. The tradition of "social" ethics that emerges in the early twentieth century does so through a tacit acknowledgment that theology is no longer social or political and must somehow be made to be so through technological means, primarily through an application to "society" via social sciences. Social ethics emerges by asking the question, what relevance can God, or theology, or the church have for the main social formative powers of civilization, which are the nation-state and the market? It is a question ably posed by the early twentieth-century philosopher Ernst Troeltsch. His work

---

6. This is such a well-known theme, argued across traditions of thought, that I do not find it necessary to develop it here once more. Those who seek a development of this theme can find it in my *Goodness of God: Theology, Church and Social Order* (Grand Rapids, Mich.: Brazos, 2001). The origins of this critique can be seen in Hegel with his critique of Kant's *Moralität*. It has been developed with significant variations by Nietzsche, MacIntyre, Lyotard, Foucault, Derrida, Kristeva, Hauerwas, Milbank, and Zygmunt Bauman, among others.

represents the high-water mark of "modern ethics." But asking this question merely perpetuates the asocial and apolitical nature of theology itself, which seventeenth- and eighteenth-century philosophers such as Hobbes, Hume, Kant, and Locke produced. They sought to police God, theology, and doctrine out of social and political matters, and they were successful. Wesley opposed them. The sixth chapter of this work, "John Wesley as Public Theologian?" uses Wesley's work to show why that question is mistaken and should not be asked.

The opening and final chapters of this work seek to show why Wesley's work cannot fit within "modern" or "public" theology. The four middle chapters invite the reader into the middle of a conversation on moral philosophy and theology. Wesley was aware of many aspects of this conversation. He read or was acquainted with the work of Hobbes, Locke, Shaftesbury, Hutcheson, Hume, Malebranche, Norris, More, and Cudworth. He did not read nor was he acquainted with the work of Adam Smith or Immanuel Kant. Yet these persons were part of an exceedingly complicated conversation that related God and goodness, doctrine and ethics, theology and politics. That conversation continues to ripple into our own times because of the important relationships between the church, the nation-state, and the market it assumed and produced. I seek to position Wesley's work within the context of that conversation. It is not essential to me that Wesley himself was fully aware of that larger conversation. The ongoing significance of his work does not depend solely on his own intentional reactions to all the various facets of this conversation, for who ever knows all the features of the conversations of which we find ourselves in the middle?

Chapter 2 examines the sources Wesley read at Oxford in his study of ethics. I do try to show some connections between these sources and his work. I am indebted to the work of historians for this chapter; it would not be possible without their work. But I do not think my argument in this chapter could be falsified according to the verification hypothesis. Even if we discover that Wesley never read Langbaine, More, Norris, or Eustachius, it would not verify that the conversation of which they were participants had no bearing on Wesley. The arguments of such persons were part of the morality of Wesley's day. The arguments and the conversation are larger than the persons who inherited and perpetuated them. Wesley seldom refers to these sources. I found no explicit reference to Langbaine or Eustachius in Wesley's published sermons, but how could that verify that the moral teaching present in such persons was not part of the culture itself? I do not trace direct causal influences, as if, for example, what Langbaine says on page 12 can be found in Wesley on page 86. Instead, I try to show how the conversation Langbaine, More, and Norris inherited was the same conversation in which Wesley was engaged. I argue in chapters 2, 4, and 5 that this inheritance was best understood as "moral theology" and that it stands opposed to the tradition that emerged in the eighteenth century known as "ethics."

Chapter 3 traces the emergence of the discipline of ethics out of the work of moral philosophers in the eighteenth century. Here is where we see the beginnings of the "mathematization" of moral knowledge. Philosophers seek a new moral foundation. Some find it in the notion of a self-authenticating intuited first principle that is universally accessible, much like what can be found in geometry. Others find it in custom, convention, benevolence, public utility, self-interest, or conviviality. Here we see the beginnings of an important transition from moral theology to ethics that begins in Wesley's era. It is a passage Wesley refused. Chapter 4, "Wesley's Moral Theology," and chapter 5, "Wesley, Aquinas, and Moral Theology" are my effort to show why and how Wesley refused that passage. His work only makes positive sense in the light of the tradition of moral theology that came before him. But at the end of his life he recognized that "ethics" would be the downfall of Christianity. He was correct, and that makes him all the more interesting to us today.

Wesley remained indebted to a medieval, dogmatic, sacramental world where the moral life depended upon friendship with God and was fundamentally oriented by the church. His world was more like that of Thomas Aquinas than like ours. I do not know if Wesley ever read Aquinas extensively. He urged the clergy to do so. He certainly read Norris who had clearly read Aquinas. They were both part of a familiar conversation that has grown unfamiliar to us. It is not their world that orients us; we are oriented by the technological world that emerged after the mathematization of knowledge. For Wesley, knowledge depended upon divine illumination and a metaphysics of participation. It was essentially linked to the Christian doctrines of the Trinity and Christology. For us, knowledge depends on bits of information that flow through our everyday life with a dazzling rapidity. But these bits of information give us our orientation in the world as surely as the church and its practices oriented Wesley and Aquinas. We cannot return to Wesley's world, nor can we recover it. I do not think we should even long for it. Nostalgia is not the point. However, orientations are not fixed. They are a function of gifts received and our cooperation with them. They are tacit social agreements that can be changed. By examining Wesley's moral theology and the practices that it assumed, I hope to present the possibility of a different kind of orientation than the technological one that seems to define church and ethics at present. I hope to convince readers that these two questions were worthy of the inquiry that consumed the past few years of my life. Might the ongoing significance of Mr. Wesley's work lie less in his work itself and more in its relationship to the changes that took place in moral philosophy and theology in the seventeenth and eighteenth centuries? Could Mr. Wesley's work have something still to teach us about how to relate God and goodness once ethics has come to an end?

CHAPTER 1

JOHN WESLEY: MODERNIST THEOLOGIAN?

My intention in this work is to revive interest in John Wesley as a "moral theologian" now that we are at the "end of ethics." As such, this work seeks to bring into dialogue two different epochs. An earlier epoch assumed that the question of the "good" entailed questions about God. God and the good were inseparable. This was Wesley's epoch, but it was replaced by a "modern" epoch where philosophers, with the assistance of theologians, separated God and the good, doctrine and morality. Eventually the "good" itself disappeared, replaced by "right." I am characterizing this later epoch as "ethics," what Hegel termed *Moralität*. My point is not to do away with ethics per se, but to build on that contemporary cultural analysis that refers to our particular moment with the expression, "the end of ethics," and to bring Wesleyan theology into conversation with it.[1]

By "ethics" I do not refer to the everyday moral practices that shape our lives in a quest for goodness. Ethics is a universal science preoccupied

---

1. I see some similarity between what I am doing here and what Zygmunt Bauman states in the introduction to his *Postmodern Ethics* ([Oxford: Blackwell, 1994], p. 2) when he writes, "The main assertion of the book is that in the result of the modern age reaching its self-critical, often self-denigrating and in many ways self-dismantling stage . . . many paths previously followed by ethical *theories* . . . began to look more like a blind alley; while the possibility of a radically novel understanding of moral phenomena has been opened." Bauman's proposed understanding of moral phenomena is by no means the same as John Wesley's moral theology. But the latter has more room to work within the radical novelty of Bauman's approach than it has found in either "modern Methodist ethics" or "the pragmatic John Wesley."

with method and the "right," as contrasted with the "good." In the modern era, ethics as a cosmopolitan, universal inquiry was thought to be greater than any confessional theology, grounded as it inevitably is in local particular communities. Ethics would adjudicate our parochial differences and bring us perpetual peace. Such was the unwarranted optimism of the modern epoch. That epoch did not deliver on its promise; no cosmopolitan ethics emerged that was able to adjudicate among competing particularities. Instead that modern epoch culminated in a technological world of information bits. Ethics gave way to technology. Many of us find this modern world incapable of receiving theological and moral arguments. Instead, utility, facts, and rights—like bits of information—seek to define (albeit unsuccessfully) our moral possibilities without remainder.

Methodist and Wesleyan theologians tended to embrace the modern epoch. It offered promise to the Wesleyan Christian tradition, for unlike forms of Christianity that were wedded to outmoded forms of thought (Catholicism, Anglicanism, Orthodoxy), Methodism has an adaptability to it that positioned it well to be relevant to the modern era. Then came the end of modernity, and what was once Methodism's promise has become its limitation. The modern Wesley, who can always be made relevant for today, now prevents this branch of the Christian ecumene from discerning the present times and speaking a theological word in them. Oddly enough, Methodism's adaptability to modernist forms of thought may very well have become a dogmatic stance that causes its adherents to refuse the necessary theological task of rethinking our tradition. Clinging to the certitudes of modernity, Methodist theologians fit our common tradition into their rigid dogmatic framework and refuse to receive the witness of Wesley and the people called Methodists outside of that framework.

Note that I said "Methodist" theologians and not "Wesleyan." For one strategy to make Methodism relevant to the modern era was to jettison Wesley altogether. His work disappeared from seminary curricula, pastors' libraries and Methodist deliberations in the latter half of the nineteenth and the early twentieth centuries. It was replaced by "principles of ethics" and "social creeds." Modern Methodist ethics either ignored Wesley altogether or received his work so formally that it lost all theological content except for something sufficiently generic, such as "moral value," "grace," or "social responsibility," which could be made compatible with Kant's "personality" or the "dignity of the individual."

When Methodist theologians did not neglect the substance of Wesley's moral theology, they tended to receive it by interpreting it through Locke's empiricism. This allows John Wesley to be a "modern theologian" who can be made relevant for today because of the pragmatic character of his work. Much of the work that relates Wesley and the moral life during the past two hundred years either interprets him as "the practical Wesley for today" or rejects the substance of his moral theology for the sake of modern Methodist ethics. Either way, a major figure of modernity— Locke or Kant—was used to mediate Wesley to us. We shall examine both positions.

THE PRACTICAL WESLEY "FOR TODAY"

In 1960 Colin Williams published *John Wesley's Theology Today*. Theodore Runyon used the same title as the subtitle of his 1998 work, *The New Creation: John Wesley's Theology Today*. These are both fine theological works that keep the tradition of Wesleyan theology alive. Williams's work is a helpful articulation of Wesley's theology for ecumenical dialogue that works against the notion that Wesley was primarily an organizer and not a theologian. Runyon's work is an effort to explain the theological foundation for the Methodist movement's social witness. All Methodist theologians are indebted to the insights of such important texts. But notice how both texts were received. Williams's 1960 text was blurbed with the following statement: "In a world caught up in a new revival of the Spirit, John Wesley's own heart-warming experience and history-making religious reforms continue to inspire and guide Christians of all denominations." What makes John Wesley's theology significant is its relevance for the new things that are happening "today." Wesley's work is relevant because of the new Spirit-inspired movements of the 1960s. Similarly Jürgen Moltmann's commendation on the cover of Runyon's *New Creation* states, "This is for me *the* Wesley book at the end of the century, with new perspectives for the next millennium." Wesley's theological contribution at both the middle and end of the twentieth century was considered to be its usefulness and applicability for the "new," which is just arriving but never quite here. This second strategy consistently correlates Wesley's theology with the "new." It is the usefulness of Wesley's work for the "new" that warrants Methodist theologians' ongoing fascination with him.

Albert Outler's 1964 publication *John Wesley* also made Wesley relevant by correlating his usefulness to the new sociological trends. The significance of this book for Wesley studies cannot be underestimated. Like Williams's earlier work, it presented Wesley as a theologian and not someone who simply led a revival movement. Outler gave us insight not only into Wesley's theology but, perhaps even more important, into Wesley's sources: Scripture, the Fathers, Christian Platonism, and the sacraments. Wesley's work was something of a *ressourcement*. But what seems to have captured the attention of Methodist theologians was the pragmatic Wesley. Outler certainly did not read Wesley in terms of the specific North American philosophical movement(s) of pragmatism. However, he defined Wesley as a "folk theologian" and suggested that his "evangelizing and theologizing . . . took its characteristic form and finish under the heat and pressures of the Revival and its needs."[2] Here Wesley appears as a reactive thinker, responding to concrete situations and adjusting theology accordingly. This fits well the North American context where pragmatism emerged from the assumption that adhering to a firm and rigid set of beliefs leads to violence and intolerance. As Louis Menand argues in his history of pragmatism, it emerged when there was "skepticism about the finality of any particular set of beliefs."[3] Pragmatism recognizes truth not in any derivation from immutable principles but in "following the correct procedures." It assumes fallibilism where we know a priori that our beliefs are potentially fallible. To begin with fixed dogma is to invite intolerance and violence. As Oliver Wendell Holmes Sr. put it,

> If you have no doubt of your premises or your power and want a certain result with all your heart you naturally express your wishes in law and sweep away all opposition. . . . But when men have realized that time has upset many fighting faiths, they may come to believe even more than they believe the very foundations of their own conduct that the ultimate good desired is better reached by free trade in ideas—that the best test of truth is the power of that thought to get itself accepted in the competition of the market, and that truth is the only ground upon which their wishes safely can be carried out. That at any rate is the theory of our Constitution.[4]

Pragmatism was a strategy of peace and tolerance that assumed that recognizing the fallibility of all our knowledge and beliefs would prevent the horrific violence found in the Civil War. But of course, as the twentieth century clearly revealed, Holmes was wrong. People were even more willing to kill others in defense of their fallible judgments than those "dogmatists" were willing to kill for their "immutable principles."

According to Menand, pragmatism emerged because key persons in North American intellectual history realized that clinging firmly to a set of core beliefs leads to violence. This was their diagnosis of the cause for the Civil War. Thus pragmatism is a tolerant proceduralism grounded in skepticism. It is in part the "translations of this individualist, Protestant ethic into social and secular terms."[5] But even more than from this so-

---

2. Albert Outler, *John Wesley* (New York: Oxford University Press, 1964), vii.
3. Louis Menand, *The Metaphysical Club* (New York: Farrar, Straus and Giroux, 2001), 441.
4. Ibid., 430.
5. Ibid., 439.

called protestant principle, pragmatism emerged from a philosophy grounded in scientism. It is the tolerance of a piece of steel that provides the basis for this philosophy. Much like steel, which can be twisted, shaped, and bent without breaking if handled properly, social organisms were assumed to have more adaptability if they are not ruled by a rigid set of doctrines.

Once the focus on Wesley's theology becomes relevant "for today" in a North American context, it is easy to see how his work can be retrospectively read as a protopragmatism. However, this may have more to do with modern theologians' fetishization of the modern than with Wesley, for it takes an imaginative act to read Wesley in terms of this pragmatist narrative where the "practical" Wesley, whose theology responds to "needs," replaces the dogmatic Wesley committed to metaphysical principles of truth and creedal Christianity. Is this imaginative act what tempts us to see him as a modern theologian preoccupied with experience, epistemology, and relevance?

Such an imaginative act is of recent origin. Perhaps a better, even if less palatable, reception of Mr. Wesley's theology is found in Leslie Stephen's 1876 publication, *History of English Thought in the Eighteenth Century*. Stephen notes the remarkable changes in moral philosophy and theology that occurred in the eighteenth century where skeptics, dogmatists, and commonsense realists vied to replace the old creedal theology that was disappearing. And he asks, "What creed could sway the passionate yearnings and the dumb instincts of the multitude? Could Hume's skepticism fill the place of the old authoritative teaching, or Reid's common sense, or Wesley's rehabilitation of ancient dogma?"[6] Modern Methodists who read Wesley as a protopragmatist might be surprised to see him read here at the end of the nineteenth century as a "dogmatic" alternative to both skepticism and commonsense realism. Our preoccupation with making Wesley relevant for today does not often include advocating the genius of Methodism as the rehabilitation of ancient dogma. However a careful reading of Wesley's works reveals that Stephen's analysis is correct. Wesley was a Christian dogmatist. This may embarrass modern theologians, but it is nevertheless true. It need no longer embarrass us, for, as James Smith has argued, "the charge of 'dogmatism' is something that cannot really stick in a postfoundationalist context."[7] Dogmatism only embarrasses us when we assume an objective, value-free rationality. At the end of ethics, such an objective rationality no longer compels. Our question is not dogma or a value-free rationality, but by which dogma shall we live?

---

6. Leslie Stephen, *History of English Thought in the Eighteenth Century* (London: Smith, Elder and Co., 1876), 1:72.

7. See his *Introducing Radical Orthodoxy: Mapping a Post-secular Theology* (Grand Rapids, Mich.: Baker Book House, forthcoming).

From Metaphysics to Epistemology: The Mathematization of Morality

Theodore Runyon, like Leslie Stephen a century before, recognizes that the eighteenth century marked a significant theological turning point. Runyon writes, "By Wesley's time . . . the traditional authorities that had guaranteed this metaphysical world were slipping and their power to convince could no longer be taken for granted." This metaphysical world was the world of medieval and Anglican sacramental grace. The truths adhered to in this metaphysical world were now under attack. An epistemological crisis resulted. In fact, epistemology was the consequence of the crisis. For as Runyon goes on to argue,

> Human consciousness would now have to participate in and be convinced by claims to the truth, whether this was through human reason, as in the case of rationalism and Deism, or through experience, as in the case of Locke and Wesley. The result was a shift *from metaphysics to epistemology*, from defining reality as supernaturally guaranteed and in principle independent of the knower to defining reality as registering on consciousness and inevitably including the knower.[8]

Modernity marks this passage from metaphysics to epistemology.

Did Wesley make this passage? Runyon says yes; Wesley, like Locke, became an empiricist who grounded knowledge in experience. But this passage from metaphysics to ethics was also characterized, as was pragmatism, by grounding philosophy and ethics in scientism. Whereas pragmatism was a philosophy suggesting that social and political forces should function more like the tolerance of steel than the application of rules from immutable principles, seventeenth- and eighteenth-century ethical thought often took geometry as its foundation. Indubitable axioms *(noema)* were identified that could found the basis for a secure and certain universal morality. Ethics would be grounded in mathematics.[9] But Wesley was clearly not tempted by the newly developing scientism. He was suspicious of it, especially of mathematics. He wrote, "So I am convinced, from many experiments, I could not study to any degree of perfection either mathematics, arithmetic, or algebra, without being a deist, if not an atheist."[10] Wesley's opposition to mathematics could merely be the consequence of his pietistic concern against wasting time. Perhaps he feared that he personally could become so enamored with mathematics

---

8. Theodore Runyon, *The New Creation: John Wesley's Theology Today* (Nashville: Abingdon, 1998), 150.

9. See Norman Fiering, *Moral Philosophy at Seventeenth-Century Harvard: A Discipline in Transition* (Chapel Hill: University of North Carolina Press, 1981), 279.

10. Sermon 50, "The Use of Money," §I.2, *Works* 2:270.

that it would consume his time and he would forget God. If so, then his opposition to the new sciences was simply the result of a pietistic anti-intellectualism. Buy why did Wesley state that the temptation to mathematics was a temptation to deism or atheism? That seems a bit harsh if his only concern was wasting time on trivial matters. Once it is recognized that significant moral philosophers and theologians in the seventeenth and eighteenth centuries were trying to found morality on self-evident axioms akin to geometry, Wesley's opposition to mathematics might also be understood in terms of a broader conversation about ethics. Even if Wesley himself did not explicitly reject mathematics for this reason—it either replaced or supplemented God as the foundation for morality—he was familiar with that broader conversation and did not seek to set forth the axioms (noema) upon which a more humanistic morality was being built in the seventeenth and eighteenth centuries.

Wesley clearly states that for him the study of mathematics is in part a temptation because he finds that it would be a form of employment that does harm to his mind. He concedes that it need not necessarily harm every person's mind; others might engage in it without danger.[11] Yet in "The Danger of Riches" and "Spiritual Idolatry" he argues that finding one's happiness in mathematics or biology, and the counsel to give ourselves wholly to them, is a form of spiritual idolatry.[12] And in his sermon "On Dissipation" he states,

> Our desires are dissipated when they are unhinged from God, their proper centre, and scattered to and fro among the poor, perishing, unsatisfying things of the world. . . .
> . . . A man may be as much dissipated from God by the study of the mathematics or astronomy as by fondness for cards or hounds. Whoever is habitually inattentive to the presence and will of his Creator, he is a "dissipated" man.[13]

Mathematics is dangerous because it diverts attention from the eternal to the empirical.

Why does mathematics tempt us to inattentiveness to the presence and will of God? Why is mathematics a threat like cards and hounds? Could Wesley have made these charges solely on the grounds that they violated the Methodist rule to avoid harm by "taking such diversions as cannot be used in the name of the Lord Jesus"?[14] Could he have failed also to recognize that seventeenth- and eighteenth-century ethics were being

---

11. Ibid.
12. See Sermon 78, "Spiritual Idolatry," §13, *Works* 3:108-9; and Sermon 87, "The Danger of Riches," §15, *Works* 3:235.
13. Sermon 79, "On Dissipation," §§10-12, *Works* 3:120.
14. *General Rules*, §4, *Works* 9:71.

grounded in self-evident axioms according to geometric principles, that mathematics was the new foundation for ethics? And that, in so doing, God was being replaced by empirical, visible realities as the basis for the moral life? Wesley knew this. He had read Henry More's *Enchiridon Ethicum* and must have been familiar with his twenty-three moral *noema*, which were More's foundation for ethics. More stated that these *noema* were based on "Being" and "Life." After listing them he wrote,

> These and such like *Sayings* may justly be called *Moral Axioms* or *Noemas*: for they are so clear and evident of themselves, that, if men consider impartially, they need no manner of Deduction or Argument, but are agreed to as soon as heard. And thus we are prepared, as with so many Touchstones, to let the inquisitive know what *Right Reason* is. For in short, *it is that which by certain and necessary Consequences, is at length resolved into some intellectual Principle which is immediately true.*[15]

Here we have a universal foundation for ethics grounded in a self-evident principle universally accessible.

For More, much like for the sentimentalists, there is a moral intuition that needed no discursive grounding, no social mediation, and no theological foundation. More even posited a new psychological faculty—the "boniform" faculty—that allowed us to immediately intuit these geometrical axioms of goodness. Did Wesley himself follow More? Is this the origin of his notion of the "spiritual senses"? I think not. Although essential elements of More's Aristotelianism and Christian Platonism can be found in Wesley, he feared that this new mathematical foundation for morality would lead to atheism. Mathematics could be dangerous because it offered a foundation for morality separate from God. Morality could be reduced to self-evident axioms that needed no discursive mediation. This opposed the ancient tradition of moral theology where grace was always mediated through social means such as sacraments, creeds, and the church. In that tradition, knowledge was discursive. To which world did Wesley belong? He clearly adhered to the medieval world of Anglican sacramental grace with its foundation in an Augustinian doctrine of illumination. He held to a metaphysics of participation where we could participate in the eternal ideas in the Divine mind. But this participation was not a priori, and therefore it was not a pure Platonism. It was mediated through Christ, who was the Eternal Idea. Thus this participation required a discursive rationality.

Wesley's rejection of a self-evident intuited axiom as the basis for morality suggests he did not make the modern passage to epistemology

---

15. Henry More, *An Account of Virtue: or, Dr. Henry More's Abridgment of Morals put into English* (London: Benjamin Tooke, 1690), 27.

as easily as is often thought. John Locke, however, clearly did. For Locke the move to epistemology is grounded in the simple ideas that experience teaches, irrespective of the mediation of language. Locke argued that these simple ideas are just there and that words cannot clarify them for us. In fact, it is our use of words that creates the problems that divide persons from each other, for we wrangle over the words without recognizing that they are always partial efforts of representation of the simple ideas experience itself teaches. If we were more careful with our definitions, suggests Locke, and did not wrangle over words, the solidarity we share through experience would alleviate conflict.[16]

Unlike Wesley, Locke thought that by following his method of reducing the rules of discourse to simple ideas, it would be possible to think "that *Morality is capable of Demonstration*, as well as mathematicks." Here, More the Platonist and Locke the empiricist find common ground. Through the careful observation of method and by an intuitive grasp of the simplest elemental features of our knowledge, morality can be as secure a science as mathematics. For Locke, this would be done through observing four rules: First, never use a word without a clear signification (that is to say, do not use a name without a clear understanding of the idea for which it stands) and do not confuse the word with the idea. Second, determine if the words used signify simple or complex ideas. The latter are composed of simple ideas, so they should then be broken down into their determinate parts. Third, the words that stand for simple ideas must not be used solipsistically but consistent with ordinary common usage. Fourth, because common linguistic usage often distorts the simple idea, care must be exercised to declare their meaning when someone is using the words peculiarly. Locke concludes, "Upon this ground it is, that I am bold to think, that *Morality is capable of Demonstration*, as well as Mathematicks: Since the precise real Essence of the Things moral Words stand for, may be perfectly known; and so the Congruity, or Incongruity of the Things themselves, be certainly discovered, in which consists perfect Knowledge."[17]

If we make the epistemological turn, morality can be mathematical. By careful attention to how it is that we know and by recognizing that the historical mediation of words misleads us, we can discover in ourselves the intuited simple ideas our words signify and from these certain building blocks construct an indubitable morality. This is the passage to modernity that Locke underwent. Wesley did not make it. His opposition to the mathematization of morality raises suspicion against it.

---

16. John Locke, *An Essay concerning Human Understanding* (ed. Peter H. Nidditch; Oxford: Clarendon Press, 1975), 125.

17. Ibid., 512-16.

To state, as Runyon does, that Locke's epistemology led to a participation of the knower in the known is problematic. It could be that Locke has an immediate intuitive grasp on simple ideas that experience teaches beneath language, but every effort to build philosophy, morality, or theology upon such an immediate experiential knowledge has failed. Although it would be the mid-twentieth century before this mathematization of morality would be finally abandoned—and as we shall see Methodists clung to it well into the twentieth century—it did not deliver what it promised. No immediate universal access to things as they really are emerged. Exactly the opposite became the consequence of the Lockean method—the knower could not know the known. The known disappeared under the power of human consciousness. What I can know are the conditions for the possibility of knowledge itself. But what I cannot know is any reality that exists separate from those conditions. The epistemological turn is the turn to the subject. Runyon cites Wesley's use of the phrase "participation in God" as evidence for his transition from the medieval and Anglican sacramental world to the modern epistemological one. But I will argue later that this phrase is evidence for the contrary. Wesley never successfully made the transition from a medieval and Anglican sacramental world to a modern epistemological one grounded in human consciousness precisely because he held to more of an ancient and medieval metaphysics of participation.

A metaphysics of participation was central to medieval theology. Augustine's and Aquinas's theology make little sense without it. But they did not invent it, they received it from Scripture (2 Peter 1:4), patristic sources,[18] and Platonic sources. Wesley's use of the doctrine of participation is not only unrelated to empiricism, it is in opposition to it. Wesley did not use the term *participate* with reference to an immediate perception of a simple idea, which we cannot adequately represent in language (as in Lockean empiricism). For him the term *participate* referred to a theological metaphysics where we can participate, via illumination, in the eternal ideas in God, which is primarily a participation in the eternal Word, the Second Person of the Trinity. This participation is not innate to human beings, it is christologically mediated through specific means. The progenitors for Wesley's doctrine of a "spiritual sense" with its metaphysics of participation and doctrine of illumination are Augustine's theory of illumination, and Aquinas's notion of the eternal ideas as developed in a certain Cartesian tradition and (related to this) Christian Platonism. This doctrine of illumination is one reason Wesley's work cannot make the

---

18. For example, Irenaeus referred to the purpose of Christ's work for us as "*ut et homo fieret particeps Dei*" ("in order that we might be partakers of God," AT) (*Adversus haereses* IV.28.2 in *Sancti Irenei, Libri Quinque* [ed. Adolphus Stieben; Leipzig: T. O. Weigel, 1848], 655).

passage to modernity well. His inability to make this transition is precisely why his theology should interest us again at the end of modernity. But to receive his work with this vision will require some significant deconstruction, for "Wesley's theology today" has become something of a fixed dogma that cannot be easily challenged without eliciting significant opposition. The "today" to which Wesley is made relevant is one characterized by epistemology, which assumes either an empiricist or idealist framework. To hear Wesley afresh, those philosophical frameworks need to be challenged.

Overcoming Epistemology with Fergus Kerr: A Dominican at Oxford Helps Methodists Understand Wesley, "Dominus Illuminatio Mea"

In his excellent analysis of nineteenth- and twentieth-century Thomisms, Fergus Kerr, regent of Blackfriars Hall, University of Oxford, notes that Thomism reemerged in Catholic seminaries as an antidote to the idealist/empiricist philosophical options that plagued post-Cartesian philosophy. Both the idealist and empiricist options (Kant and Locke come readily to mind) assume a skepticism toward the existence of the world outside our mind.[19] Far from a robust participation in the world as it is, both positions distance us from any acknowledgment that we can know or have the world as it is. This led to a radical solitude of the individual self, with the assumption that all the self has is an individual experience that can be communicated to others only with difficulty through something as contingent, finite, and untrustworthy as language. Both idealist and empiricist epistemologies assumed a "subject-centered self" who observes objects "which one apprehends initially in the images, impressions, sense data, or other representations of them which we make, or they force on us." In contrast to this, argues Kerr, Thomism "has a non-subject-centered conception of the self: the objects out there in the world become intelligible in the act of awakening the intellectual acts on our part which manifest our intelligence."[20]

Although Kerr is basically correct about the errors in post-Cartesian philosophy, there were theologians developing Descartes' work along lines similar to Thomas Aquinas precisely on the point of the "awakening of intellectual acts" coming by participation in the Triune life.

---

19. In the next chapter I will argue that Wesley's reworking of the kind of Cartesianism he found in the work of persons like Malebranche, Norris, and Cudworth avoids in part the criticism Kerr rightly levies at the post-Cartesian tradition.

20. Fergus Kerr, *After Aquinas: Versions of Thomism* (Oxford: Blackwell, 2002), 27.

Malebranche, Norris, and Cudworth—despite the Cartesian problems in their work—appealed to the doctrine of the Trinity as that which allows us to know the world. Wesley's doctrine of participation was influenced by their work and inasmuch as it incorporated this understanding of the awakening of intellectual acts it harks back more to Thomas Aquinas than to either empiricism or idealism.

Two key themes in Aquinas's understanding of knowledge are (1) awakening and (2) participation. These themes are what make his work significant in a post-Cartesian era. Our mind is not angelic in nature, intuiting knowledge as does the divine mind. Such a form of "Augustinian illumination" can lead to the problematic Cartesianism where the divine and human mind are not adequately differentiated (one sees this to a greater degree in Malebranche and More than in Cudworth and Norris). By contrast, a model of knowledge stressing (1) awakening through act[21] and (2) participation both in the divine act and in the horizontal creaturely activity of everyday life avoids the errors of both idealism and empiricism. I believe that Wesley's theology requires these two Thomistic (and biblical and patristic) themes. The centrality of 2 Peter 1:4 for the moral theology of both Aquinas and Wesley cannot be overemphasized. Wesley found these themes in Scripture and the Fathers, yet he also inherited them from an unlikely source: the unorthodox Cartesian philosophy of Christian Platonism. It is the significance of the latter that allows his work to avoid the twin modern errors of idealism or empiricism.

Rather than positing a gap between mind and world that needs to be mediated with sense-images, Aquinas assumed a participation of the knower in the known that would have been unintelligible to Locke. As Charles Taylor notes, this is only possible as long as the ancient metaphysics of forms, or the *eidos*, is still intact, for only as mind participates in the divine ideas can it at the same time participate in the form of the known.[22] If no such "form" is present, no participation is possible. If everything is only a singular concrete entity, including each subject, then I as a subject cannot participate in the chair before me except through a very strange use of the term *chair*.

The assumption of such forms makes no sense in Aquinas without his theological doctrines of God and creation. In this sense, the mind and things are not in opposition (as with empiricism and idealism) nor are they naively viewed as identical. They are "assimilated" to each other. We need not assume that our mind simply conforms to things in the world as they are, or reverse the polarities and assume (à la Kant's Copernican

---

21. Which seems to me to be yet another form of Augustinian illumination.
22. Charles Taylor, *Philosophical Arguments* (Cambridge, Mass.: Harvard University Press, 1995), 3.

revolution) that the things of the world conform to our mind. Instead, as Kerr notes, "On Thomas's view, articulating as it does the doctrine of creation in terms of the metaphysics of participation, the object, in being known by the subject, is brought more clearly into the light and to that extent its nature and destiny are fulfilled."[23]

Wesley does not present us with as sophisticated an account of human action and a metaphysics of participation as does Aquinas, but the tendency of Wesleyan theologians to read Wesley in terms of Lockean empiricism has misled us from seeing how his work continues the medieval and Anglican sacramental world that assumed the ancient metaphysics of participation. Our end is happiness and holiness. Our knowledge of the world entails a "pious participation" in the use of all things for the glory of God. This is how the knower participates in the known and vice versa. But for Wesley, following Malebranche, Norris, and Cudworth, this metaphysics of participation is primarily linked to Christology and the Trinity. These dogmas make our knowledge of the world possible.

Wesley is less of a modernist theologian than we may have assumed. (Although, as we shall see, elements of modernity, particularly in understanding the freedom of the will, are clearly present in his work.) He is not concerned with epistemological matters. He did not seem burdened by the need to come up with some theory that would relate our mind to the world. Instead, he presents us with a "spiritual sensorium" that uncritically mixes an Augustinian theory of illumination (mediated through Cambridge Platonism) with the sensibility of knowledge plundered from Locke, which Wesley assumed did not conflict with Aristotle. Wherever he saw conflict between Locke and Aristotle, Wesley sided with Aristotle. The result is something much more like Aquinas's work than anything that follows from the significant philosophical changes that occurred in the eighteenth century with the options it bequeathed to us. This other inheritance has been too quickly accepted by Wesleyan theologians because of our preoccupation with making Wesley's theology relevant for today. It is a dangerous inheritance to accept, for Runyon is correct that beginning with the eighteenth century (and even a century earlier) the medieval and Anglican metaphysics Wesley still embodied was being overthrown.

The inheritance that overthrew a metaphysics of participation assumed morality could be grounded in something immanent in humanity. It sought self-evident axioms in experience as the new scientific basis for ethics. At the end of modernity we now clearly see that such an ethics failed. This immanent, humanist ethic is coming to its end, and we can see

---

23. Kerr, *After Aquinas*, 31.

what Wesley only dimly saw: the rise and fall of humanism where God would be policed out of human affairs in the name of morality. In 1789, toward the end of his life, Wesley wrote,

> Thus almost all men of letters, both in England, France, Germany, yea, and all the civilized countries of Europe, extol "humanity" to the skies, as the very essence of religion. To this the great triumvirate, Rousseau, Voltaire, and David Hume, have contributed all their labours, sparing no pains to establish a religion which should stand on its own foundation, independent on any revelation whatever, yea, not supposing even the being of a God. So leaving him, if he has any being, to himself, they have found out both a religion and a happiness which have no relation at all to God, nor any dependence upon him.
>
> It is no wonder that this religion should grow fashionable, and spread far and wide in the world. But call it "humanity," "virtue," "morality," or what you please, it is neither better nor worse than atheism. Men hereby wilfully and designedly put asunder what God has joined, the duties of the first and the second table. It is separating the love of our neighbour from the love of God. It is a plausible way of thrusting God out of the world he has made.[24]

Note Wesley's emphasis on both discursive rationality and a theological metaphysics in this important quote. Knowledge of morality, humanity, and virtue is not self-evident; revelation, including torah, mediate it to us. As we shall see, this mediation is essential for Wesley's moral theology. Jesus is the mediation of torah in Wesley's theology. Wesley also recognizes the threat a humanistic morality poses to a theological metaphysics—it develops virtue and morality without any reference to even the *being* of God.

Is it too much to say that Wesley saw the beginnings of what Nietzsche would diagnose as the situation of Western civilization in the next century? Dostoyevsky was wrong. It is not the case that if God is dead everything is permitted. Quite the contrary, as Nietzsche recognized, "Those who have abandoned God cling that much more firmly to the faith in morality."[25] It was morality and virtue that killed God, making God irrelevant for everyday human action. God is replaced by a human will to power that became its own basis for ethics and politics. It also came to fruition in technology. What is surprising is how quickly Methodist theologians forgot Wesley for this other religion, a religion where god is dispensable.

I began by suggesting that there are two dominant strategies for relating Methodist theology and ethics, one of which is to make Wesley

---

24. Sermon 120, "The Unity of the Divine Being," §§19-20, *Works* 4:69.
25. Friedrich Nietzsche, *The Will to Power* (ed. Walter Kaufmann; trans. Walter Kaufmann and R. J. Hollingdale; New York: Vintage, 1968), 16.

relevant for "today." This strategy dominated Wesleyan theology from the mid-twentieth century until today. As problematic as that strategy is, it is preferable to the strategy that dominated the end of the nineteenth and beginning of the early twentieth centuries, which was to neglect Wesley altogether in order to make Methodism relevant to modernity. For that older strategy, Wesley's theology as well as the Anglican liturgy and doctrine he bequeathed to us, were obsolete. They were to be discarded for the sake of the new and improved. Wesley had to be forgotten. In so doing, theologians sided with the very forces Wesley resisted: the mathematization of morality on a priori humanist grounds. This strategy of neglecting Wesley altogether made Methodist ethics nonresistant to the culmination of the mathematization of morality into the forces of technology, which orient the modern world much as the church oriented Wesley's world.

MODERN METHODIST ETHICS

The modern era ends with the dominance of technology, which is characterized by the repetition of the obsolete and the emergence of the "new and improved." These notions allow technology to shape being, yet the recurring cycle of obsolescence/new creation is itself part of a historical tradition. As Martin Heidegger suggested, technology is the completion of the Western metaphysical tradition, a tradition that ends in nihilism. Nihilism is not essentially negative, it is liberation toward the new and its repetition. For Heidegger it was Nietzsche who first saw this (and was thus the last metaphysician).

Christianity is also about new creation, so it need not simply set itself over against nihilism with its technological fascination. The latter can easily be seen as a simulacrum of a Christian eschatology. Yet nihilism is a temptation and should not be uncritically embraced by Christians. For technology not only assumes a never-ceasing liberation toward the new, it also assumes a death of god, which is not christologically understood. (Christianity too recognizes that one of the Trinity suffered and died, but it interprets it christologically, allowing that God remains God and thus cannot literally suffer and die. God remains impassable.) Nihilism's death of god puts theology out of work. Thus to embrace technology as the end of Western metaphysics is to deny theology any shaping force in history. As Heidegger argued, when Christianity seeks reconciliation with the modern world and its technological fascination, it "repudiates ever more decisively its former history-shaping force."[26] The more Christianity

---

26. Martin Heidegger, *The Will to Power as Knowledge and as Metaphysics* (vol. 3 of *Nietzsche*; ed. David Farrell Krell; trans. Joan Stambaugh, David Farrell Krell, and Frank A. Capuzzi; San Francisco: Harper & Row, 1987), 241.

becomes relevant to the modern, the more it is evacuated of any significant orienting power by technological forces. Like a virus that works on one's operating system, mimicking its functions, nihilism and its technological fascination overtakes Christianity, rendering it inoperative. Heidegger seems to have thought this was inevitable, for Christianity itself was simply part of the tradition of Western metaphysics. But Heidegger was wrong.

To make Wesley's witness relevant today may unwittingly prove Heidegger correct and bear witness that only technology orients us now. (Is this not borne out in The United Methodist Church's recently trademarked evangelistic television and radio campaign: "Our hearts, our minds, and our doors are always open"?) Methodism's desire for relevance to the modern merged technology, religion, and ethics to such a degree that they are nearly indistinguishable. I intend to demonstrate the convergence of ethics and technology within the Wesleyan tradition by noting what occurs when Methodist theologians develop ethics as a systematic, scientific discipline in the latter part of the nineteenth century without reference to Christian doctrine. Such an ethics succumbs to technology. It only furthers the orienting power of technology and underwrites the death of god. Although few theologians uncritically accept the ethics presented below, its foundation in scientism/pragmatism is still with us, especially in our reception of Wesley's work. We have not yet developed adequately the tradition of medieval and Anglican sacramental theology still residually present in the Wesleyan tradition because we accommodate scientism/pragmatism. That tradition of moral theology provides a different orientation altogether, which could allow us to avoid scientism without falling prey to (Heidegger's) obscurantism.[27]

Technology as the philosophical foundation for modern living emerges during that moment when philosophers proclaim the death of god. Humanity posits its own values, and they become the conditions for our existence. Such values assume technology's orienting power, which divides reality between facts and values. Science gives us *facts*, the way reality is. Theology, like morality, is *valuational*; it tells us how we would like the world to be. It can be brought to bear on reality either after science has done the real material work or insofar as it secures its basis in a factual substrate.

The philosopher Albert Borgmann offers a compelling alternative to this fact/value rationality.[28] He avoids defining technology solely in

---

27. See Simon Critchley, *Continental Philosophy: A Very Short Introduction* (Oxford: Oxford University Press, 2001), 95-122.

28. See Albert Borgmann, *Technology and the Character of Contemporary Life* (Chicago: University of Chicago Press, 1987). Though his focus is technology, a careful reading will see "God" appearing at the margins of this work.

terms of a scientific or "natural" causality that must bracket out God. Neither does he define faith and morality solely in terms of a causality grounded in a transcendental "freedom" immune from science or natural reason. Avoiding this all too common nature/freedom distinction, he situates the question of technology within a deictic explanation that runs counter to the apodictic analysis the nature/freedom distinction assumes.

What is deictic explanation? Borgmann's contrast between a hearth and a furnace illustrates it well. A hearth is not simply a device to offer a product, in this case heat. The hearth, unlike a furnace, is inseparable from its context. To see how a hearth orients a home, one has to see it within its context; the furnace needs no such appearance in order to make sense of it. In fact, the furnace is normally concealed, because in the technological era the machine that makes the product possible is less important than the product itself.

Deictic explanation discloses how we *take up* everyday life, seeing its patterns, shapes, and forms and allowing its orienting power to appear. Borgmann reminds us that the term *orientation* arose from the way cathedrals once shaped daily life. They were built pointing toward the east, bearing witness to where our hope was directed—toward the homeland of Christ who would one day return. But such orientation no longer shapes daily life. Even the deictic explanation that disclosed such shaping power disappears and is difficult to reclaim. It is replaced by apodictic analysis, grounded in scientific laws. But apodictic analysis conceals how and what shapes existence. To discuss the hearth using the technical language one would use to describe a furnace would prevent us from seeing what the hearth is. Poets would not compose odes to a furnace. It still has an orienting power, but one that seems to resist deictic explanation.

Borgmann finds deictic explanations to have nearly disappeared from intellectual life, including ethical analysis. Particularly is this the case as ethicists try to produce an explanatory method grounded in social-scientific principles. Calculations, self-evident axioms, rational choice—these are the foundations which orient (so we assume) social life. As Borgmann notes, "there is today no subject matter for the social sciences that would call for deictic explanations. The traditional focal things and events of religion, art, and daily practice have lost their commanding places in our world, the firmness of their contours, and their orienting force." Our lives are more oriented by interstate highways than they are by cathedrals.[29] Is this not the consequence of the modern passage from a metaphysics of participation to epistemology? Are poets, philosophers, or theologians needed to show us how an interstate highway orients us? All we need is a computerized map.

---

29. Ibid., 72. And interstate highways are constructed to give access to malls and other business attractions. The very flow of our daily life is oriented toward these things.

Why have focal practices of art, religion, and philosophy lost their orienting power? Why are they often "explained" in terms of the social facts that make them possible rather than viewed as forces of theological significance shaping us in the first place? And why has Protestant ethics, of all disciplines, embraced these explanations? Perhaps because ethics itself became an apodictic science trying to explain, predict, and control human behavior. Once ethics was based on geometric premises, it easily lent itself to become merely a support to the orienting power of technology. Despite the difficulties Heidegger's work poses for theology, it helps us see the convergence between technology and ethics. It helps us see where modern moral philosophy ends. In so doing, we might be able to see the freshness of something like Wesley's moral theology.

Ethics as Technology

Heidegger was one of the first philosophers to address the question of technology, although he may not have done so if Max Weber had not given his 1919 lecture (one year before his death) in Munich on "the inner calling of science." Weber found that the certainty of the scientific worldview made dangerous incursions into morality and religion, so he sought to unmix facts and values. The factual thinking behind the technological marvel of a streetcar, whereby one does not need to know how it functions but simply that everything has been calculated and can be trusted, intrudes into values, leading to false promises of an objective foundation for how one should live one's life. Philosophers construct morality on the same factual premises attempting to give a direction to the moral life so it will unfold along a path, much like the streetcar follows its well-laid tracks.[30]

Weber argued that facts and values needed to be "unmixed." Science should penetrate into the natural causality of all things, but values should proceed through a different analysis by way of the freedom found in "the mystery of personality."[31] Weber did not desire to turn back from the science that held forth so much promise in the early stages of the technological era, and he recognized that this meant theology had become irrelevant. God could no longer be thought of as present in the techno-

---

30. See Rüdiger Safranski's *Martin Heidegger: Between Good and Evil* (trans. Ewald Osers; Cambridge, Mass.: Harvard University Press, 1998), 90.

31. This of course continues Kant's third antinomy and argues for it such that each form of causality (nature/freedom) should remain independent of the other. This had tremendous influence on Troeltsch's analysis of the church's social teachings and in turn greatly influenced the development and strategy of "the principles of Christian ethics" in the Wesleyan tradition. For as we shall see, this "mystery of personality" becomes the ground for the development of Methodist ethics from the latter part of the nineteenth through the mid-twentieth centuries.

logical era. Nietzsche was right: "God is dead." If there were a place for God and theology in technology, then it would have to be in the arational space of the individual soul with its commitment to values and its basis in personality. As Rüdiger Safranski puts it, "Max Weber calls for honesty. Facts should be faced, even unpleasant ones—in a world that we can rationally penetrate and technologically manage, God has disappeared. If he still exists, then he does so only in the soul of the individual, who must be prepared 'on his own account' to make the 'sacrifice of the intellect' and believe in him."[32] One can still have god in the era of technology, but at the price of reason. Weber recognized the problem the mathematization of morality produces. But his response is to construct an impenetrable domain of "value" (also called *Geist* or spirit) where morality and theology can proceed without reason.

Weber's work sets the stage for Heidegger's first foray into thinking about technology. His first lecture as a privatdozent, given in 1921, was entitled "The Idea of Philosophy and the Worldview Problem." He challenged the easy assumption that things can be seen simply because we have a worldview about them. Heidegger asks the students what they see when they come into the lecture hall and see a lectern. He notes that they do not first have a theory of perception that they then apply, but that they see the lectern "in an orientation . . . which presents itself to me directly, without any mental detour via a grasping of things. Living in an environment, it means to me everywhere and always, it is all of this world, it is worlding."[33] We never simply *perceive* a lectern, we discover we are already oriented by it. Our world has been shaped and formed such that by seeing the lectern we already see an entire world. His point is not to reconcile or unmix facts and values, but to raise a question prior to the question of factual or valuational causality. In this first lecture he calls this "worlding." The objects we can see only appear against a background of being itself that we too often fail to see precisely because of the fixation on the objects. Do we not see in this first lecture the seeds for what will become Heidegger's most significant contribution to philosophy, the ontological distinction where everyday "things" like tools, people, Bach's fugues, the earth itself appear only when Being itself disappears?

Heidegger was convinced that Western philosophy was only capable of seeing the everyday things, while forgetting the question of Being. In fact, "Being abandoned beings."[34] What does this mean? The things of life are

---

32. Safranski, *Martin Heidegger*, 91.

33. Quoted in ibid., 95.

34. "Everywhere and always machination, cloaking itself in the semblance of a measured ordering and controlling, confronts us with beings as the sole hierarchy and causes us to forget Being. What actually happens is that Being abandons beings: Being lets beings be on their own." Heidegger, *Nietzsche*, 3:181.

no longer viewed in terms of their position within life as a whole. They are viewed solely in terms of a subject/object relation based on representation. The subject/object relation is not mere subjectivity. It is not that the ego defines the world through mere willfulness as if I could make things whatever I wanted to make them. Instead, everything becomes an *object* thought within the conditions of calculability, accessibility, and representation—conditions we ourselves posit. Subjectivism and objectivism are not two competing positions; like objectivism and relativism they mirror each other. As Heidegger put it, "the essence of subjectivism is objectivism, insofar as everything becomes an object for the subject. The nonobjective—the nonobjectival—too is determined by the objective, by a relation of opposition to it."[35] *Gegenstand* (opposition) makes possible the subject/object relation and the change in the "beingness of being" that defines the modern era through representation. This represents the end of modernity and the completion of metaphysics. It is a technological conclusion. Objects appear to subjects (who are themselves objects) to be represented as accessible, calculable devices for human use. "Value" is Western destiny.

Heidegger found Nietzsche to be the great Western thinker who brought metaphysics to its closure, for he identified the essence of Western metaphysics, the essence of being, as the "will to power."[36] This is not a lust for violence, but "value positing." We posit our own life, our own power, by way of commanding its enhancement and preservation. This is nihilism, not merely as a negation of everything that came before (although it includes such negation) but primarily as the recognition that the highest values—truth, goodness, beauty—devalue themselves. They no longer matter; they do not ground our activities, and thus they do not permit us to *understand* our changed environment. They are, after all, values that we posit, and values are the conditions by which we make sense of everyday life.

Because the old values devalue themselves, we need to posit *new* values. This is the task of the "overman." He is not an individual. There is no technological messiah we await. The overman is the essence of humanity that "in the *history* of nihilism thinks itself in a modern way, that is to say, wills itself." This new human essence is defined by mastery, which is not an arbitrary coercion over things, but "submitting oneself to a command for the sake of the empowering of the essence of power." This is what it means to humanize the world. It is to "feel ourselves more and more masters within it." This metaphysical character of mastery comes to closure

35. Ibid., 3:221.
36. Heidegger distinguished between "thinkers" and "researchers." Thinkers have one thought that they think through completely. Researchers merely assemble the thoughts of others and present them to their audience. See ibid., 3:5.

with the machine. "Mechanization makes possible a mastery of beings that are everywhere surveyable, a master that conserves—and that means stores—energy."[37]

"Nihilism," writes Heidegger, "does not strive for mere nullity. Its proper essence lies in the affirmative nature of a liberation."[38] Surely this is why Heidegger penned his famous phrase, "The essence of technology is by no means anything technological."[39] By this he meant technology cannot be rightly discerned solely with regard to its products; technology is not just about the invention of new things and their instrumental use, it is the culmination of a philosophy of human liberation. But for what are persons liberated? For *nothing* but freedom itself. This is nihilism.

Technology is a summons to a new kind of being because the old values devalue themselves, always becoming obsolete. New values are posited, including values whereby we store energy for our own uses. These values are the conditions for our life, which are not given by anything other than the will to power of our own being. Therefore, if the technological question is based on the fear that our technology will finally exceed our control, and thus it calls for ethical mastery, we simply repeat the moment of nihilism that is modernity's end. If we call for a new ethic that takes into account our changed situation, we remain oriented by the very technology we seek to master. Why would we need a new ethic if we were not already nihilists? That is to say we witness to the fact that in our changed context the old values—truth, goodness, beauty—have devalued themselves and need to be replaced and renewed, just like the energy we constantly seek to store up for our own sake.

Neo-Protestant Ethics

As a modern, scientific discipline, much of neo-Protestant[40] ethics adopted a technological orientation that implicitly and explicitly rejected the ancient metaphysics of participation and doctrine of illumination. In so doing it rejected the tradition of moral theology. Neo-Protestant ethics became preoccupied with founding morality on something immanent to human nature, something we could be sure we knew. It is grounded on epistemological certitude that looks for simple axiomatic truths. It is both subjective and objective at the same time. This neo-Protestant tradition emerged in the nineteenth century following in the wake of Immanuel

---

37. Ibid., 3:217, 228, 230.
38. Ibid., 3:204.
39. Martin Heidegger, *The Question concerning Technology* (trans. William Lovitt; New York: Harper Torchbooks, 1977), 35.
40. Luther, Calvin, and Wesley were not neo-Protestants. By the latter term I primarily refer to Protestant ethics developed in a Kantian tradition.

Kant's critique of causality and freedom. Science would have its secure foundation in nature, but morality might escape such a foundation through a different conception of causality, found in a transcendental freedom. However, these two forms of causality could not be reconciled, as Kant noted in his third antinomy. It sets the limits within which much of the history of Protestant ethics emerged in the nineteenth century.

In *The Critique of Pure Reason*, Kant developed two forms of causality: nature and freedom. The former explained science, the latter morality and religion. Kant's assumption that both of these forms of causal explanation worked in their separate spheres and yet could not be reconciled, led him to distinguish between a phenomenal and noumenal realm. Natural causal explanation worked in the phenomenal realm and rendered intelligible science. Free causal explanation worked in the noumenal realm and made possible morality and religion. But the price for morality and religion's intelligibility was its policing to one of these independent realms.

After Kant two possibilities emerged if theologians sought to mediate theology by way of causal (apodictic) explanation. Theology could be "natural" and made relevant by a causal explanatory framework consistent with modern science. Here ethics is grounded primarily in sociology or biology, or a merger of both. Or theology could retreat to a "noumenal" realm and draw on revelation, consciousness, experience, or feeling as a privileged source of knowledge of God free from encroachment by a natural or scientific framework. Either of these modern strategies insured that theology could only be marginal—dare one say, sectarian—when it came to issues of philosophy, politics, and economics (including technology). Once Kant's third antinomy provided the epistemological conditions for any possible knowledge of God and morality then these two alternatives constantly resurfaced as the only theological possibilities.

Some theological ethicists (Protestant and Catholic) accepted Kant's basic causal division and developed Christian ethics on scientific terms. Current forms of "natural law" ethics that develop an ethics without any particular theological themes would be examples. Others accepted Kant's distinction and developed ethics based on the causality of freedom. Here ethics is grounded in a subjective self-certainty such as the mystery of personality or human dignity. Still others accepted Kant's dualistic causality but sought to reconcile his basic division through some form of dialectical reasoning—by offering us a science of personality. This seems to be the strategy of Schleiermacher's influential Christian ethics. But none of these options escapes technology's orienting power.

In John Shelley's introduction to Schleiermacher's lecture notes on ethics, he explains Schleiermacher's ethics as "the process through which nature gradually becomes the organ of reason." Schleiermacher sought to resist the division between nature and freedom by relating them dialectically. Ethics became something more basic than either, in that ethics became the metaphysical ground by which freedom and nature were to be reconciled through dialectic. Reason and nature engage each other until finally the flux that is nature is mastered by reason. Shelley notes that this dialectical process is "most literally visible . . . in a work of sculpture or in the development of technology, whereby raw materials are given shape and/or organized in such a way as to perform useful functions for human beings."[41] Ethics is technological.

For Schleiermacher, ethics offers access to the "primordial consciousness," which is the essence of religion, equidistant with dogmatic theology. In other words, both ethics and theology can direct us toward that primordial consciousness.[42] Ethics does not need dogmatic theology for its own intelligibility; it is an independent source for religious experience. Schleiermacher did argue that Christian ethics was inseparable from the two focal points of Christology and pneumatology, and it could only make sense as the customs of that community we call "church." Yet in contrast to the Catholic principle, the Protestant principle assumed "no obedience to the Church," but is grounded on "that which each individual demands of himself."[43] This secure interior space, which has come to be known as "metaphysics of presence," Kant designated "personality."[44] Today it often goes by the name of "experience." It is no surprise that as the scientific discipline of ethics works itself into the Wesleyan tradition in the latter part of the nineteenth century it does so through the alien notion of the "supreme significance of the moral personality."[45]

Borden Parker Bowne, a Methodist philosopher, offered the Wesleyan tradition its first *scientific* ethics and produced a tradition preoccupied with "ethics" through the publication of his *Principles of Ethics*. This tradition gave rise to the centrality of the "Social Principles," which are still used for confirmation in many Methodist churches, although the basic doctrinal teachings are neglected. This shows the ongoing influence of this tradition. Bowne's work represents a complete rupture with Wesley's moral theology. Even though he was no empiricist, Bowne sides completely with modern scientism and the necessity for theology to be relevant to it. Similarities between his scientific ethics and the geometric foundation of morality by the seventeenth-century moral philosopher

---

41. Friedrich Schleiermacher, *Introduction to Christian Ethics* (trans. John C. Shelley; Nashville: Abingdon, 1989), 22-23, 44-46.

42. Ibid., 47-48.

43. Ibid., 58.

44. Immanuel Kant, *Religion within the Limits of Reason Alone* (trans. Theodore Green and Hoyt H. Hudson; New York: Harper Torchbooks, 1960), 23.

45. Borden P. Bowne, *The Principles of Ethics* (New York: Harper & Brothers, 1892), v.

Henry More are readily found. However, where More had twenty-three moral noema, Bowne (like Kant) reduces the self-evident axiom to a single imperative. Ethics is a law-ruled discipline where experts apply universal ideals to a chaotic and recalcitrant nature. Bowne's ethics is scientific, but he also followed Kant in arguing that radical evil limits what the scientific approach can achieve. He writes, "When science has done its best, and when the evil will has been finally exercised, there will still remain, as fixed features of earthly life, physical and mental decay, bereavement and death; and none can view a life in which these are inevitable as having attained an ideal form."[46] Bowne could not foresee the possibility that the scientific task of morality could conquer death and decay, but its task is to do all it can to tame nature through freedom by the application of universal law.[47]

In many respects Bowne follows Schleiermacher. He presents ethics as a system of laws grounded in the concept of duty (contra Schleiermacher, who still grounded it primarily in the good and was thus more open to the ancient tradition). Even more so than Schleiermacher, Bowne's systematic ethics is technological in the sense identified by Heidegger. Bowne insisted that moral laws were not subjective but objective. Moral value is not simply subjective. But recall Heidegger's claim that in nihilism, "the essence of subjectivism is objectivism, insofar as everything becomes an object for the subject." For Bowne moral norms are "objective." They exist outside of our willing, even though the "goodwill" is the source of morality. Nevertheless the end willed by the goodwill is grounded in the constitution of our human nature; it is the "well-being" that defines natural, human existence.[48] Thus no metaphysics of participation is present or necessary. All that is needed is a metaphysics of freedom. Nature, as the ground of our moral constitution, needs enhancement by means of freedom. The aim of moral activity "is to lift the natural to the plane of the moral by setting the stamp of the free spirit upon it."[49] Here is the subject/object dichotomy that characterizes the end of Western metaphysics as technology. Nature is a chaotic flux that reason must tame. Bowne refers to this natural chaotic flux as the predatory character of tribalism.[50] It is that excess of nature that refuses rationalization. This tribalism has been rationalized to some extent by industrial civiliza-

---

46. Ibid., 74.

47. Bowne wrote, "Our moral task is seen to be to develop this life into its ideal form; and ethics is forbidden to call anything common or unclean which life involves as one of its component factors" (ibid., 76).

48. As Bowne puts it, "Morality has an objective as well as a subjective aspect. Objective, or material right is founded in the nature of things, and is altogether independent of the agent's motives" (ibid., 143).

49. Ibid., 39.

50. See ibid., 156.

tion, but it is not yet complete. Only the application of moral ideals through a universal critical reason will finally accomplish the necessary moral progress. How this differs from the will to power is not easy to discern.

Methodist theologians such as Edgar Sheffield Brightman and Albert C. Knudson continued the science of ethics introduced by Bowne into the Wesleyan tradition. In 1933 Brightman published his *Moral Laws*. He begins his work with the distinction between descriptive sciences based on facts and normative sciences based on values, reproducing the subject/ object dichotomy. Morality should be a normative science grounded in law. While "virtue" has little or no place within such a science, law is fundamental. Law allows for an objective standard, which, at the same time, makes human freedom to appropriate and apply the law subjective. These laws provide a basis for ethics to be applied to the conflicting "moral data" that emerge from social, political, and economic analysis. "Ethics is based," states Brightman, "on this fact of purposive control by rational principles."[51] Brightman lays out eleven laws by which the moral ideal can be applied to the conflicting mass of data for purposes of human mastery. Unlike Schleiermacher, Christology, pneumatology, and ecclesiology play no role in Brightman's scientific ethics. And whereas Schleiermacher had allowed both ethics and dogma to offer us equal access to the primordial consciousness of religious experience, Brightman (following Kant more closely) makes ethics logically prior to dogma. The truth of the latter depends on the truth of the former.[52] Ethics is considered a more universal category than theology. Brightman's work represents the high-water mark of the accommodation of Methodist theology to ethics as technology.

Albert C. Knudson continued this tradition of the logical priority of ethics to theology in his *Principles of Christian Ethics*. Although he recognized that a "sharp line . . . between Christian ethics and Christian theology is gradually disappearing," he nevertheless states that "in a sense . . . the permanent element in Christianity is its ethical teaching."[53] If the line were disappearing, it is because ethics is replacing theology. Knudson does bring Jesus back into the conversation. However, the Jesus to whom he appeals is someone for whom "the autonomy of the individual was . . . a fundamental presupposition."[54] For Knudson, like Brightman, ethics is

---

51. E. S. Brightman, *The Moral Laws* (New York: Abingdon, 1933), 13, 70.

52. See ibid., 265-66.

53. Albert C. Knudson, *The Principles of Christian Ethics* (New York: Abingdon, 1943), 34-35. Knudson dedicates his book to E. S. Brightman.

54. Ibid., 43. Knudson also states later in his work that Jesus' profoundest contribution to ethics was his bringing to light "the infinite value of every personality in the sight of God" (ibid., 79).

grounded primarily in freedom. It offers a new source of causality into the natural flux of life that allows us to shape institutions and persons. They both accept the modern assumption of a liberty of indifference as the crucial moral faculty of the soul. The will must always be free to choose irrespective of the movement of the intellect, which means that it must have the power to suspend judgment even on judgments it has already made. This constitutes a significant shift in the understanding of practical reasoning. As we shall see below, Wesley may very well have set this direction for Methodist thought. He adopted the "liberty of indifference" to avoid a theory of predestination. He appears unaware how this conflicts with other aspects of his understanding of human action.

Knudson and Brightman develop the notion of a liberty of indifference in a direction Wesley could not have countenanced. For them, freedom is more basic than God. The capacity to choose between good and evil is projected even onto God. As Knudson puts it, "God himself as a moral being must distinguish between good and evil and must be metaphysically capable of choosing either."[55] This conception of God undermines traditional Christian and Wesleyan language where God is perfect, immutable, and impassable and instead makes "choice" a divine attribute. God could not have been defined by "choice" prior to the twentieth century. But once the subject/object dichotomy of technological thinking predominates, then even moral goodness becomes an object that God as subject must have the freedom to choose or reject. As we shall see, this understanding of ethics completely capitulates to the very Hobbesian reality Wesley rejected through the influence of persons like Malebranche, Cudworth, and Norris.

Knudson's principles of Christian ethics assume that the moral task is to produce unity in a world of conflict. His notion of ethics fits not only the technological era but also the liberal political theory that goes with it. In fact, like Hobbes, he finds the state of nature to be a state of war. Moral principles provide rights to individuals against this state of conflict and chaos. But Knudson also applies this political theory to God. Thus he states, "The only way in which the idea of a moral universe can be maintained is by ascribing moral responsibility to God and a limited independence to man. As Creator of the world, God is a responsible Being, and we his creatures have rights over against him as well as duties to him."[56] That God does not want us to be passively dependent is certainly true, but Knudson posits rights against God without acknowledging any problems this poses for a reasonable theology. Why do we need to secure

---

55. Ibid., 82. Of course, if God is capable of choosing evil, then the freedom to choose is more basic to our being than God, and God is no longer worthy of our worship.

56. Ibid., 180.

ourselves against God unless God is like other finite causes, so limited by the possibility of good and evil that God cannot finally be trusted?

Unlike more reasonable expressions of the Christian faith where God is understood in terms of the grammar of simplicity, perfection, and immutability, Knudson's ethics require a different grammar altogether to speak of God—the grammar of choice, freedom, and individual responsibility. Once God chooses between good and evil, we need rights to secure ourselves against God because a subjective will to power and an objective moral law are more basic to existence than the goodness of God. But this is nihilism, for here is a clear example of how the highest values devalue themselves. If we claim for ourselves "rights" against God, we claim power over God as well. Knudson concludes, "The highest in man is a revelation of divine truth and the divine will."[57] That statement can be read as showing us something Knudson may not have intended to say. What is divine truth and divine will other than that which is highest in human beings?

For Bowne, Brightman, and Knudson, ethics is technology, and it has completely replaced Wesley's moral theology. Ethics is a scientific discipline of mastery that sets freedom in opposition to nature. Thus, it is also a discourse of liberation and accessibility. It liberates from previous dogmatic stances toward a universal accessibility of self-actualization and well-being grounded in the nature of human being. Admittedly, some later Methodists have resisted these developments. In particular, Paul Ramsey, one of the most important Methodist ethicists in the twentieth century, worked his way out of this ethics to begin the process of recovering moral theology. However, those who argue that the first task of ethics is to adopt and learn social sciences in order to read the facts, and then apply the values of theology after the "facts" present reality, still maintain this other tradition. As previously noted, the centrality of the "Social Principles" as definitive for the Christian life perpetuates this tradition. It initiated a "scientific" discipline of ethics into Wesleyan theology that converges with technology. This notion of ethics does not suit us well at the end of modernity when technology orients our lives so thoroughly.

While the tradition of liberal Methodist theology from Bowne to Knudson represents an influential shaping force on Wesleyan ethics, it is certainly not the only such force. Consider Richard Watson, who included the essay "Man as a Moral Agent," in his 1858 *Theological Institutes*. Although his work does not bear the marks of the science of personality seen in Boston Personalism, it establishes morality solely on the basis of God's will and neglects an essential element of John Wesley's ethics, namely that "will" alone is insufficient as the basis for the moral life. It

---

57. Ibid., 283.

was this nominalism in Hobbes and Locke that the Cambridge Platonists rejected in favor of the importance of reason and truth as a basis for morality instead of mere willfulness. But Watson follows Locke more closely than did Wesley. He writes,

> He is a moral agent who is capable of performing moral actions; and an action is rendered moral by two circumstances,—that it is voluntary, and that it has respect to some rule which determines it to be good or evil. "Moral good and evil," says Locke, "is the conformity or disagreement of our voluntary actions to some law, whereby good or evil is drawn upon us from the will or power of the law-maker."[58]

Here we see that technology's subject/object distinction was present early on in Methodist ethics. The development of an ethics of obligation grounded in will was not first introduced by Bowne, Knudson, and others. The seeds for this kind of ethics were already present in Locke and developed by Watson.

Another key influence on the development of the discipline of ethics within the Wesleyan tradition—through persons such as Paul Ramsey, Philip Wogaman, Robin Lovin, and (to a lesser extent) Georgia Harkness—was Reinhold Niebuhr. Bowne was a contemporary of Niebuhr. As Niebuhr's particular approach to Christian ethics ascended, that represented by the tradition of Bowne, Brightman, and Knudson diminished. Is Niebuhrian ethics less "technological" than the initial development of ethics by Bowne, Brightman, and Knudson? I think not. The only doctrine that Niebuhr developed with care was anthropology. It forms the basis for all his other work and it remains caught in the two forms of causality—nature and freedom—that form the basis for the rise of modern ethics in the first place. Niebuhr does not reconcile these two forms of causality as Kant began to do in his third critique. Rather, like Schleiermacher, he sought a dialectical resolution. The result is that Niebuhr ontologizes a struggle between nature and freedom that cannot be overcome. Agonistics receives dogmatic status. Niebuhr began *The Nature and Destiny of Man* with the assertion: "Man has always been his own most vexing problem. How shall he think of himself?"[59] The vexing problem is that if we think of ourselves entirely in terms of nature we do not do justice to our rational faculties that transcend nature. If we think of ourselves in terms of those transcendent rational faculties, we do not do justice to our embeddedness in nature. This vexing problem—our location within both a transcendent realm of rationality and freedom and an

---

58. Richard Watson, "Man A Moral Agent," in Thomas A. Langford, ed., *Wesleyan Theology: A Sourcebook* (Durham, N.C.: Labyrinth, 1985), 57.

59. Reinhold Niebuhr, *Human Nature* (vol. 1 of *The Nature and Destiny of Man: A Christian Interpretation*; New York: Charles Scribner, 1941), 1:1.

immanent realm of nature, inclination, and instinct—generates all of Niebuhr's anthropology and makes tragedy necessary.

For Niebuhr, "Nature supplies particularity but freedom of the spirit is the cause of real individuality." This ontological structure, caught between nature and freedom, vitality and form, the "natural fact of a particular body" and the "spiritual fact of self-transcendence" is irremediable. As he puts it, "No philosophy or religion can change the structure of human existence." This unchanging structure is the source for the possibility of evil because it tempts us to misunderstand ourselves in two directions: idealism or naturalism. Both lose a proper interpretation of the human self, either to the universality of transcendent rationality and freedom or to the immediacy of nature and vitality. Only by providing an interpretation that gives unity to the relation of vitality and form can the temptation be avoided. This is what the Christian view of anthropology seeks to do. But Niebuhr claims that all it can do is provide an interpretation that makes sense of the unity of the two. It cannot overcome the contradiction the two represent that tempts us toward evil.[60]

Niebuhr's theological ethics does not move us beyond the subject/object dichotomy of modern technological thinking. It only critiques liberalism in that it argues that the dichotomy between nature and freedom can never be reconciled. We are not going on to perfection. Any disagreement between Niebuhr and the Boston Personalists or Social Gospelers is within a broader agreement as to what ethics is, a reconciliation of the freedom/nature distinction. The extent of the difference between them should not be exaggerated. Brightman could also recognize limitations on human perfectibility by adopting Kant's "radical evil."

Ethics became a discipline of human mastery, where freedom engages nature in order to overcome it, to serve the values that we ourselves posit. As theologians adopt this modernist ethics, they abandon an older tradition of Christian moral thought which I will call "moral theology." We will return to this critique in the final chapter after we have looked at Wesley's moral theology. Only then will we be able to see that Wesleyan perfection and Niebuhrian fallibilism are irreconcilable.

Contradicting Heidegger

Is Heidegger correct? Is it true that Christianity's reconciliation with "the modern world . . . repudiates ever more decisively its former history-shaping force?"[61] Is it true that the more Christian theologians seek relevance to the modern world the more irrelevant Christian theology must

---

60. Ibid., 1:54-55, 69.
61. Heidegger, *Nietzsche*, 3:241.

become? On this point I think he was correct. Ethics became the discipline by which Christian theologians sought to reconcile religion and the modern world. God and goodness, doctrine and ethics, truth and love were rendered asunder. The Methodist tradition of ethics assumes that rights, justice, or values are more universal categories than the Christian doctrine of God. This is not a shift within Wesley's theology, nor is it merely making his work relevant for today. It represents a repudiation of Wesley's moral theology. It is a reconciliation effected through the development of a scientific ethics that eschews substantive theological doctrines.

The introduction of "ethics" into Wesleyan theology proves Heidegger correct. Ethics as "value positing" based on objective laws becomes all the more necessary once God is dead. Such an ethics fits well the technological era where the task at hand is to use the freedom of our will to power to enhance our own lives and transform the chaotic flux of nature through a search for some elusive authentic self. Is this the inevitable outcome of Western metaphysics, and did Christianity itself participate in the negation of those values that summons us to a constant revaluation? Is this the only possible reading of our technological world? No. Heidegger's account of Christianity was reductionistic. In fact, this modernist ethic can only arise once significant theological doctrines are repudiated. Western metaphysics ends in technology *in opposition to* Christian theological claims, not because of them. There is no single Western metaphysics. A metaphysics of freedom is not a logical consequence of a metaphysics of participation.

Heidegger's thesis contains significant problems, even beyond his poor reading of Christianity. As Borgmann notes, his reading of technology is an unstable blend of a substantivist approach where technology determines our being and a call for persons to take the freedom to be participants in their technological destiny.[62] In his essay, "Only Theology Overcomes Metaphysics," John Milbank has challenged Heidegger's reading of a common tradition of Western metaphysics emerging from Plato through Christianity to Hegel and culminating in Nietzsche. Heidegger viewed this metaphysical tradition as "ontotheology" where God (or reason, logos, and so forth) and being are conceived univocally. God is understood in terms of the *causa sui*, the self-caused cause, and thus God is bound to the chain of causation as the first being among others. Ontotheology inevitably leads to statements such as we saw in Knudson: "The highest in man is a revelation of divine truth and the divine will." Yet contra Heidegger, Milbank denies that Plato, Aristotle, and much of Christianity embodied this kind of metaphysics. Ontotheology first occurs with Suarez who regards "ontology/

---

62. Borgmann, *Technology*, 40.

metaphysics as first and foremost a science of what constitutes 'being' taken as a possible object of knowledge which is *unproblematically comprehensible* without reference to any non-material or absolute beings." Only then does God become *causa sui*—"univocally conceived as of the same type as a finite cause."[63] Thus modernity does not fulfill but invents "Western" metaphysics. And what needs to be overcome is not Christianity but the misreading of Christianity that modernity is, and that misreading is perpetuated in much of what constitutes "ethics."

Clearly what we find in early twentieth-century Methodist ethics are not focal practices that show us the Christian life but the repetition of modernity. We do not find a deictic explanation but an apodictic one. In fact, Knudson stated unequivocally that aspects of the Christian life such as "creedal profession, church membership, sacramental symbols, ascetic practices, emotional experiences, modes of worship, sabbath observance, and even peculiarities of dress and speech . . . are all obviously too superficial or external to constitute or represent its essential or distinctive nature."[64] Yet these are precisely the kind of focal practices that can fund a deictic discourse that we have all but lost. Moreover, these specific practices were central to the nature of Methodism. When "ethics" was introduced into Wesleyan theology it facilitated their disappearance. Has our very embrace of ethics (including that troublesome expression "social ethics") as the essence of the Christian faith disoriented us from the very focal practices and things that could provide the Wesleyan tradition a shaping force within our technological environment? I shall argue that Wesley's ethics can only be understood in terms of a common ecclesial life based on practices such as the Eucharist, a common doctrinal confession, and the General Rules. It is no surprise that Wesley's work disappears when "ethics" becomes the essence of Methodism.

Our technological environment will not disappear, and its presence is by no means an unmitigated evil. There is no pure or radical evil, that is an invention of recent origin.[65] Our choices are not technological determinism or ludditism. But to fail to recognize that technology has replaced the church as that which orients our lives is to refuse to discern the times. To refuse to see how "ethics" has become inextricably related to the culmination of Western philosophy in this technological orientation is a refusal to "know ourselves." And to refuse to raise the question how this ethical, technological orientation relates to the death of god is to shirk our theological responsibility. The permanence of technology need not mean the irretrievable loss of focal practices with their orienting power. In fact,

---

63. John Milbank, *The Word Made Strange* (Oxford: Blackwell, 1997), 40-41.
64. Knudson, *Principles of Christian Ethics*, 162.
65. See the first chapter in John Milbank's *Being Reconciled* (London: Routledge, 2003).

the end of modernity is a moment of great opportunity to see more clearly what could not be seen till now. As Borgmann notes, "the technological environment heightens rather than denies the radiance of genuine focal things."[66] Precisely because of the dominance of our technological environment we should be able to see better the significance of focal things and practices than those who did not live at the end of modernity. They could not appear to them as they can to us, and that makes them all the more significant. It also provides no excuse for theologians and leaders in the Wesleyan tradition to forget focal things and practices in favor of technological devices.

Borgmann contrasts focal things with technological devices. The latter work by concealing themselves in order to make their commodities present. A furnace offers heat, but we only notice the furnace when it breaks down and fails to provide its commodity for us. A focal thing, however, requires a practice within which it can prosper.[67] The Latin word *focus* means hearth, fireplace, altar, home, family. A focal thing assumes the kind of presence the hearth once represented. A focal practice is a family meal; a technological device is the commodity put forward by a fast-food restaurant. A focal practice is catechism, the sacrament, learning and confessing the Creed; a technological device is the "Igniting Ministries" campaign sponsored by The United Methodist Church, or the megachurch and its church growth rules.

While both focal things and technological devices are only made possible against the background of a practice, the focal thing depends upon the human embodiment of the practice more so than does the technological device. The former needs reality, the latter only virtuality. It does not matter who prepared the fast food or who cleans up after it. I do not need to know their names. Nor does it matter whether the actors in the "Igniting Ministries" commercials are obedient members of the church, what creeds they confess, or how they live their lives. Both offer a commodity where the "device" that operates it can be concealed or replaced without consequences. But the practice of preparation and cleanup is intrinsic to the family meal as a focal thing, as is the embodiment of human reality in catechism, sacramental practice, or learning and confessing the Creed.

The Direction of a Conclusion: A Medieval and Anglican Sacramental Metaphysics

How can we remember focal things and practices and be less fascinated by technological devices? If we do not remember focal things or if we

---

66. Borgmann, *Technology*, 196.
67. Ibid.

think they can be replaced by technological devices without consequence, we will reinforce the orienting power of technology—the interstate that takes us to the mall will form our lives more thoroughly than the church with its expectant witness looking for Christ's return. Our churches still stand and bear within them an intentionality toward a nontechnological orientation. Their very presence is a "focal thing" that bears witness to the "new creation" Christ will bring even when our people no longer know the reason why they face the direction they do. The witness of those who came before us, those who were not bound by the repetition of obsolescence and the new and improved, offers us a different orientation that we might still see even though we have nearly lost deictic explanations. That witness is also present—even in Wesleyan ethics—in the residual tradition that I shall call "moral theology." The latter assumes the medieval and Anglican sacramental world that Runyon rightly diagnoses as disappearing in the eighteenth century. But it never disappeared or we could not speak of it today. It is the world to which John Wesley witnessed and is at least residually present in the tradition that bears his name. As long as his resources are ours, that world cannot entirely disappear from the Wesleyan traditions.

The systematic and social-scientific study of ethics sought to render obsolete an older tradition of moral theology, but it was unsuccessful. The latter did not disappear, not even in Bowne, Brightman, and Knudson. Traces of it remain, and they can help orient us. Rather than ethics as that which guides us, moral theology can help us see better the difference between deictic and apodictic discourse. Moral theology, unlike ethics, depends upon the common life of the church—a common worship, life, and discipline—for its intelligibility. Ethics, however, always underwrites the superiority of the state which is supposedly more universal, more global than the church.[68] Moral theology is characterized by virtues, holy tempers, and the centrality of desire. It subordinates the place of law, duty, and obligation to these ends. As Aquinas put it, law directs human acts to virtuous ends. Law, duty, and obligation are not ends in themselves, but point us to something greater, something that we must see: the vision of God.[69] Ethics is primarily constituted by duty, obligation, disinterestedness, and nonpreferential loves that assume universality and

---

68. It should come as no surprise that Knudson subordinates the church to the state's authority; for this goes part and parcel with ethics as technology. Knudson writes, "All societies, the church included, are subordinate to [the state's] authority. . . . In this respect the church is under the control of the state; and if its existence should threaten or seem to threaten the security and unity of the state, the state would regard itself as justified in destroying the church or so restricting its activities as to render it harmless." Knudson does then give the church "a certain moral authority" to subject the state to "moral criticism" (Knudson, *Principles of Christian Ethics*, 249).

69. Kenneth Kirk's much neglected work, including his *Vision of God*, is an excellent place to begin to recover the tradition of moral theology, which would suit well our Wesleyan tradition.

accessibility. It focuses on methods and procedures for insuring equal access that take us away from desires for the local and particular in favor of an abstract universal. Moral theology assumes we must first love and adore the everyday, particular focal things before we can be moral. They orient our lives, and that requires preferential and particular loves. If I do not love my children more than all other children in the world, I will not know how to love my neighbor and her children. If I do not know how to love my spouse forsaking all others, then I will not know how to be a good neighbor to the spouses of others. If I do not know how to love God first, I will not know how to love at all. And if I do not know how to love Jesus and his church with the particularity of the people he called into it (including the specificity of the Methodist tradition), I will not know how to love God.

Ethics is grounded in the philosophical tradition of fallibilism. It begins by assuming that every form of knowledge must be held tentatively, for it could be wrong and will probably be proved to be so in the future. It always seeks a critical distance from the everyday. Likewise, every form of moral knowledge must also be held tentatively, for any account of the good could potentially be different. This tradition of ethics assumes that all moral norms, like skyscrapers and superhighways, are social constructions and therefore subject to change. Moral theology is more akin to infallibilism and perfection. It assumes that without truth error could never be known. It begins with the assumption of a truth given and known without the admixture of error, and this provides the possibility for the necessary humility and repentance our finitude requires. Likewise, goodness makes possible the knowledge of evil, but not vice versa. The Wesleyan doctrine of perfection and the Roman Catholic doctrine of infallibilism will always be anathema to "ethics." But within the practice of moral theology, they are necessary if we are to refuse nihilism and cease to bear witness to the (post)modern dogma that the highest values always and inevitably devalue themselves. It is technology that summons us to that witness. It is one we must refuse. This refusal is not for the sake of any authoritarian rule by those who claim to know the true or the good, although this is something we must always be on the watch against. But fallibilists can be as prone to authoritarian rule as those who still hold forth the possibility of truth known without error, or goodness performed without evil. For fallibilists can be tempted toward the will to power that constantly negates and posits, only to negate and posit again. Those striving for perfection, or acknowledging an unrevisable truth, recognize that they participate in something other than negation and value positing. Moral theology is a focal practice that assumes we must learn to confess how our lives do not embody the truth and goodness that is disclosed to us but which we ourselves do not posit. For that reason it has an orienting power that causes us to face a different direction than the constant movement technology produces and its handmaid ethics seek to reinforce. By receiving Wesley's witness in terms of this tradition of moral theology and recognizing that he did not make well the passage from a medieval sacramental to a modern epistemological world, we will be able to understand better the nature of his theology and its significance for us today.

CHAPTER 2

JOHN WESLEY: MORAL THEOLOGIAN?

Chapter 1 suggested that Methodist theologians developed a tradition of "ethics" either by ignoring Wesley altogether or receiving his work through a modernist framework. This either-or does not represent the entirety of the Methodist tradition. Robert Cushman's work, for example, offers a significant alternative.[1] But inasmuch as Methodist theologians adopted this tradition of ethics, they accommodated the spirit of Wesleyan theology to eighteenth-century developments Wesley himself rejected, for Wesley thought that God and the good, or doctrine and ethics, were inextricable. He did not seek a new foundation for morality in self-evident principles anyone could intuit. Nevertheless, Wesley's moral theology was soon to be eclipsed by new developments in moral philosophy.

As Leslie Stephen ably noted in his 1876 *History of English Thought*, theology and ethics went through a divorce in the eighteenth century. Philosophers declared the old theological synthesis between God and goodness dead and sought a new foundation for ethics. While some, such as Hume, were content to see "God" disappear, or at least receive a lesser role in ethical matters, others sought new means to make God relevant to the good. All were of one mind that with or without God ethics itself would and should remain. Philosophers looked to the body both

---

1. See Robert E. Cushman, *Faith Seeking Understanding: Essays Theological and Critical* (Durham, N.C.: Duke University Press, 1981), esp. 69-70, where he notes, "Wesley makes no sharp divorcement between nature and grace." He then points in the direction of both a doctrine of illumination and a metaphysics of participation, although it is underdeveloped.

individually and corporately as the new foundation for ethics. They proposed reason, conscience, sentiment, a boniform faculty, a moral sense, and utility as new moral foundations. Those philosophers such as Locke and Kant who maintained God's relevance primarily did so on the basis that moral actions required a final judgment. "God" ensured that moral acts received due justice in the next life, a justice not always found in this one. This provided a necessary link between moral approval and disapproval and expected consequences of actions. Even those who divorced theology and ethics could agree that "God" was a useful fiction to keep the vulgar masses moral. Common people had religion; the educated knew its true essence—ethics.[2]

Not everyone welcomed the divorce between God and ethics. Wesley certainly did not. If the options were Locke or Hume, Wesley sided with Locke. But those were not the only options. Wesley accepted one role for God still permitted in the eighteenth century: God as the final judge who insures the link between utility and moral approval or disapproval. But Wesley also drew on a more ancient tradition that related God and the good more decisively. This is the tradition of moral theology, a tradition Thomas Aquinas definitively shaped.

"Moral theology" contrasts well with a modern ethics based on scientific principles. Whereas modern ethics depends on the divorce between theology and ethics, the tradition of moral theology assumed their identity. Nevertheless, the term itself is modern. It did not exist before the Counter-Reformation at the end of the sixteenth century, when it emerged as part of a Thomistic renaissance, which used Aquinas's theology to counter Protestant theology.[3] In this light, it is somewhat anachronistic to call Thomas Aquinas a "moral theologian" and set his work against a modern "ethics." Perhaps it would be less anachronistic to contrast scholastic theology and scientific ethics, but even that has limitations in that it is now well documented that modern scientific forms of knowledge occurred because of certain late medieval scholastic developments and not in spite of them. In other words, the passage from a medieval to a modern world involved less rupture than was once thought. Moreover, the theoretical differences between various schools of moral philosophy in the seventeenth century were not based on a scholastic versus modern distinction, but on a scholastic voluntarism as opposed to a more Thomistic intellectualism.[4] Modernity is a variation on scholastic voluntarism.

---

2. John Locke, *The Reasonableness of Christianity* (ed. I. T. Ramsey; Stanford, Calif.: Stanford University Press, 1958), 60-61.

3. John Mahoney, *The Making of Moral Theology: A Study of the Roman Catholic Tradition* (Oxford: Clarendon Press, 1987), viii.

4. See Norman Fiering, *Moral Philosophy at Seventeenth-Century Harvard: A Discipline in Transition* (Chapel Hill: University of North Carolina Press, 1981), see esp. 91.

LIBERTY OF INDIFFERENCE

Scholastic voluntarism led to modernist forms of thought centered on the arbitrary power of the will, giving rise to modern political, market, and educational institutions where the will and its preferences rather than truth or goodness establish social bonds. A central issue in the transition to these modern institutions was whether one thought of the will as rational appetite, as did Aquinas, or whether one followed Scotus and Suarez and thought of the will in terms of a "liberty of indifference." Is the "will" a reasonable desire led by a true understanding, or is it a faculty, a bare power of choice independent of the understanding?

We do not know how thoroughly acquainted John Wesley was with this important debate, but it was present in the sources he read, especially in the work of John Norris and Ralph Cudworth. And, as will be shown, Wesley insisted that clergy should be knowledgeable of the metaphysical thought of Aquinas and Scotus as well as Malebranche and Clarke. Would he advocate this for others if he himself were not cognizant of these debates? His father, Samuel, must have been acquainted with these arguments for he tells us in verse that he studied Suarez under Charles Morton, whose influence as a moral philosopher was significant both in England and in the newly emerging United States.[5]

Morton associated the liberty of indifference with popery and Arminianism. He contrasted this with his own Reformed position, which referred to the will as "rational spontaneity." Liberty of indifference is based upon a teaching by Duns Scotus concerning the case of Buridan's ass. Buridan's ass was placed between two bales of hay, each at equal distance. Because there was no reason for the ass to choose one bale of hay over the other, the ass was incapable of decision. It lacked a freedom of will that would allow it to choose when there was no necessity to do so, when the understanding provided no truthful judgment that one choice was better than another. Scotus argued that humans could make a decision in this case because they possessed an arbitrary power of free will, a liberty of indifference, which beasts did not.[6]

This famous case led to the development of a scholastic voluntarism that rejected the Thomistic assumption that the will is rational desire. The latter, building on Aristotelianism, found that "will" names the reality whereby a moral agent follows the last dictate of practical reason. The will was not a faculty waiting to be actualized through choice, it was a reasonable desire ordered to truth and moved by goodness. Without this ordered movement of truth and goodness there could be no desire and

---

5. Ibid., 214.
6. Ibid., 114.

thus no will. But if the will followed the last dictate in a strict syllogistic form, how could we be genuinely free to choose one thing rather than another especially when there was no compelling reason to do so? Would not the truth of the last dictate compel obedience? How then could the will be free?

Morton understood popery and Arminianism as a form of scholastic voluntarism. His Reformed "rational spontaneity" rejected a position similar to Thomism and developed in late scholasticism, which allowed for a distinction between the specification and the exercise of the will. For Aquinas the will cannot be *specified* by evil, otherwise it would be irrational and not bound to the good and the true. Nevertheless the will can *exercise* its activity such that it is ordered toward that which is less than good, which is evil. As *rational* desire, the will participates in God's good order such that it can only—of necessity—be specified by an apparent good. Only the good specifies the will, but in its exercise the will has the power to suspend judgment. So in its exercise, although not its specification, the will could suspend the natural movement toward the good or cease to will against evil.

As David Gallagher explains it, the exercise of the will "refers to the fact that a power is actually eliciting an act." This exercise simply means that the will is willing. This is a power in the agent. However, the specification of the will "refers to the act's being directed to one object or another." The intellect orders the will toward such an object. The object gives an action its specification. But this does not produce determinism where the exercise of the will is necessitated by its specification. The purpose of distinguishing exercise from specification is to insure the voluntary nature of human action. Gallagher explains how this occurs in Aquinas:

> Is there any act that the will must necessarily exercise? To this, Thomas says no. It may seem that for a given object, there must necessarily be some act either toward or away from it, and, in this sense, the will must exercise its act. But since the will's act depends upon the intellect's presentation of the object, and because the will can command the act of the intellect, it is possible, for any given proposed act, simply to will to cease thinking about the object and so to obviate all acts in its regard.[7]

It is important to recognize that for Aquinas the specification and exercise of the will are not two distinct acts, they are parts of the same act. But it is the will's exercise that allows for the possibility of evil. This preserves

---

7. David Gallagher, "The Will and Its Acts," in *The Ethics of Aquinas* (ed. Stephen Pope; Moral Traditions Series, ed. James F. Keenan; Washington, D.C.: Georgetown University Press, 2002), 75-76.

the goodness of God's created order and allows him to speak of evil as a function of human willing and not as a consequence of the ontological conditions of human existence. In late scholastic moral theology, the will's specification and exercise become distinct acts. Late scholastic voluntarists emphasize the latter, which is a power of the agent to will or not to will. This arbitrary power of the will, the "liberty of contradiction" or "suspension of exercise," becomes a bare power not to be moved by the truth of objects, which is the liberty of indifference.

This emphasis on a liberty of indifference provides the basis for the modern notion of the freedom of the will, which John Locke developed and to which John Wesley appeals whenever he explains anthropology. Thus the debate over moral agency in the seventeenth and eighteenth centuries is not simply scholasticism versus modernism. It is better characterized by a scholastic and modern voluntarism versus a scholastic and modern intellectualism. The former leads to empiricism, the latter to the philosophy known as Cambridge Platonism.

Locke's empiricism rejected innate ideas; knowledge is not recollection of what we already have. Instead knowledge results from "searching and casting about."[8] Understanding begins from "sensation" when the mind perceives the qualities from bodies.[9] Precisely because the will is not moved of necessity by innate ideas, its power is to "order the consideration of any *Idea*, or the forbearing to consider it."[10] The will is not free per se for Locke. The will is nothing but a power or ability to choose. But Locke posited a faculty of the soul antecedent to will that he called "liberty." The will is a power of motion. Liberty comes even before this. It is the condition for the possibility of moving or not moving at all. As Locke puts it, *"Liberty* . . . is the power a Man has to do or forbear doing any particular Action, according as its doing or forbearance has the actual preference in the Mind, which is the same thing as to say, according as he himself *wills* it."[11]

If the will is drawn into some motion by the consideration of ideas, it is not yet free. It is only free if a power of liberty precedes this motion so that at any moment the agent has the freedom to act or not to act. This locates freedom at a different place in practical reasoning than in Aquinas. For him freedom occurs within the context of a truth always already intuited by the intellect. Freedom was not more basic than truth. Locke's position necessitates a certain detachment of the agent from the workings of will and intellect. Our liberty always stands outside any attachment to the true

---

8. John Locke, *An Essay concerning Human Understanding* (ed. Peter H. Nidditch; Oxford: Clarendon Press, 1975), 50-52.
9. Ibid., 105, 137.
10. Ibid., 236.
11. Ibid., 241.

and the good. They no longer specify the will's movement. Instead an antecedent power called "liberty" moves the will.

The Christian Platonism of persons like Norris, Malebranche, and Cudworth also rejected innate ideas but they maintained a more traditional rendering of practical reason. Their "intellectualism" did not set forth understanding as recollection of something everyone already possessed. Nor did it posit an unmediated intuitionism. Nor did they argue that knowledge arose from experience of objects through sensation, first perceived by the understanding. Knowledge emerged from "ideas" that were not innate but were primarily in the mind of God. Only as we participate in God's mind can we gain understanding. Such participation only occurs christologically. But this understanding required "illumination." This maintained a more traditional rendering of practical reasoning because here the good is not to be achieved primarily by a foundational liberty that chooses for it and can always also choose against it. Instead the will pursues the good only as the understanding discovers, or is discovered by, truth.

The division between voluntarism and intellectualism appears to lead to empiricism and Christian Platonism. As true as this is, even here the division should not be too thoroughly drawn. Hume cited Malebranche more than any other person in his *Treatise of Human Nature*, even though he sought to establish empiricism as the ground for all our perceptions. But Malebranche's work was also significant for the development of Cambridge Platonism against empiricist trends. Wesley inherited both traditions. His anthropology referred to "liberty of indifference," and his theology resembled Cambridge Platonism with its doctrine of illumination grounded in Christology and Trinity.[12] He quoted the Thomistic thesis "there is nothing in the understanding that is not first in the senses" and also argued for the necessity of participation and illumination to understand anything well.

This only surprises us if we assume we must choose between empiricism and intuitionism. That is a modern division Wesley could not have known. Aquinas himself held to an "empiricist" (note the scare quotes) account of knowledge coupled with the insistence that we only know because our mind participates in the Ideas in the mind of God. Nevertheless Wesley is on the border of being a modern theologian, or to be more precise, Wesley inherited trends in scholastic voluntarism. However Samuel Wesley, under the tutelage of Morton, would have been taught to reject this liberty of indifference in favor of Morton's "rational spontaneity." This was more similar to Thomism and Aristotelianism, for Morton taught that the will followed the last dictate of practical reasoning—but spontaneously, not of necessity. The will spontaneously

---

12. The seal of Oxford University says, "*Dominus illuminatio mea*" ("Lord illumine me").

obeyed the dictate on rational grounds. Thus the will did not act arbitrarily based on a power of indifference even if it neither acted of necessity.[13]

WHAT MORAL PHILOSOPHY DID WESLEY KNOW?

Did Wesley know the debates concerning scholastic voluntarism, the liberty of indifference, rational spontaneity, and a more intellectualist Thomist and Aristotelian account of the will? Did John Wesley know the influential work of Charles Morton, his father's teacher? He does not make any specific reference to Morton, but shows some awareness of these important issues, albeit not always to his credit. In fact, he defends a kind of scholastic voluntarism that uses the same terms of the debate that Charles Morton rejected, a "liberty of contradiction." In setting forth his anthropology Wesley wrote,

> I am conscious to myself of one more property [of soul], commonly called *liberty*. This is very frequently confounded with the *will*, but is of a very different nature. Neither is it a property of the will, but a distinct property of the soul, capable of being exerted with regard to all the faculties of the soul, as well as all the motions of the body. It is a power of self-determination which, although it does not extend to all our thoughts and imaginations, yet extends to our words and actions in general, and not with many exceptions. I am full as certain of this, that I am free with respect to these, to speak or not to speak, to act or not to act, to do this or the contrary, as I am of my own existence. I have not only what is termed a "liberty of contradiction," a power to do or not to do, but what is termed a "liberty of contrariety," a power to act one way or the contrary. . . . And although I have not an absolute power over my own mind, because of the corruption of my nature, *yet through the grace of God assisting me I have a power to choose and do good as well as evil.* I am free to choose whom I will serve, and if I choose the better part, to continue therein even unto death.[14]

Both Samuel Clarke and John Locke talk about an aspect of the soul that they call "liberty." They describe this faculty as more basic than the will. Not surprisingly, we also find in Wesley's thought a strain of this same scholastic voluntarism in his description of the soul. His use of it is both confused and deleterious. It is confused because he suggests that freedom is both a natural faculty of the soul and a result of God's grace.

---

13. Fiering, *Moral Philosophy*, 234.

14. Sermon 116, "What is Man?" §11, *Works* 4:23-24 (italics added). The difference between a liberty of contradiction and contrariety comes from Gerard Langbaine's *Philosophiae moralis compendium*, 24. He uses it to distinguish the specification and exercise of an act according to the scholastics' terminology.

But as his sermon "On Conscience" shows, this is an interesting confusion.[15] Wesley rejected the common position of someone like Butler to make natural conscience itself the universal basis for morality. Conscience was not conscience without grace, and thus it required revelation from Word and sacrament, for that is how grace is mediated in Wesley precisely because he adheres to the claim that there is nothing in the intellect that is not first in the senses.

Although the confusion is interesting, this anthropology is also theologically harmful. In this quote God's grace gives us a freedom of indifference, including a power to work evil. How can God's grace be the cause for evil? Surely Wesley did not intend to suggest such a thing, but his own language suggests this (see italics in quotation). It betrays a nominalism at work in his theology, which is worse than Pelagianism; it is the beginnings of the modern will to power with its assumption that if the will is to be truly free it must be capable of a radical evil. It is evidence that Wesley simply did not see the serious problems he introduced into theology even if he rightly deplored their consequences. This is also why Methodists must do as Wesley said and not always as he did. We must draw on the broader theological sources of the catholic church, without which we will quickly deteriorate into the worst form of sectarianism. Wesley alone can never give us our theological compass.

Wesley also stated that the study of these questions—questions of metaphysics and natural philosophy—were essential for the clergy. In his 1756 "Address to the Clergy" he noted nine acquired endowments that would lead to a competent share of knowledge for the clergy.[16] The fifth such endowment was "some knowledge of the sciences," which he divided into logic, metaphysics, and natural philosophy. Metaphysics was the second part of logic. It was not necessary for the clergy but "highly expedient" for two reasons. First, "In order to clear our apprehension, (without which it is impossible either to judge correctly, or to reason closely or conclusively,) by ranging our ideas under general heads." Second, "In order to understand many useful writers, who can very hardly be understood without it."[17] Wesley then encourages the clergy to question their own competence in metaphysics by asking,

> Do I understand metaphysics; if not the depths of the Schoolmen, the subtleties of Scotus or Aquinas, yet the first rudiments, the general principles, of that useful science? Have I conquered so much of it, as to clear my apprehension and range my ideas under proper heads; so much as

---

15. See Sermon 105, "On Conscience," *Works* 3:480-90.

16. I am indebted to Kenneth Oakes, "Temporality as Rupture & Remainder: Wesley, Pinnock, and St. Thomas," *Wesleyan Theological Journal* (forthcoming 2004) for directing my attention to this address and its significance.

17. "Address to the Clergy," §I.2, *Works* (Jackson) 10:483.

enables me to read with ease and pleasure, as well as profit, Dr. Henry More's Works, Malebranche's "Search after Truth," and Dr. Clarke's "Demonstration of the Being and Attributes of God?" Do I understand natural philosophy?[18]

Wesley claimed the works of Aquinas, Scotus, Malebranche, More, and Clarke were highly expedient for the clergy. But he himself never placed these persons nor their ideas "under general heads" or presented a "clear apprehension" of their basic ideas. We can certainly find evidence that he assumed their arguments throughout his work, but not that he did so with the care that he charged the clergy with doing in his address to them. Once again, we must do as Wesley said and not necessarily as he did.

In fact, Wesley adopted a variety of positions from these various schools that appear from our vantage point at the end of modernity as contradictory. He did not seem to be aware of the significant differences between these thinkers. I think there are three reasons for this. First, Wesley lived through these debates, which began in the seventeenth and continued into the eighteenth century. The positions may not have been as clearly discernible in the midst of the discussion as they may appear to be now, although even now it is difficult if not impossible to trace clear lines of similarity and difference among the competing schools. Second, Wesley would not have had access to the materials we do in order to sort through these various positions. Third, despite his counsel to others, Wesley was not an attentive philosopher. He did not examine his sources carefully. And this does not make him a pragmatist, it makes him on occasion careless in the use of his sources.

Nevertheless, Wesley's focus on the sacraments, the common confession of the church, and the discipline of the General Rules allowed him to receive these various sources better than his philosophical skills would have otherwise allowed him to do. Wesley was not a profound philosopher, but he was a faithful church theologian. He received these sources within the context of the church's tradition and that gave him a richer context than he would have had if he only received these works through his own philosophical skills. He did not need to receive them in an architectonic system with a well-established epistemology because he still had a world oriented by the church's practices.

---

18. Ibid., §II.1.(5), 10:492. For Wesley natural philosophy treats of two topics: God and creatures, or invisible and visible beings. Natural philosophy originated with Aristotle and was preserved by Arabian philosophers. However, for Wesley, natural philosophy transgresses when it seeks knowledge of God and invisible beings.

After discussing the usefulness of natural philosophy to explain visible, creaturely beings, Wesley wrote in his essay "Of the Gradual Improvement of Natural Philosophy" (§24, *Works* [Jackson] 13:487):

> What remains of natural philosophy is, the doctrine concerning God and spirits. But in the tracing of this we can neither depend upon reason nor experiment. Whatsoever men know or can know concerning them, must be drawn from the oracles of God. Here, therefore, we are to look for no new improvements; but to stand in the good old paths; to content ourselves with what God has been pleased to reveal.

If Wesley were aware of the debates between scholastic voluntarism and the intellectualist school, he did not always enter into them well. He had to know something of these debates. His Oxford diary lists the authors Langbaine, More, and Eustachius for his study of "ethics."[19] He also regularly read the work of John Norris. These seventeenth-century philosophers intentionally developed ethics grounded in "heathen" virtue. Wesley knew at least the moral philosophy of Langbaine, who followed Aquinas and Aristotle, and Eustachius, who followed Suarez. He also studied and advocated aspects of the peculiar Platonism of Henry More's ethics, as well as the Thomism of John Norris. In what follows I will lay out the basic moral philosophy of Langbaine, More, and Norris in order to place Wesley's work in the context of discussions about the relationship between God and the good of which we can be assured he had some knowledge.

Gerard Langbaine

Wesley certainly knew some Aristotelian moral philosophy. He tutored students using Gerard Langbaine's *Philosophiae Moralis Compendium, Juventutis Academicae Studiis*. Langbaine's work is a brief commentary on Aristotle's *Nicomachean Ethics*. He noted in his preface that he is indebted to Aristotle above all other thinkers for his moral philosophy.[20] He divides philosophy into two parts: *instrumentalis* and *principalis*. The first investigates ideas more so than cognition of things and is thus concerned with logic. In other words, it does not need to refer to any particular thing. The second examines the cognition of things. There are two parts to this: a speculative and a practical investigation. Speculative *principalis* is concerned with physics, metaphysics, and mathematics. Practical *principalis* is more properly called "ethics" and is examined under either *poesis* or *praxis*. The former examines the good as it inheres itself in the effect of a thing, and thus examines *effectionem*. The latter examines the good not so much in itself but from the operation of *animus agentis*. Thus the good is not simply an aesthetic category that inheres in things, it is also a practical activity which is contingent on human action. This practical philosophy has three subsets: ethics, politics, and economics. Ethics is the activity of acquiring happiness. Politics is the activity of acquiring public happiness and economics is concerned with the family. Thus the "ethics" Wesley knew and taught fit within a medieval framework that looked like this:

19. This was confirmed to me by Richard Heitzenrater in correspondence dated October 5, 2002.

20. *"cui pro veritate tam pertinaciter adhaereo et debeo"* ("to whom for the truth one adheres tenaciously and is indebted," AT) in Langbaine, "Praefatio," *Philosophiae Moralis Compendium* (London: Richard Sare, 1698), 2. (The pages of the preface are unnumbered.)

Instrumental Philosophy (Logic)
Principal (First) Philosophy
Speculative Principal Philosophy (physics, metaphysics,
    mathematics)
Practical Principal Philosophy
Poesis
Praxis (ethics, politics, economics)

It is worth noting that *politics* is not here what it is for Hobbes and Locke. It is not an autonomous discipline ruled by power and interests. It is a subset of practical philosophy understood as the pursuit of happiness. All the pieces to this framework assume the others. That Wesley assumed something like this framework in his own moral theology can be seen by his consistent criticism that Locke neither understood nor adequately developed logic. As we shall see, Wesley assumed that one must know the essence of something, insofar as it could be known, in order to know its practical significance. This should be kept in mind when we pose the question in the last chapter of whether Wesley had a "political" ethic. "Politics" for him was unthinkable without first recognizing our teleological ordering toward happiness.

Wesley knew and used Langbaine's work to instruct others in ethics. How he used it, and whether it influenced him, requires careful attention because there are no explicit references to Langbaine in Wesley's published sermons. But this is not surprising, for Langbaine's work is a basic textbook of Aristotle's ethics for youth. The question is whether the ideas contained in this basic ethics textbook influenced Wesley. An answer requires outlining Langbaine's Aristotelian moral philosophy and noting connections to Wesley.

After laying out his philosophical division and locating the subject matter of ethics, Langbaine discusses the good. Quoting Aristotle, he defines the good as *"quod omnia appetunt"* (what everyone desires).[21] If this is the good, then there can be no liberty of indifference. We are never indifferent in our desires but always desire under the category of the good. The good may be only an apparent good, but without the good there is neither will nor desire. Inasmuch as Wesley adopted the liberty of contrariety (following Scotus and Locke) he rejected the Aristotelian and Thomist assumption that the will is rational desire. However, for Langbaine, like Aristotle, Aquinas, and Wesley, the highest good is happiness. Early in his career Wesley stated that the true Christian life, grounded in love, would bring happiness in God. The significant question for him was, "Are you

---

21. Ibid., 6.

happy in God? Is he your glory, your delight, your crown of rejoicing?"[22] This is a consistent Aristotelian-Thomistic theme throughout his work. It is the heart of the Christian moral life. In 1789 he was setting forth the same position, "as there is one God, so there is one religion and one happiness for all men."[23] Wesley clearly follows the tradition of moral theology in that all human action takes place under a common telos: the desire for happiness. This is the good. He sides with Aquinas against Aristotle in finding that common telos to be our participation in God. Holiness and happiness go together. In spite of efforts to make John Wesley an *agape* deontologist, he was without a doubt a teleological thinker.[24]

Wesley did not necessarily learn this from Langbaine, for such teleological thinking was common prior to the divorce between theology and ethics in the eighteenth century. Langbaine simply gives a classic Aristotelian-Thomistic presentation of it. He notes that there is the good as an end and the good as a medium to an end. Following Aristotle closely, Langbaine argues that there is also a *summum bonum* (highest good). It is that under which all human action occurs. He inquires in what it consists, mentioning the same possibilities Aristotle raised—wealth, honor, pleasure, the contemplative life. He concludes like Aristotle that it is "happiness."

Here happiness is not quantifiable pleasure, as it will become with the utilitarians. It is a supravalent good under which all human action proceeds. Thus it entails the notion of the will as rational desire. The will does not stand continually naked between arbitrary decisions in some complete realm of freedom; it is always already ordered to a reasonable good. The will cannot be other than this for it is not an interior "faculty"; it is desire, which is always for some "thing." Wesley clearly thought of the moral life in terms of happiness in this sense, and not as a utilitarian. But thinking of the moral life in this sense conflicts with his anthropology grounded in a liberty of indifference. For the latter does not need to conceive of the will as desire. In fact, with the latter, the will is grounded in a neutral, objective faculty called "liberty," which is a power always to suspend judgment and act in a way other than a practical judgment would entail.

Wesley was attracted to this "liberty" for good reason. Both Hobbes and Spinoza were interpreted by Wesley's favorite thinkers as offering a complete determinism that refused to recognize the distinction between soul and matter. This distinction allowed for a human being to be a self-moving agent, for if matter were all there was then determinism naturally

---

22. Sermon 2, "The Almost Christian," §II.9, *Works* 1:141.
23. Sermon 120, "The Unity of the Divine Being," §1, *Works* 4:61.
24. See Ron Stone's *John Wesley's Life & Ethics* (Nashville: Abingdon, 2001), 215.

followed. Samuel Clarke defended "liberty" against Hobbes and Spinoza on the basis that they made thinking and willing mere "effects and compositions of figure and motion." Clarke stated that Locke also made "thinking to be an affection of matter." Against these materialists Clarke advocated the kind of liberty of indifference we saw in Wesley (and in Locke as well). For Clarke, both God and human agents always have a liberty to act one way or another—the liberty of contrariety. Clarke states that the essence of liberty is "having a continual power of choosing whether he shall act or whether he shall forbear [from] acting."[25] This creates two difficulties in Clarke's metaphysics; difficulties we also find in Wesley. First, he must distinguish between God's metaphysical and moral attributes. The former have a necessity to them: God cannot be other than God. But for God to be a moral agent, God must also always have a power of choice to be or act other than God has chosen or acted.[26] This forces Clarke to posit (in nominalist fashion) an absolute power behind God's ordained power. It also requires that he reject an understanding of the will as rational desire.[27]

Clarke explicitly rejected the argument for "the necessity of the will's being determined by the last judgment of the understanding."[28] For the sake of a liberty that could oppose Hobbes, Spinoza, and Locke, he rejects the Aristotelian-Thomist synthesis and posits liberty as more basic to the will than thinking of it under the natural desire for the good that brings happiness. He does not seem to take seriously the alternative position, like one finds in Norris and Cudworth, where the will has an intellectualist orientation that does not entail determinism. This recognizes a convergence between Aristotelianism and Platonism, a convergence that Aquinas already made.

Langbaine is more of an Aristotelian than Wesley in that Langbaine separated rather decisively Aristotelianism and Platonism/Cartesianism. Langbaine states that the *summum bonum* does not consist in the "bare naked idea of the good as in Plato nor in virtue before its habituation as the Stoics suggested," nor Descartes' notion of virtue as seen.[29] The latter is quite interesting, for we know that Wesley was well acquainted with

---

25. Samuel Clarke, *A Demonstration of the Being and Attributes of God* (ed. Ezio Vailati; Cambridge Texts in the History of Philosophy, ed. Karl Ameriks and Desmond M. Clarke; Cambridge: Cambridge University Press, 1998), 74.

26. Clarke writes, "God is, by necessity of nature, a free agent, and he can no more possibly cease to be so than he can cease to exist. He must of necessity every moment, either choose to act or choose to forbear [from] acting because two contradictories cannot possibly be true at once" (ibid., 75).

27. See ibid., 72-75.

28. Ibid., 73.

29. Langbaine, *Philosophiae Moralis Compendium*, 8-12 (AT). For how closely Langbaine is following Aristotle, see *Nicomachean Ethics*, 1094b to 1096a.

the work of John Norris, who presented Malebranche's Cartesianism to the English-speaking world. As we shall see, this mixture of Cartesianism, Platonism, and an Augustinian theory of illumination had tremendous influence on Wesley's work that is in tension with his emphasis on a liberty of indifference.

The Christian Platonism is much more determinative than any specific incorporation of Eastern Orthodox thought in Wesley's work. Wesley's doctrine of deification and metaphysics of participation are present in the Platonic/Cartesian sources prominent in the eighteenth century, which we know he read. Specific references to it are readily found. However, Langbaine's ethics sets an Aristotelian account of the good against a Platonist and Cartesian one and suggests that the good is not to be found in any vision of it as an "idea" but in the practical activity that leads to happiness. Wesley's moral theology is a combination of Aristotelianism and the Christianized Platonism/Cartesianism that emerged from persons like More, Malebranche, Norris, and Cudworth. The "idea" of the good and practical activity are not set in opposition.

Having identified happiness as the *summum bonum*, Langbaine then explains virtue by giving Aristotle's definition: "*Operatio animae rationalis secundum optimam et perfectissimam virtutem, in vita perfecta*" (an activity of the rational soul according to the best and most perfect excellence in a perfected life).[30] Like Aristotle, Langbaine's definition of virtue assumes that it "renders good the thing itself of which it is the excellence and causes it to perform its function well."[31] In other words, virtue assumes a capacity for an activity that allows a person to fulfill his or her proper function *(ergon)* in life. The fact that Wesley links happiness and holiness as the proper end of the Christian moral life reflects this Aristotelian understanding of virtue.

Langbaine then explains the principles of human action and how they contribute to virtue. The first principle of human action is the intellect, which has a speculative and practical component. He discusses will, the sensible appetite, and the affections. Throughout his discussion he moves from Aristotle to Aquinas. He develops Aquinas's teaching on the passions of the concupiscible and irascible appetites, listing them approximately as they appear in the *prima secundae* of *Summa Theologica*. He lays out six passions of the concupiscible appetite: *amor, odium, fuga, desiderium, gaudium, dolor*. He then presents five passions of the irascible appetite: *spes, desperatio, timor, audacia, ira*.[32] He then presents the virtues proper, beginning with prudence, which is the intellectual virtue that is

---

30. Langbaine, *Philosophiae Moralis Compendium*, 13; see *Nicomachean Ethics*, 1106a 15-18.

31. Aristotle, *Nicomachean Ethics* (trans. Martin Ostwald; Indianapolis: Bobbs-Merrill/ Library of Liberal Arts, 1962), 41.

32. Langbaine, *Philosophiae Moralis Compendium*, 27.

also "necessarily connected to the moral virtues."[33] Prudence is the only intellectual virtue Langbaine discusses. After discussing the passions, he moves on to the moral virtues. The first one he discusses is piety. It is discussed first because it is a virtue directed primarily to God. It is related internally (to the soul) through the passions of love and fear, and externally (to the body) through prayer and acts of thanksgiving. Its excess is superstition and its defects are the indecorum of fanatical schisms and impiety such as atheism.[34]

The centrality of the virtues of piety and devotion is commonplace in the sources Wesley read, as we shall see in Norris. It is precisely what prevents the divorce of theology from ethics. All the practical virtues emerge from the duty of piety. Without fulfilling our obligation to God, we cannot fulfill our obligation to neighbor. This is also evidence of the ancient tradition of moral theology where the two tables of the Ten Commandments were correlated with specific virtues, gifts, and beatitudes. When Wesley challenges the modern ethics of Rousseau, Hume, and Voltaire, he does so by appealing to this older tradition. Wesley wrote that they sought to ground ethics in "'humanity,' 'virtue,' 'morality,' or what you please." But in doing so they severed theology and ethics. "Men hereby wilfully and designedly put asunder what God has joined, the duties of the first and the second table."[35] Knowledge of God and knowledge of ethics, love of God and love of neighbor, are wedded together in Wesley, and divorce is impossible. This flies in the face of nearly every significant moral philosophical movement in the eighteenth century, except certain forms of Cambridge Platonism.

Langbaine then develops the virtues *ad hominem*, which come under the genus of "probity." There are twelve such virtues: prudence, courage, temperance, justice, liberality, magnificence, magnanimity, modesty, gentleness *(mansuetudo)*, truth, mildness *(lenitas)*, and urbanity or civility. This is followed by a lengthy discussion of justice and then mention is made of the heroic virtues as well as the intellectual virtues. Langbain's work concludes with an index that outlines the various virtues.

Wesley knew and used Langbaine's work. It was a common presentation of the moral life and would have been noncontroversial. Many of these virtues can be found in Wesley's work, and he never attacked them or this language as a "pagan" morality that keeps one from faithfulness, as Luther did. Luther wrote, "Then there is [Aristotle's] 'Ethics,' . . . which is accounted one of the best, but no book is more directly contrary to God's will and the Christian virtues. Oh, that such books could be kept

---

33. Ibid., 45.
34. Ibid., 52-53.
35. Sermon 120, "The Unity of the Divine Being," §20, *Works* 4:69.

51

out of the reach of all Christians!"[36] Wesley could state, "Some great truths, as the being and attributes of God, and the difference between moral good and evil, were known in some measure to the heathen world; the traces of them are to be found in all nations." However, all such heathen virtue was still short of true virtue because it lacked two crucial elements. First it was unaware that the eternal Son of God was the propitiation for sin. Second that the Spirit of God worked to renew us in the image of God.[37] This reveals two Thomistic themes in Wesley's work that are interwoven: (1) grace perfects nature, and (2) the moral life cannot be adequately understood without the doctrine of the Trinity. "Nature" was part of God's good created order, even though Wesley fully embraced the doctrine of total depravity. "Nature" bore the image of God when it was restored by grace. Grace made a proper understanding of nature possible. For this reason, Wesley consistently links a right understanding of the moral life with a right understanding of the doctrine of the Trinity. In the light of the latter the former becomes intelligible.

Henry More

More so than Langbaine, Henry More drew on "heathen" morality. Benjamin Tooke's introduction to More's work states, "he did purposely meditate how to expose, to the Eyes of the Christian World, What a holy and sanctifi'd sense of Virtue even the Heathens had. . . . For (alas) we of this Age, scorn to be subject, either to the Name or Exercise of Virtue."[38] Although More and Norris are indebted to an Augustinian theory of illumination for human knowledge, neither follows Augustine in finding pagan virtues to be "splendid vices" (nor did Augustine himself).

More's ethics divides into two parts. The first part is "knowledge of happiness" and the second is the "acquisition of it."[39] He draws explicitly on Aristotle in his development of happiness, which More associated with pleasure, albeit the higher pleasures, as the utilitarians will do. Happiness is "that pleasure which the mind takes in from a sense of virtue and a conscience of well-doing and of conforming in all things to the rules of both."[40] More allows a significant place for pleasure in the moral life; we take pleasure in the exercise of virtue. But this poses the same problems to More that it will pose to the utilitarians. If morality is grounded in happiness

---

36. As quoted in Fiering, *Moral Philosophy*, 10.
37. Sermon 85, "On Working Out Our Own Salvation," §§1-2, *Works* 3:199-200.
38. Henry More, *An Account of Virtue: or, Dr. Henry More's Abridgment of Morals put into English* (London: Benjamin Tooke, 1690). See More's "Epistle to His Reader," 6. (The pages of the epistle are unnumbered.)
39. Ibid., 3.
40. Ibid., 4.

as pleasure, why is it that the baser pleasures, which appear strong and instinctual, are not worthy of pursuit? This question was answered theologically in Wesley and Aquinas. More answers it similarly, but by positing a *"Boniform Faculty of the Soul,"* which is "of that divine Composition and supernatural Texture, as enables us to distinguish not only what is simply and absolutely the best, but to relish it, and to have pleasure in that alone."[41] This boniform faculty is an oddity in moral philosophy—an invention of More, by which he explains why it is we find pleasure in virtue rather than vice. Drawing upon Plotinus, More argues that the life of virtue helps one "behold the Beauties" and thus produces "Joys that cannot be uttered." The result is a *"Blessed Disposition of the Soul."*[42]

Having explained where virtue is and what it produces, More then defines it: "Virtue *is an intellectual Power of the Soul, by which it over-rules the animal Impressions or bodily Passions; so as in every Action it easily pursues what is absolutely and simply the best."*[43] For More it is important to distinguish virtue as an intellectual power from virtue as a habit because virtue is the internal cause that makes the essence of a thing, and not its external cause as habit would be. Therefore virtue is located in an intellectual power of the soul, which should be called *"the very Eye of the Soul."*[44]

Here we see a common seventeenth- and eighteenth-century concern against using the term *habit* to explain virtue. *Habitus* had already lost its more Greek notion of "character" and become something laboriously routine. The moral life could not consist simply of such habits, for they are not necessarily meritorious. They are external matters about which one might be compelled. Virtue becomes separated from habituation and becomes intellectualized in More. This leads to a peculiar doctrine of illumination and to a rigid internal/external distinction. It is not in the external exercise of the good that virtue consists, but in an inner disposition found in the soul. Wesley clearly inherits this external/internal distinction. He can speak of a "spiritual sense," quite similar to More's boniform faculty, which works "inwardly."[45] But he can also insist on external actions as necessary for the cultivation of a proper inward disposition. This is why he speaks of the "duty of constant communion." Whether or not one is inclined or disposed to regular communication at the Lord's table, Wesley counseled each of the Methodists to "obey God and consult the good of his own soul by communicating every time he can; like the first Christians, with whom the Christian sacrifice was a constant part of

41. Ibid., 6
42. Ibid., 9.
43. Ibid., 11.
44. Ibid., 14.
45. Sermon 45, "The New Birth," §II.4, *Works* 2:193.

the Lord's day's service. And for several centuries they received it almost every day." Without this, he argued, a Christian has no piety.[46] Wesley suggests, contra More, that the external practice of daily communion will both strengthen and be a sign of the virtue of piety. Wesley was not finally able to separate the external and the internal. Here is where he resists the acids of modernity most effectively.

More's Platonism is found in his metaphysics of participation, which is essential for true virtue. Because virtue is an intellectual power in the boniform faculty of the soul that pursues the simply and absolutely best in every action, the human agent must participate in the divine mind in order to know what the best is. This participation occurs through right reason. More wrote, "For *Right Reason, which is in Man, is a sort of Copy or Transcript of that Reason or Law eternal which is registred in the Mind Divine*."[47] Wesley's work is replete with the language of "copy" and "transcript." For him, these terms are almost always used for the Trinitarian procession of the Son from the Father. More hints that this "right reason" has a christological determination, but never says it quite as directly as does Malebranche, Norris, Cudworth, and Wesley. More calls right reason the "Interpreter between God and Man."[48] In other words, for More our mind already participates through reason in the divine mind. This is not a function of practice or habituation, but is natural. Our mind shares in the ideas of the divine mind only mediated by reason. It seems to be an immediate participation we possess through creation. It is not mediated to us, nor is it discursive as it will be for Wesley.

Wesley develops a similar interpretation of eternal law in his "Original, Nature, Properties, and Use of the Law." Eternal law is the "right reason" upon which Christianity is based. But Wesley gives it a christological interpretation that requires a practical mediation of this law through Christ's flesh for us to participate in it. He explains the use of the law by Paul in Romans 7:12 in language strikingly similar to More's "right reason":

> Now this law is an incorruptible picture of the high and holy One that inhabiteth eternity. It is he whom in his essence no man hath seen or can see, made visible to men and angels. It is the face of God unveiled; God manifested to his creatures as they are able to bear it; manifested to give and not to destroy life; that they may see God and live. It is the heart of God disclosed to man. Yea, in some sense we may apply to this law what the Apostle says of his Son—it is "the streaming forth" or outbeaming "of his glory, the express image of his person."

---

46. Sermon 101, "The Duty of Constant Communion,"§1.4, *Works* 3:430; cf. §II.4, 432.
47. More, *Account of Virtue*, 15.
48. Ibid., 14.

> ... The law of God is all virtues in one, in such a shape as to be beheld with open face by all those whose eyes God hath enlightened. What is the law but divine virtue and wisdom assuming a visible form? What is it but the original ideas of truth and good, which were lodged in the uncreated mind from eternity, now drawn forth and clothed with such a vehicle as to appear even to human understanding?
>
> ... The law of God (speaking after the manner of men) is a copy of the eternal mind, a transcript of the divine nature; yea, it is the fairest offspring of the everlasting Father, the brightest efflux of his essential wisdom, the visible beauty of the Most High.[49]

After what "manner of men" is Wesley speaking in this quote if not the Christianized Platonism of More? In this intriguing quote, Wesley brings together Platonic themes, including a reference to all the transcendental predicates of being—truth, goodness, and beauty—with scriptural quotations in an explicitly christological and trinitarian framework. It represents something Wesley learned from More and other seventeenth- and eighteenth-century philosophers who were bringing together Platonism and Christianity in post-Cartesian perspective. But it also represents a specifically Christian theological rendering of their Platonism. The true, good, and beautiful are not simply to be found in a direct participation of our mind in God's mind. Instead, they are found in the visible presentation of the one who "inhabiteth eternity." They are *seen* only in their mediation in Jesus' incarnation, which is received by faith. This is not something More explicitly sets forth. However, it resembles the Platonism and Christianity in Norris, who developed Malebranche's unorthodox Cartesian philosophy for an English context.

John Norris

John Norris was not a moral philosopher, as were Langbaine and More. However, his work certainly bears the signs of the tradition of moral theology. He begins his most significant work, *Reason and Religion*, by arguing, as did Aquinas, that God is the "most *Intelligible*, as the most *Intelligent* Being in the World." In other words, God is the most knowable of all beings. God is not hidden from us, incapable of being known. God as the fullness of being is the most intelligible of all being. But this poses problems for us. In a sense, God is too knowable, for God is the brightness of light that blinds. "God is *too intelligible* to be here clearly understood by an *Imbody'd* understanding; and too great a Light hinders vision, as much

---

49. Sermon 34, "The Original, Nature, Properties, and Use of the Law," §§II.3-6, *Works* 2:9-10.

as Darkness."[50] There is then no "clear and distinct knowledge" of God precisely because God is so intelligible that our sensible forms of understanding betray us. Yet following Exodus 33, Norris writes that we can glimpse God's "back-parts" and that is sufficient for "true Piety and Devotion."[51]

Much as we saw with Langbaine, Norris finds the beginning of virtue in piety or devotion. He quotes Aquinas to define devotion. It is *"a will readily to give up ones self to all those things which belong to the Service of God."*[52] Devotion is the heart of the moral life, for it includes "faith, hope, love, fear, trust, humility, submission, honour, reverence, adoration, and thanksgiving."[53] These virtues are the duties that we owe God. They bear a striking resemblance to the list of virtues, or "holy tempers," that Wesley names throughout his work. These virtues characterize Christ's human righteousness and can become inherent in us. They are: faith, hope, love, humility, resignation, reverence, meekness, and gentleness.[54] Of course, these lists are biblical and that is the key text Norris, Wesley, and Aquinas shared.

Norris insists that we not separate knowledge and devotion, intellect and will, or reason and religion. This also entails that we should not separate doctrine and ethics. In *Reason and Religion* he holds all of these together. He writes, "But still Knowledge has a *natural* aptness to excite Devotion, and will infallibly do it if not hinder'd by some other cause." Thus, "the more knowing and considering, still the more devout."[55] The moral life (devotion) is not primarily a function of the will but of knowledge. Piety does not arise from sincerity but from truth. Norris recognizes that theology and ethics must be held together. His influence on Wesley on this point is what makes Wesley's work so important at the end of modernity. Knowledge and vital piety, reason and religion, theology and ethics, truth and goodness cannot be finally separated.

Following Nicolas de Malebranche, Norris is more than suspicious of sense knowledge, and here is where Wesley and Norris do part company somewhat, just as Malebranche parts company with Aristotle on this point. Wesley conceded with Aquinas, *"Nihil est in intellectu quod non fuit prius in sensu"* (There is nothing in the understanding which was not first perceived by some of the senses).[56] But Wesley did not celebrate this fact,

---

50. John Norris, *Reason and Religion: or, The Grounds and Measures of Devotion, Consider'd from the Nature of God, and the Nature of Man. In Several Contemplations*, 2nd ed. (London: Samuel Manship, 1693), 4-5.
51. Ibid., 6.
52. Ibid., 8.
53. Ibid., 7.
54. Sermon 20, "The Lord Our Righteousness," §II.2, *Works* 1:452-53.
55. Norris, *Reason and Religion*, 10-11.
56. Sermon 117, "On the Discoveries of Faith," §1, *Works* 4:29.

he did not put it forth positively. As it did for Aquinas, this reality posed a problem in Wesley; how can we know God, who is not an object of the bodily senses, when all our knowledge is mediated through such senses? God is not an object in the world that can be sensed. If our knowledge is first in the senses then how can we know God? Both Wesley and Aquinas taught that God could only be known through a supernatural gift. We do not have empirical knowledge of God. The empiricism that prioritizes sense-knowledge entails that knowledge of God requires something more than nature, something more than sense objects. It requires a gift of illumination.

This is why Wesley rejected innate ideas. He accused Francis Hutcheson, whose work he constantly pillories, of setting forth the position of innate ideas.[57] Wesley argued that this led to atheism, even though Wesley knew Hutcheson was no atheist. It led to atheism because it implied that humanity, as it was, contained all it needed in order to be drawn to the good. It is not idealism per se that Wesley rejected. His metaphysics of participation was a species of idealism. It is the innate character of the ideas that he rejects, for if the ideas are innate, human nature contains all it needs within itself. It does not need the supernatural gift of illumination. Like Malebranche and unlike Descartes, Wesley rejects *innate* ideas for a metaphysics of participation. Unlike Malebranche, but like Aquinas, he argues knowledge is first "sensible."

This leads Wesley's interpreters to read him as a Lockean and empiricist.[58] But to argue that there is no knowledge in the intellect, which is not first in the senses, does not commit one to an empiricism in opposition to idealism. As Aquinas held both, so did Wesley, and even Malebranche could state that we only know things because of the senses, even if objects in the world were not the efficient causes of sensation. All our knowledge was only possible because our mind participated in the ideas of God. The priority of sensible knowledge and a metaphysics of participation need not be set against each other.

For Norris sensible knowledge is primarily a source of error, for sensibility does not provide us with what really is but only "*shadows* and *phantasms*."[59] What is real are ideas, even before "natures." This leads to a Platonism that privileges essence above existence—even in God. For this reason Norris denies that God should first be defined in terms of being absolutely perfect. He does not deny that God is being absolutely perfect, but he refuses to put "being" and "perfection" terms together. Like Clarke he distinguishes too sharply between metaphysics and morals. Norris

---

57. See ibid. (with its n. 2).
58. See Outler's comment in ibid. n. 3.
59. Norris, *Reason and Religion*, 27.

writes, "Now that to be a Being absolutely perfect, is not the *first conceivable* in God; but supposes something before it in the Divine Nature, is plain from hence, because it may be proved *à priori*, or by way of a *causal dependence* from something in the same Divine Nature."[60] In other words, there must be something prior to being "absolutely perfect" for the latter is a characteristic that is virtually and potentially, but not formally and explicitly, in the notion of God. God's name as "I am" is the formal conception of God, and this is an idea of God before it is even an existence such as perfection would entail.

Norris separates God's essence and existence in order to defend a theological Platonism against an Aristotelianism. He writes,

> This must of necessity be allow'd, whatever the *Peripateticks* remonstrate to the contrary. Things must exist in *Idea* before they do in *Nature*, otherwise 'twill be impossible to give an intelligible account of the *stability of Science*, and of propositions of *Eternal* Truth. . . .
>
> And now that the Essence and Idea of God does consist in this *Being it self*, or this *Essence* of *Being*, will be further confirm'd from this Consideration, That as all other Universal Natures or Essences are nothing else . . . but the Intellect of God, which as variously imitable, or participable, exhibits all the general Orders and Natures of things; so this Being it self, or this Essence of Being, what can it be else, but the very Essence of God, containing in it the whole Plenitude and Possibility of being, all that is, or can be?[61]

But here Norris has confused categories. He is correct that when it comes to created being, essence precedes existence if we are not to posit an eternal creation. But Norris seems to say more. He suggests that even the "idea" of God must come before God as absolutely perfect, and thus he distinguishes God's metaphysical and God's moral attributes. He then argues that from the essences of things flow all their attributes and perfections. Thus the first general attribute of God is being "absolutely perfect."[62] Yet we now have God as "being" posited as a subjectum to which God as "being absolutely perfect" can adhere. A hidden essence of God is posited behind God's existence, which creates theological problems. For if God can be distinguished from God like this, then how can we know that God as being itself is the same as God as being absolutely perfect? In other words, can perfection be an attribute God possesses? Does Norris's doctrine of God resemble the anthropology of scholastic voluntarism we witnessed in Clarke and Wesley, where liberty is prior to goodness?

---

60. Ibid., 14.
61. Ibid., 24-25.
62. Ibid., 27.

John Wesley, like most other eighteenth-century theologians, was pre-occupied with God's attributes and especially God's "perfections." He was thoroughly traditional in his understanding of them. He found truth in ancient Greek metaphysics. In his sermon "Catholic Spirit" Wesley posed a much quoted question as to the heart of catholic unity: "My only question at present is this, 'Is thine heart right, as my heart is with thy heart?'" This often-quoted expression is seldom carried on into what John Wesley states next, which is in fact rather troubling, because it is too close to Norris's peculiar version of God's being. Wesley states, "The first thing implied is this: Is thy heart right with God? Dost thou believe his being, and his perfections?"[63] Wesley states that the first thing necessary for Catholic unity is to believe God's "being and his perfections." Why does this come first? Why would not the Trinity be the first thing implied, or Christ's atoning work? Instead, this metaphysical form of knowledge is the first thing Wesley requires for a "Catholic spirit." If one is to join hands with him, one must first believe God's "being and perfections."

Knowing how frequently he read Norris, one cannot help suspecting that this peculiar expression ("his being and his perfections") reflects Norris's influence. Wesley does not use the expression God's "being absolutely perfect," as was common. He separates "being" and "perfec-tions" as did Norris and Samuel Clarke. For them this separation signified a distinction between God's metaphysical and moral attributes. Is that what it meant for Wesley? In explaining this first thing implied for Christian unity, Wesley lists God's perfections as "eternity, immensity, wisdom, power; his justice, mercy and truth."[64] These perfections are sim-ilar to the ones noted by Samuel Clarke in his *Demonstration*.

Clarke distinguished between God's metaphysical and moral attributes to insure that a sovereign liberty most defines God. Clark argues that the metaphysical attributes have a different kind of necessity than the moral.[65] After mentioning God's existence, he then discusses the meta-physical attributes of eternity, infinity (or immensity), intelligence, unity, liberty, and omnipotence. Another shorthand way of explaining these is eternity, immensity, wisdom, and power—which is identical to Wesley's listing of the metaphysical attributes. Clarke then discusses the moral attributes of goodness, justice, truth, and perfection. We find a list similar to Wesley's own as the first essential for Christian unity.

Why would Wesley think that these metaphysical and moral attributes are the first thing necessary to join hands with him? Why would he begin with the metaphysical and moral attributes before Trinity and

---

63. Sermon 39, "Catholic Spirit," §I.12, *Works* 2:87.
64. Ibid.
65. Clarke, *Demonstration*, 86.

Christology? They are the second essential Wesley sets forth. To take hands with him, one must also properly answer the question, "Dost thou believe in the Lord Jesus Christ . . . and him crucified?"[66] It could be that these first two essentials are Wesley's effort to bring together reason and revelation. We must know *that* God is, but such knowledge is not yet sufficient. It is merely knowledge of God's existence. We must know more. We must know *who* this God is that is. We must know God's essence, which we cannot know without knowing Christ. In classic fashion, the *de Deo uno* of Wesley's first essential assumes and renders intelligible the *de Deo trino* of his second essential.

These essentials and their attributes bear some resemblance to what came before in Christian tradition, especially to Aquinas's discussion of God in the *prima pars* of the *Summa Theologica*. He begins with the one God, which is essential to the doctrine of the Trinity, and discusses God's existence—we can know *that* God is, but not *what* God is (God's essence). He then notes God's simplicity, perfection, infinity, immutability (including impassability), eternity, and unity. However, Aquinas never separated God's "metaphysical" and "moral" attributes. And when he discusses the Triune Persons, Aquinas does so under the categories "Knowledge" and "Power." The former is a reference to the Son and the latter to the Holy Spirit. When Wesley invokes God's perfections as "wisdom" and "power," they do not seem to have the trinitarian reference that Aquinas gave them. Would this trinitarian reference have been common knowledge in Wesley's day, or had the reference to "Knowledge" and "Power" become mere attributes of God's "being"? Could Wesley assume that when we speak of God's wisdom and power we are speaking of the Holy Trinity?

Wisdom and power do not seem to function as trinitarian references in Clarke, but they still did in Norris. Clarke makes no trinitiarian references when discussing God's wisdom and power. Reason and revelation are distinct in his demonstration; they are two separate sources. He can speak of God's attributes without speaking of the Trinity, and he can speak of revelation as something completely other than, even added onto, these attributes discovered by reason alone. Such was not the case with Norris. Despite his odd argument separating God's being and God's perfections, Norris clearly read God's wisdom christologically. This is the main point in his treatise *Reason and Religion*. He insisted that religion, by which he meant devotion, did not require a fanatical abandonment of reason precisely because the only way to make sense of how we know anything is through our participation in God's ideas. Norris began his argument by quoting the *prima pars* of Aquinas's *Summa Theologica*, question fifteen—

---

66. Sermon 39, "Catholic Spirit," §I.13, *Works* 2:87.

"For 'tis impossible that God should make a World with Counsel and Design, unless he make it according to something, and that can be nothing else but something existing within himself, something in this *Ideal* and *Archetypal* World." Norris then comments, "And what if I should further say, that this Ideal World, this Essence of God consider'd as variously exhibitive and representative of things is no other than the Divine [Logos], the Second Person in the ever Blessed Trinity."[67] He acknowledges that this is a Christianized Platonism, but it is one that is necessary to avoid the antitrinitarian thought of socianism. Not to defend Platonism per se, but "so great a guard is true *Platonism* against *Socinianism*."[68] Norris used Platonism, as did Aquinas, to make sense both of the Christian doctrine of the Trinity and *creatio ex nihilo*. Here is where Norris distanced himself from Descartes.

Norris agrees with the "schools" that "*the Truth of every thing is its conformity to the Divine understanding*." This is a Thomistic understanding of truth that one finds in part in both Descartes and Malebranche. But Descartes' blunder, according to Norris, was how he conceived of the divine intellect, for he described it as "conceptive," that is, dependent on things rather than "exhibitive."[69] And then following Aquinas quite closely Norris wrote "Power and Wisdom is not any thing really different from the Essence of God."[70] This is a clear trinitarian reference, and only after it can Norris, like Aquinas, explain God's omnipotence. It is not a power to be able to do anything, but "a Power of doing whatsoever is *possible* to be done." Thus God's omnipotency is "a Power of doing whatever involves no repugnancy or contradiction," which is only "not being."[71] But "not being" here is not a bare existence, it is not being as the Triune God. The Second Person of the Trinity is the archetype that defines what it is reasonable for God to be. This poses no limits on God unless we posit a hidden God of absolute liberty behind the God who is to be, who can "choose" to be or not to be. But that is not freedom, it is bondage.

Wesley's anthropology emulated this bondage. Here he was an early modern in that his position was similar to scholastic voluntarism. But Wesley's doctrine of God was free of such an arbitrary God precisely because he held so firmly to the Christian teaching on the Trinity. For Wesley, the "law of God," upon which the creation of all things depends is defined as "all virtues in one," the "original ideas of truth and good," and "supreme, unchangeable reason" or "the everlasting fitness of all things." But most of all it is Jesus Christ. "What is the law but divine

---

67. Norris, *Reason and Religion*, 84-85.
68. Ibid., 91.
69. Ibid., 92.
70. Ibid., 105.
71. Ibid., 113-16.

virtue and wisdom assuming a visible form?" This law is "a copy of the eternal mind, a transcript of the divine nature . . . the brightest efflux of his essential wisdom."[72] Given this description of Christ, Wesley's reference to God's wisdom as an essential for Catholic unity cannot but be read as a christological and trinitarian theme. His first and second essentials for Catholic unity do not divide reason and revelation. And Wesley explicitly uses these themes to avoid any nominalistic tendencies. He explains the significance of how this law provides the basis for justice:

> It is exactly agreeable to the fitnesses of things, whether essential or accidental. It clashes with none of these in any degree, nor is ever unconnected with them. If the word be taken in that sense, there is nothing *arbitrary* in the law of God: although still the whole and every part thereof is totally dependent upon his will, so that "Thy will be done" is the supreme universal law both in earth and heaven.[73]

Although Wesley does not reference any specific work in this sermon, one cannot read it without seeing the influence of the kind of theology present in Malebranche, Cudworth, and Norris. But this theology does not fit well with the liberty of indifference that characterized Wesley's stated anthropology. It presumes an understanding of human nature in terms of our participation in the life of God. As Norris put it, our true privilege is "the Honour to be Hypostatically United with the *[Logos]* the Second Person of the B[lessed] Trinity."[74] Such a participation assumes our will is drawn to Christ, who is the fitness of all things. It cannot assume that our will must remain grounded in a more basic liberty that can suspend judgment in its proper ordering to this end. That would make a capacity for liberty more basic to our being than Christ's grace. It is this great *privilege* to be partakers of the divine nature that allows us to discover ourselves to be holy and happy.

WESLEY'S PRACTICAL REASON

My argument in this book is not that John Wesley was an explicit Thomist, it is that Wesley's work makes more sense when placed in the context of the conversation Thomism represents, which I characterized as "moral theology," than when placed in the context of "ethics," which developed after the divorce between God and the good in the eighteenth

---

72. Sermon 34, "The Original, Nature, Properties, and Use of the Law," §§II.4-6, *Works* 2:9-10.

73. Ibid., §III.5, *Works* 2:12.

74. Norris, *Reason and Religion*, 137.

century. Wesley still assumes it necessary to bring Christianity into conversation with Aristotelianism and Platonism. The Platonist themes above are obvious, but they always serve the doctrine of the Trinity. It is a Christian Platonism Wesley inherits and uses. But unlike Norris, Wesley embraces Aristotle's practical reason with its syllogistic logic. In fact, he favors Aristotle's language on how the mind works over Locke and does not find Locke doing anything different than Aristotle already did. Where Locke differs from Aristotle, Wesley sides with Aristotle. He writes,

> The operations of the mind are more accurately divided by Aristotle than by Mr. Locke. They are three, and no more: Simple apprehension, judgment, and discourse. It seems Mr. Locke only gives a new name to simple apprehension, terming it perception. Of judgment and reason, he speaks in the Fourth Book. Discerning, comparing, compounding, abstracting, are species of judgment. Retention, or memory, refers to them all.
> Complex ideas are most awkwardly divided (I fear, chiefly through affectation of novelty) into modes, substances, and relations. . . . How much clearer is the vulgar division of beings into the ten classes called "predicaments," or into the two,—substances and accidents![75]

Wesley defends Aristotle's categories against Locke's novel division of human understanding. He consistently chides Locke for failing to understand or use Aristotle's syllogistic logic.[76] This logic was the basis for Aristotle's "practical reasoning." It begins with the question, what makes you happy? In other words, what do you desire? It then assumes a major premise such as obedience to God is the good that makes one happy. It is followed by a minor premise such as the duty of constant communion is an instance of the major premise. The result is an action.[77] This can be outlined, drawing on Wesley's sermon, "The Duty of Constant Communion," as follows:

Happiness and holiness as our true end (intuited by the intellect, simple apprehension)

Major premise: Happiness is found in obedience to God.

Minor premise: Constant communion is an instance of obedience to God.

---

75. "Remarks upon Mr. Locke's 'Essay on Human Understanding,'" *Works* (Jackson) 13:456.

76. Cf. ibid., 460.

77. See Alasdair MacIntyre, *After Virtue* (Notre Dame, Ind.: University of Notre Dame Press, 1982), 160-61.

Result: True prudence, piety, and wisdom can only be infused in those who attend the Lord's Supper.[78]

Freedom can be exercised within this account of practical reasoning only after point three. Freedom cannot change the first three points; they "specify" the object of the will. Although Wesley does not use that Thomistic language, he clearly assumes it in this sermon. It is only after number three that the will can exercise its power to ignore the truth of the first three points. But this would be less the will's free exercise than its sinful rebellion, for once the intellect presents the first three points to the will then its freedom is most marked by the fact that it has no choice but to attend to the result in point four. This is why Wesley argues against every hindrance that might not result in the action point four entails.

This account of practical reasoning assumes the necessity of discernment at the level of the minor premise. Here is where "judgment" occurs. The major premise presumes "simple apprehension." In other words, given that happiness is what I desire, I then apprehend that obedience to God will bring happiness. Thus Wesley correlates happiness and holiness. However, for Wesley this simple apprehension will require illumination, for without it my understanding will not be healed so that I can see what my true end is. Once my mind is illumined and I apprehend that obedience to God is good, then I will need to judge whether this particular instance falls within the major premise. The duty of constant communion represents one such instance. The term *discourse* reflects the fact that all of this does not happen instantaneously through some immediate intuition. Practical reasoning occurs discursively. Although I am free in the process of discernment at the level of the minor premise, once I have discerned that the minor premise falls within the major premise then an action follows necessarily. Here is where Locke and Aristotle part company. Locke's insistence on liberty as more basic than will implies that if I am to be truly free then I still have a capacity to move my will or refuse to move my will once I have judged that a particular instance falls within the major premise. His metaphysics of freedom renders void a metaphysics of participation. In the latter, the key is not to choose for the good, but simply to participate in it and not choose against it.

Wesley affirms Aristotle's syllogistic reasoning against Locke, but he also affirms Locke's liberty of indifference without recognizing how this distorts Aristotle's practical reasoning. If the agent remains detached after

---

78. Note how Wesley refers to the duty of constant communion: "In a word: considering this as a command of God, he that does not communicate as often as he can has no piety; considering it as a mercy, he that does not communicate as often as he can has no wisdom" (Sermon 101, "The Duty of Constant Communion," §II.5, *Works* 3:432).

discernment and judgment, then rationality cannot be practical. It will always be theoretical, for I must, in every moment, choose to move my will or refuse to do so. This turns the will into an instrument I possess rather than the internal and external movement of rational desire for which I am responsible, but over which I am only partly in control. If I desire something that is not good or fail to understand the truth before me, then my actions will result from that wrong desire and understanding. I am responsible for the actions that follow even though the failure results less in the choice I make than the desire and understanding that informs such a choice.

Wesley explicitly uses this kind of practical syllogism in his sermon "The Duty of Constant Communion." The sermon begins with the assumption that reasonable people will fear God and seek God's favor. The major premise is that "it is the duty of every Christian to receive the Lord's Supper as often as he can." The minor premise uses discursive reasoning to explain instances where people have the opportunity to receive the Lord's Supper but fail to recognize it as an instance of obedience. Having shown that objections to receiving the Lord's Supper in these particular instances are a failure to recognize when one should pursue the good of obedience, Wesley concludes by asserting that "no man who does not receive it as often as he can has any pretence to Christian prudence."[79] Here the practical and intellectual virtue of prudence is related to the syllogistic logic laid out in the sermon. Prudence is the name for the virtue that fulfills well Aristotle's practical reasoning. Wesley seems to assume that if the syllogism works, the Christian only has one response: attend the Lord's Supper as often as possible. He does not assume that if the syllogism works it is still necessary for the Christian to suspend judgment and choose whether or not to attend the Lord's Supper. Wesley objects to this kind of reasoning. For instance he has no time for persons who refuse to attend because they do not find it meaningful or have not had sufficient time to prepare themselves. Such reasons signify the absence of the virtues of piety and prudence. But how does this fit with Locke's very different account of reasoning that suggests a suspension of judgment as necessary if one is freely to undertake any action? It does not. Wesley did not see what Locke saw. Locke's account of liberty does not fit Aristotle's syllogistic reasoning. Locke and Aristotle differed more significantly than Wesley assumed.

Wesley sided with Aristotle's syllogism against Locke, but failed to see how Locke's position was a more devastating critique of Aristotle than Wesley recognized. Here is where Thomas Aquinas assists Wesley because of his understanding of the will as rational desire. For Aquinas

---

79. Ibid., §II.21, *Works* 3:439.

65

the will does not stand on its own as a faculty to suspend judgment. It only makes sense in terms of his doctrines of God and creation, which is similar to the intellectualist school found in Norris and to which Wesley was also indebted. This is why Aquinas can refer to the will as "rational appetite." However, with the modern turn to the subject, the will stands alone. It is no longer thought of in terms of rational appetite. Once this occurred, a number of dualisms emerged in moral philosophy that continue to define modern ethics. Theory and practice became more fully separated than ever before, such that some moral philosophers eschew any notion of theory, contemplation, or doctrine at all.

Both the Puritan and the so-called eighteenth-century "sentimentalist" school of moral philosophy fall into this category. (American pragmatism should certainly be seen as, in part, the heir of these schools of thought.) Both react against the "schools," but nevertheless remain indebted to the late medieval teaching of a liberty of indifference in doing so. Other schools emerge that react against this nominalist strain of thought, particularly as it is developed in Hobbes. They so stress theory or contemplation that they lose the significance of sensibility altogether. Certain exemplars of Cambridge Platonism could be cited here. The result is a basic dualism between will and understanding where each faculty works with little to no reliance on the other. This led to other troubling distinctions in moral philosophy and theology such as: either the good or the true, love/knowledge, affections/reason, heart/head, piety/doctrine, pietism/scholasticism, gospel/law.

Throughout the seventeenth and eighteenth centuries, contending schools of thought played one side of these pairs against the other. The result was increasing incoherence and fragmentation in what constituted a reasonable moral life. But the significant shift that occurs in the eighteenth century is the vanquishing of the second pole of these dualisms by the first. Kant's basic understanding of morality that only a goodwill determines goodness; Shaftesbury, Hutcheson, and Smith's appeal to moral sentiments; Locke's empiricism; and Hume's claim that reason is a slave to the passions—all of these emerge out of the vanquishing of the intellect by the will. A transition occurs from the will understood as rational appetite to the will understood as basically indifferent grounded in an arbitrary liberty. The former assumed that the will was not a faculty for choosing irrespective of reason as much as it was rational deliberation. The good and the true—morality and doctrine—could not be decisively separated. But in the eighteenth century they are separated; theology and morality divorced. As Leslie Stephen put it, once "the vision of God becomes faint," then the important question that emerged was "should morality survive theology?"[80]

---

80. Leslie Stephen, *History of English Thought in the Eighteenth Century* (London: Smith, Elder and Co., 1876), 2:1-3.

BEFORE GOD AND GOODNESS DIVORCED: THE WILL AS RATIONAL APPETITE

Should the "good" survive without God? On what foundation is it secured once God does not provide such a foundation? Why did this question emerge in the eighteenth century? It is not the case that the good was always conceived theologically. Philosophical inquiry into the good existed before the specificities of Christian doctrine were forged. Augustine, Anselm, and Aquinas could find witness to the good in pagan philosophy, even if it still needed conversion. Nevertheless, a significant shift occurred in the eighteenth century, where theology and morality not only divorced but philosophers began to wonder if morality could survive at all. Some suggested that theology would be a hindrance to morality's survival.

One significant factor for the divorce between God and goodness was the compartmentalization of all our knowledge into disciplines and faculties. This is a time of breaking things down into their simplest elements to examine how they are actually constructed. In so doing, the narrative wholeness of life itself gets lost. Vivisection helps scientists determine causal connections between component parts, but it does so at the expense of life itself. Breaking down every whole into its simplest ideas, especially when it came to knowledge, morality, and language, destroyed the kind of knowledge morality itself required. This can certainly be seen in the technological developments in morality where a desperate search for a single foundation for the moral life reveals that the latter has already become so unstable that it can no longer be salvaged. Thomas Aquinas's work can guide us at precisely this point. He did not posit the will as a "faculty" and seek to reduce morality to its simplest component parts. He recognized that morality could not be found by searching internally. It only made sense within the context of creation and creation's God, moving all things to their proper end.

Aquinas began his discussion on whether the intellect moves the will with an objection from Augustine.[81] It would seem according to Augustine that the intellect does not move the will, for, as he states, "*The intellect flies ahead, the desire follows sluggishly or not at all: we know what is good, but deeds delight us not.*" Augustine's argument here will be the argument against Aquinas and Aristotle in seventeenth-century English-speaking moral philosophy. They cannot account for the perversity of the will. If the will is rational deliberation, then how can it be free either to obey or disobey the dictates of practical rationality? If a practical syllogism ends in an action, then the will seems bound by the intellect. This

---

81. *Summa Theologica*, I-II.9.1.

becomes even more significant in the twentieth century with its advocacy of "radical evil." But this conflicts with an older tradition.

If the will is *rational* desire, then once it knows the true good, it will pursue it of necessity. But Augustine seems to suggest that the will has a perversity of its own. It can will against a true good that the intellect knows. Aquinas's response to this objection is not to advocate an optimistic account of human beings as naturally inclined to the good without the possibility of moral failure. That optimistic nineteenth-century anthropology emerges, ironically enough, out of the anti-intellectualist romanticism that emerged out of scholastic voluntarism. For Aquinas, the movement of the will depends on actualizing the power of the soul, which is in potentiality. But it is in potentiality in two ways. It can either act or not act, and that is a power in the subject. It can also act with respect to "this or that action," which is a function of the object, by reason of which the act is specified. That which moves the will is the good; it has "the nature of an end" and is "the object of the will." If there were no good, there would be no movement, there would be no will. The will here is not some faculty that can choose to move or not move itself through an autonomous self-determination. The will is rational desire that is moved by the good. But the good as the object that moves the will does so "after the manner of a formal principle, whereby in natural things actions are specified, as heating by heat."

In other words the movement of the will is not simply arbitrary; it is not a mere will to power—a bare ability to do one thing or another or to do nothing at all. Instead, the good that moves the will does so through a formal principle, which is to say that just as heat is specified by its ability for heating, good is specified by its formal principle, which for Aquinas is "universal *being* and *truth*." The good moves the will toward that which truly is, even as heat heats.[82] In this way the intellect moves the will. It cannot be other than this any more than we could say that fire cools. The good is desired as a formal principle that cannot be otherwise. It specifies the will's action. But this is not determinism, for the desire that the good elicits from the will must yet still be ordered by an agent through his or her exercise of will.

Does this then rule out the possibility of a perverse and fallen will? The will in its exercise can disregard a truth seen, but a truth seen cannot cease to specify the will. The will does not have the power to posit its own values. The will, simply by being will, moves toward truth and goodness and can never completely turn from it. It is always already "specified." Thus, there is no "radical" evil in Aquinas like there will be in Kant and his

---

82. Ibid.

modern heirs—Brightman and Niebuhr. But the intellect does not of necessity see or know the truth, and thus the will need not be moved of necessity by the intellect. Moreover, there is no single causal direction between the will and the intellect in Aquinas. For he also stated, "The will moves the intellect as to the exercise of its act; since even the true itself which is the perfection of the intellect, is included in the universal good, as a particular good."[83] Even though the intellect specifies the good under which the will moves, the will exercises the movement that allows the intellect to specify the object. No simple deduction occurs from the theoretical vision of the intellect to the practical determination of the will. The will is moved by what the intellect sees and knows, but the intellect is likewise moved by what the will loves.

This is what is meant by "rational appetite." One can only know what one loves and one can only love what one knows. And if we ask which comes first—knowledge or love—then we seek to separate reason and appetite and make one more primal than the other. They can only be separated under a certain aspect, that is, through classifying human action under a particular aspect. When it comes to the determination of an act, the intellect moves the will. When it comes to the exercise of the act, the will moves the intellect. This aspectual differentiation is possible because, for Aquinas, any particular act is not simply a brute fact. That would be the mere exercise of the act. It also, at the same time, participates in a universal essence that renders the existence of the act possible, just as the essence can only be known by the particular existence. This essence is the formal determination, and it is this that scholastic voluntarism, and nominalism, rejected.

Aquinas develops the moral life in terms of a pursuit of the good closely linked to truth where the will is understood as rational appetite. This entails that doctrine and ethics are not finally separable. In opposition to this, modern scientific ethics separates the good and the true such that one would not need to know anything to be good, for there is finally nothing good but a goodwill. A person could be ignorant of truth and still be good. The measure of goodness becomes something like sincerity or authenticity. This notion of the good assumes the will as the center of the moral life and divides it from the intellect. It rebels against the schools (particularly scholastic "intellectualism"), but not because they piled distinction upon distinction—that was a problem that could easily be remedied. It rebelled against the schools because they assumed that the intellect moved the will. This did not sit well with the renewed emphasis on sin, nor did it allow for a pursuit of the good solely based on the will, sentiment, or nature. It is the severing between the good and the true that characterizes modern ethics, and it is a severing indebted in part to the loss of the will as rational appetite.

---

83. Ibid., ad. 3.

Is John Wesley better understood as a moral theologian or a modern "ethicist"? I think the answer is obvious. Wesley's reflections on the moral life bear much more similarity to Thomas Aquinas than to Immanuel Kant or John Locke. That should be obvious, but its significance should not be underestimated. Aquinas was not a moral theologian who grounded "ethics" in "theology." Nor were Kant and Locke philosophical ethicists who bracketed God out of ethical matters. Nevertheless, rupture occurred in Wesley's days as to how God and goodness were to be related. Sifting through the complexity of how this happened is not easily done—even two centuries after the fact. Understanding the intellectual relationships among Hobbes, More, Shaftesbury, Cudworth, Clarke, Locke, Malebranche, Hutcheson, Smith, Wesley, Hume, and Kant is not easily done. It is more like walking into the middle of several conversations taking place simultaneously, than it is following a carefully laid out road map.[84] I use the expression "from moral theology to ethics" only as a way to begin to enter into that conversation. "Moral theology" signifies the place of departure, a place Wesley was firmly located. "Ethics" signifies the place to which the conversation was headed, a place Wesley resisted.

---

84. Some helpful secondary works on these various relationships are Stephen, *History of English Thought* and Isabel Rivers, *Reason, Grace and Sentiment: A Study of the Language of Religion and Ethics in England 1660–1780* (2 vols.; Cambridge: Cambridge University Press, 1991–2000).

CHAPTER 3

FROM MORAL THEOLOGY TO ETHICS

"Moral theology" refers to what eighteenth-century moral discourse shifted away from, which I think can be best described in terms of the tradition exemplified in Thomas Aquinas where doctrine, ethics, spirituality and philosophy cannot easily be distinguished.[1] *Ethics* refers to that science of human action that emerged in the eighteenth century in persons such as Kant and Locke where doctrine, philosophy, and ethics were intentionally distinguished for the sake of ethics. I am using these terms as a shorthand reference for a significant shift in the eighteenth century, which can be termed "from moral theology to ethics." This is a bit simplistic and could easily lead to misunderstanding. I am not arguing that there was some secular scientific conspiracy against theology. Theologians contributed as much to this shift as did philosophers. In fact, the shift would most likely not have been possible if it were not for Martin Luther's refusal to see anything worthy in the "pagan" virtue tradition. This set in place an opposition between reason and revelation, or nature and faith, that still hampers us today where theologians and ethicists take sides with one at the expense of the other. It could be that Martin Luther's efforts to purify theology of ethics were more responsible than any philosopher's attempts to purify ethics of theology for the autonomous development of ethics.

The Reformation certainly led to the development of a different moral language, which in many ways exhibited a rupture with that which came

---

1. See Servais Pinckaers, *The Sources of Christian Ethics* (trans. Mary Thomas Noble; Washington, D.C.: Catholic University of America Press, 1995).

before and which took the work of Aquinas as emblematic for what needed to be defeated. As Alasdair MacIntyre has argued, "It is, therefore, not just that Aquinas' Christian Aristotelianism and Luther's Christian fideism are based on alternative and competing metaphysical schemes; it is also the case that they are providing an analysis of and insight into different moral vocabularies."[2] For MacIntyre, the key to this different vocabulary is the rise of the "individual" as the decisive factor in considering moral agency. Machiavelli and Luther join forces in the development of this new ethics, and its eventual outcome is Hobbes. MacIntyre notes,

> It is, by now at any rate, clear that following the age of Luther and Machiavelli, we should expect the rise of a kind of moral-cum-political theory in which the individual is the ultimate social unit, power the ultimate concern, God an increasingly irrelevant but still unexpungeable being, and a prepolitical, presocial timeless human nature the background of changing social forms. The expectation is fully gratified by Hobbes.[3]

Of course without Hobbes there would be neither Locke nor the rise of empiricism. But as MacIntyre tells the story it is not just Hobbes that is a natural consequence of the transition that begins with Luther's new moral vocabulary. If we start with Luther we will naturally end up with Kant. More than any other figures from the philosophical tradition, Kant's transcendental idealism and Locke's empiricism provide the current understanding of "ethics." Although significant differences exist between them, and both sought to provide an apology for the Christian faith, the consequence of these two major voices is an inevitable divorce between theology and morality.

The synthesis between God and the good found in moral theology and necessitated by understanding the will as a rational appetite was undone in the seventeenth and eighteenth century. God and the good divorced, even when they still lived in the same house. MacIntyre does not find much potential in the tradition of Christian Platonism to stand against this trend with its logical consequences in Hobbes, Locke, and Kant. Christian Platonists were incapable of recognizing moral disagreement because they assume the Platonic thesis that a condition of having grasped a moral concept is that one should have grasped the criteria for its correct application, and such criteria are ambiguous. Therefore true moral disagreement is impossible, it is only a function of incorrect reasoning.[4]

---

2. Alasdair MacIntyre, *A Short History of Ethics* (New York: Macmillan, 1966), 125.
3. Ibid., 130.
4. Ibid., 161.

But this takes Henry More, with his mathematization of morality, as the exemplar for Cambridge Platonism. It overlooks altogether the rich synthesis of theology and morality found in Malebranche, Norris, and Cudworth that is much more than an a priori mathematization of morality. Their work does not contribute to the divorce that occurred between God and the good. Wesley saw this divorce occurring toward the end of his life and spoke vociferously against it. Throughout his life his work assumed, and depended on, an indissociable bond between God and the good, doctrine and ethics. To understand the significance of this bond, we must see the moral alternatives that existed during his life with which he was and was not familiar. My point in this chapter is not just to trace causal lines that influenced Wesley's moral theology (although I will do some of that), I want to bring his work into conversation with the complex moral discourse that occurred in and before his day in order to show the significance of his moral theology. The main contributors to that discourse were Locke, Kant, Hobbes, Hume, Shaftesbury, Malebranche, Hutcheson, and Adam Smith.

At the risk of being too simple, let me suggest that the seventeenth and eighteenth centuries saw four major movements in moral philosophy that related, or failed to relate, God and the good: (1) God was subordinated to the good (Locke, Kant); (2) the good was developed without and/or in opposition to God (Hobbes, Hume); (3) God was indifferent to the good (Smith, the sentimentalists); and finally, (4) God and the good were necessarily combined (Malebranche, Cambridge Platonism). This fourfold distinction is simplistic in that the lines of influence run across all of these positions. By far the most long-lasting movement subordinated God to the good, assuming the latter was a more universal category than the former but that the former was still necessary to have the latter. Locke (1632–1704) and Kant (1703–1791) both assumed this. Although Locke's empiricism and Kant's transcendental idealism could be viewed as opposed to each other on many points, when it came to how God and the good related, their work was similar.

The work of Thomas Hobbes (1588–1679) and David Hume (1711–1776) was more radical than that of either Kant or Locke. God was no longer needed for the good and possibly dangerous to it. If we were to have goodness, "God" must be carefully regulated if not rejected. Although Hobbes and Hume differ significantly from Kant and Locke as to how God and goodness relate, Locke's work would not have been possible without Hobbes. Likewise Hume's would not have been possible without Hobbes, Locke, Shaftesbury, and Malebranche. Hume was in conversation with all of these philosophers, drawing upon and critiquing their work. He has been referred to as "Malebranche without God." Kant's work, which had a place for God, would not have been possible if Hume had not awakened him from his "dogmatic slumber." For the sentimentalists (Shaftesbury [1617–1713], Hutcheson [1694–1746], and Smith [1723–1790]) God and the good remained related, but which God and how they were related differed significantly among them, let alone in relation to those positions they opposed such as Locke's empiricism. Locke's work gave rise to the deist theology of Toland and Tindal, yet Locke was no deist. The sentimentalists opposed Locke's empiricism, yet their use of "God" resembled deism more so than Locke. For them "God" ensured harmony out of antagonism. Similar to Kant and Locke, God provided the conditions for the possibility of morality but without any direct bearing of theology on ethics. Ethics worked well based on a natural moral sense, but if pressed where this sentiment came from, "God" could provide an answer rather than Hume's constant conjunction. Cambridge Platonism has unfortunately been tied to latitudinarianism. This is unfortunate because persons such as Malebranche (1638–1715), Cudworth (1617–1688), and John Norris (1657–1711) used Platonism and Christianity to wed God and the good closely together. And unlike the sentimentalists, the "God" so wedded was not a unitary power of providence but the Holy Trinity. Wesley's thought wove in or rejected many of the themes represented in the contrasts between these various figures.

GOD SUBORDINATED TO THE GOOD (KANT AND LOCKE)

With the exception of the Christian Platonists, nearly every major movement of moral philosophy in the eighteenth century sharply distinguished between faith and reason, nature and supernature. Locke, Kant, Hobbes, and Hume made this distinction. Hobbes and Hume did so to protect morality and politics from theology. Locke and Kant did so to protect faith from critical rationality. Both wrote books that sought to explain Christian faith in terms of reason, but both did so by positing a realm outside of reason where faith securely existed. In *The Critique of Pure Reason*, Kant argued that he challenged reason in order to make room for faith. He gave us the limits of reason so that an arational remainder could emerge, a remainder about which one could not say anything substantive. This arational remainder was faith. Nevertheless Kant, like Locke, also provided an account of religion within the limits of reason alone.

Locke's *Reasonableness of Christianity* drew on a threefold account of the relationship between reason and faith, which he laid out earlier in his *Essay concerning Human Understanding*. Faith could be "according to reason," "contrary to reason," and "above reason." But only the first and third are legitimate forms of faith. For Locke, faith is based on revelation through some extraordinary way of communication, primarily by miracles.[5] His work appears less subject to subordinating God to the good than does that of Kant, but this appearance is misleading. Even though Locke appears to defend a rather traditional account of Christianity, it is done within the context of his philosophy of simple ideas. He does not need any essential Christian doctrines such as the Trinity to explain the faith. What he needs is some positive "fact" like a miracle. This fact then becomes evidence for God, making the idea of God reasonable on empiricist grounds. But it is Locke's empiricism that allows the idea of God to be possible; it is not God who allows our knowledge of the world to be intelligible. The result is the same as one finds in Kant. God is useful, but by no means essential, to goodness.

Kant states unequivocally that while morality does not need theology for its intelligibility theology does need morality in this regard. In his preface to the first edition of *Religion within the Limits of Reason Alone*, he writes, "So far as morality is based upon the conception of man as a free agent who, just because he is free, binds himself through his reason to unconditioned laws, it stands in need neither of the idea of another Being over him, for him to apprehend his duty, nor of an incentive other than the law itself, for him to do his duty."[6] For Kant, morality is grounded primarily in freedom, not the good or God. God provides neither a necessary foundation for morality nor any proper incentive to it. Unlike Locke, Kant does not argue that future rewards and punishments should be an incentive to morality. We should do our duty for duty's sake. However, like Locke, "God" is primarily necessary because of the moral usefulness of a future judgment. This allows for a potential unity between happiness and obligation that one does not always see in this life. Kant's ethic is nevertheless a disinterested one: one does one's moral duty solely from the obligation to obey the moral law in its unconditional and universal nature and not because of the promise of reward. We have no evidence that Wesley ever read Kant, but as we shall see, this idea of a disinterested ethic was popular in England in Wesley's day. He saw it in Hutcheson and strongly opposed it as a subtle form of atheism. He did so primarily because he recognized that it destroyed the teleological nature of moral theology. Wesley did not oppose a disinterested ethic on the basis of Locke's argument that morality required the incentive of future rewards.[7]

---

5. John Locke, *The Reasonableness of Christianity* (ed. I. T. Ramsey; Stanford, Calif.: Stanford University Press, 1958). See Ramsey's introduction, 10.

6. Immanuel Kant, *Religion within the Limits of Reason Alone* (trans. Theodore Green and Hoyt H. Hudson; New York: Harper Torchbooks, 1960), 3.

7. See Locke, *Reasonableness of Christianity*, 48.

He opposed it because it lost the goal of the moral life, which is the conjunction of happiness and holiness.

Locke was clearly more willing than Kant to bring in God's final judgment as an incentive for moral obligation. He was also willing to see Jesus as the lawgiver who required obedience for those incapable of using reason to discern the moral law. In his defense of revelation as a basis for morality Locke wrote,

> It should seem, by the little that has hitherto been done in it, that 'tis too hard a task for unassisted reason, to establish morality, in all its parts, upon its true foundations, with a clear and convincing light. And 'tis at least a surer and shorter way, to the apprehensions of the vulgar, and mass of mankind, that one manifestly sent from God, and coming with visible authority from him, should, as a King and law-maker, tell them their duties, and require their obedience, than leave it to the long, and sometimes intricate deductions of reason, to be made out to them.[8]

The revelation of Jesus is useful for the vulgar masses who do not understand morality's true foundation, which appears to be unassisted reason. Locke's moral philosophy is not teleological, for these incentives are not the basis for the moral action. It should still be accomplished irrespective of future rewards and punishments; that is why the obligation still holds even though the rewards are merely held on credit.

Kant, more so than Locke, emphasizes the obligation to do one's duty for its own sake. Kant states, "for its own sake morality does not need religion. . . . when it is a question of duty, morality is perfectly able to ignore all ends, and it ought to do so."[9] He argues against any final *telos*, such as friendship with God, that pulls one's desires toward itself and makes one happy such as Aquinas and Wesley suggest. Instead, the will must be completely its own master. The will is not rational deliberation; it is always free to do other than what it has done. Morality depends on the obligation to do one's duty irrespective of whether one is rewarded or intending to achieve some end or whether it brings happiness. Yet he does not deny an end altogether; an end is possible if it is "taken not as the ground but as the [sum of] inevitable consequences of maxims adopted as conformable to that end." So Kant concludes, "Morality thus leads ineluctably to religion, through which it extends itself to the idea of a powerful moral Lawgiver, outside of mankind, for Whose will that is the final end (of creation) which at the same time can and ought to be man's final end."[10] In other words, although one cannot begin with God and then develop a morality, one can begin with morality, with the need for

---

8. Ibid., 60-61.
9. Kant, *Religion within the Limits*, 3-4.
10. Ibid., 4-6.

the freedom to act in accordance with a universal law, and then see the necessity of the idea of a powerful moral Lawgiver who both gives a universal moral law and insures our freedom to do our duty. Morality comes first; God comes second. God makes sense only after we first have an independent morality. God still had a role to play in Kant's ethics, but always only out in the future.

Kant and Locke agree more than might be expected on how God and the good relate. This is surprising because Kant's idealism was a response to errors he saw in Locke's empiricism. He challenged Locke's claim that metaphysical problems were primarily problems of common experience, and if we were just more attentive to the simple ideas that our language tried to name, metaphysical problems could be resolved. Kant wrote,

> In more recent times, it has seemed as if an end might be put to all these controversies and the claims of metaphysics receive final judgment, through a certain physiology of the human understanding—that of the celebrated Locke. But it has turned out quite otherwise. For however the attempt be made to cast doubt upon the pretensions of the supposed Queen (metaphysics) by tracing her lineages to vulgar origins in common experience, this genealogy has, as a matter of fact, fictitiously been invented, and she has still continued to uphold her claims.[11]

Kant thought that we could not move beyond certain metaphysical problems if we assumed, with Locke and Hume, that our knowledge was a posteriori, arising from common experience. Kant's Copernican revolution in metaphysics challenged Locke's primacy of experience for human understanding. Kant asked whether our mind gave rise to the things in the world rather than simply tabulating them from experience. For Kant this means that we could not know things in themselves, that is, objects in the world as they truly are. Instead, we only know them as we give them their intelligibility. In other words, our knowledge does not conform to objects, but objects conform to our knowledge.[12]

This led to another important division in seventeenth- and eighteenth-century philosophy: "a priori" or "a posteriori" knowledge. The empiricists assume the latter; Kantian idealism, Cartesianism, and Cambridge Platonism the former. This is why the Christian Platonists held, contra Hobbes, Locke, and Hume, a strong doctrine of illumination and a metaphysics of participation. Wesley held positions in both camps and did not seem to recognize the difficulties this produced. He denied any innate ideas in human knowledge and accepted Locke's understanding of the mind as a *tabula rasa*, which produced ideas after its reception of sense

---

11. Immanuel Kant, *Critique of Pure Reason* (trans. Norman Kemp Smith; New York: St. Martin's Press, 1965), 8.

12. Ibid., 22.

impressions. For instance, in his sermon "The Imperfection of Human Knowledge," Wesley challenged Platonism when it suggested that the knowledge of God was "stamped on every human soul." "The truth is," he wrote, "no man ever did, or does now find any such idea stamped upon his soul. The little which we do know of God (except what we receive by the inspiration of the Holy One) we do not gather from an inward impression, but gradually acquire from without." For Wesley, this is biblical, based on Romans 1:20 where the invisible is only known through the visible.[13] But is this empiricism? Is it evidence that Runyon is correct in his reading of Wesley as working from a modern empiricism where knowledge arises from experience? Outler states that this quote shows how Wesley "follows [Christian Platonists] since 'our knowledge of God and the things of God' are not 'empirical' but rather intuitive."[14] But it is difficult to see how this quote coheres with Christian Platonism. It seems to fit better with Theodore Runyon's directly opposed claim: Wesley's "view of reason's operations is based on an empirical model, and he denies to reason the direct intuitional capabilities ascribed to it by Descartes, the Cambridge Platonists, and the Deists."[15] How can two Methodist theologians who both carefully read John Wesley come to such opposing conclusions? The problem might not be with the interpreters but with Wesley's work itself. Perhaps he held inconsistent positions on metaphysical matters. Or perhaps we have not carefully analyzed the complex arguments in the eighteenth century to see that the debate was not empiricism versus intuitionism or experience versus innate ideas. We may have wrongly assumed that the options were either empiricism or the intuitionism of innate ideas.

The seventeenth-century debate concerning innate ideas emerged from Descartes' second meditation. He raised the question as to what it is we know of a piece of wax when it is melted. His answer was that it was nothing perceived by means of the senses because there was no longer anything to perceive. Nor is it merely the ability to imagine via the understanding alone. Instead,

> the perception of it, or the action by which one perceive it, is not an act of sight, or touch, or of imagination, and has never been, although it seemed so hitherto, but only an intuition of the mind, which may be imperfect and confused, as it was formerly, or else clear and distinct, as it is at present according as my attention directs itself more or less to the elements which it contains and of which it is composed.[16]

---

13. Sermon 69, "The Imperfection of Human Knowledge," §I.4, *Works* 2:571.

14. See ibid. n. 14.

15. Theodore Runyon, *The New Creation: John Wesley's Theology Today* (Nashville: Abingdon, 1998), 15.

16. René Descartes, *Discourse on Method and The Meditations* (New York: Penguin, 1986), 109-10.

Locke challenged this argument in the first book of his *Essay on Human Understanding*. His empiricism assumes the mind as a blank slate that contains nothing until furnished by sense knowledge of particular objects. But intuitionism and empiricism were not the only two options. Malebranche's Christian Platonism rejects Descartes' innate ideas as well. His unorthodox Cartesianism, which influenced John Norris and John Wesley, did not assume that the human mind contained a secure innate idea. Instead, the human mind participated in the ideas in the divine mind and through that participation alone could a human subject properly attend to sensible objects in the world. The rejection of innate ideas did not entail Lockean empiricism.

One reason Wesley has been interpreted as a Lockean empiricist is precisely so he can be relevant to Enlightenment thought, which allowed us to speak of "John Wesley today." Theodore Runyon, drawing upon the work of George Croft Cell and Richard E. Brantley, argues that to understand Wesley's doctrine of regeneration "we must first examine how he adapted John Locke's method of empiricism to explain how knowledge of spiritual reality is possible."[17] Runyon and others see Wesley as a Lockean, drawing on a form of empiricism at a time when transcendental forms of truth were being called into question. Brantley developed a strong Lockean thesis in his interpretation of Wesley. He stated,

> My thesis, in short, is twofold. First, Locke's theory of knowledge grounds the intellectual method of Wesley's Methodism. And second, Wesley's Lockean thought (i.e., his reciprocating notions that religious truth is concerned with experiential presuppositions, and that experience itself need not be non-religious) provides a ready means of understanding the "religious" empiricism and the English "transcendentalism" of British Romantic poetry.[18]

Unsurprisingly, Brantley draws a "parallel between Wesley's conversion and such resurgences of empiricism as that of A. J. Ayer, whose 'verification principle' demanded that 'for a proposition to have meaning we must adduce some human experience by which its truth or falsity may be tested.'"[19] The evidence for this Lockeanism in Wesley comes primarily from his denial of innate ideas and his insistence that we must have a "clear apprehension" of things before we make a judgment about them.[20] Why this is not Cartesian or Hobbesian rather than Lockean is unclear. Whoever argued against clear apprehension in the philosophical

---

17. Runyon, *New Creation*, 72.
18. Richard E. Brantley, *Locke, Wesley and the Method of English Romanticism* (Gainesville: University of Florida Press, 1984), 2.
19. Ibid., 5.
20. Cf. ibid., 7.

tradition? Locke certainly did use this expression in his epistemology, but so did Malebranche. The term alone does not offer much evidence to indict Wesley of empiricism.

Once Wesley is read as an empiricist then he becomes more pragmatic and less dogmatic than previous forms of Christianity. As Runyon put it, "The point was to make *experience* a reliable source of knowledge and grant it a place of authority alongside the traditionally accepted authorities—Scripture, tradition, and reason. This is why Locke found it necessary to abandon Descartes' notion of innate ideas."[21] This is a somewhat odd way of putting it, for empiricism assumes that reason arises from experience. The standard definition of empiricism is "the theory that experience rather than reason is the source of knowledge."[22] Empiricism does not put experience alongside reason as two different sources. At least in Locke, it suggests that we neither need illumination prior to understanding sensible objects, nor do we have a "reason" prior to sense objects that allows us to make sense of them. This is why he refers to the mind as a *tabula rasa*. Thus, if Wesley is an empiricist, reason and experience cannot both be reliable sources of knowledge.

Wesley's defense of spiritual senses against the Cartesian and Platonic notion of innate ideas is seen as evidence that his epistemology was Lockean.[23] The result of course, and this I fear is what is really at stake in this argument, is that Wesley becomes an Enlightenment liberal always relevant to "today." As Brantley puts it, "It is an indication of my view of Wesley that the blend of English mind and religious temper with which he was endowed assured him a place in the Enlightenment of which Locke's theological as well as philosophical *Essay* was a major manifesto."[24] But this interpretation of Wesley overlooks entirely too much evidence as to his theological doctrines of participation and illumination as necessary for knowledge.

This interpretation also is challenged by Wesley's stated opposition to key Lockean ideas. Wesley published a series of extracts from Locke's *Essay*, with some critical comments, in the *Arminian Magazine* from 1782–1784.[25] Among these extracts were Locke's critique of the mistaken notion of liberty (which he sees as "freedom to play the fool") and his emphasis on the constant pursuit of true and solid happiness as the highest perfection of intellectual nature. They also included Locke's notion of

---

21. Runyon, *New Creation*, 73.
22. D. W. Hamlyn, "Empiricism," *Encyclopedia of Philosophy* (8 vols. in 4; New York: Macmillan, 1967), 1:499.
23. Brantley, *Locke, Wesley*, 7.
24. Ibid., 17.
25. The series of extracts began in *Arminian Magazine* 5 (1782): 27 and ran through 7 (1784): 316.

the liberty of indifference, his complex ideas of substances, and reflections on human understanding. Wesley provides little commentary on most of these extracts. However, in 1784 he offered a number of criticisms. In each of these criticisms Wesley sides with the more ancient/medieval account of human understanding than with Locke's empiricism. Wesley wrote,

> In reading over the second volume of Mr. Locke's Essay, I was much disappointed: It is by no means equal to the first. The more I considered it, the more convinced I was, 1. That his grand design was, (vain design!) to drive Aristotle's Logic out of the world, which he hated cordially, but never understood: I suppose, because he had an unskilful master, and read bad books upon the subject. 2. That he had not a *clear apprehension*. Hence he had few *clear ideas*; (though he talks of them so much;) and hence so many confused, inadequate definitions. I wonder none of his opponents hit this blot.[26]

Wesley then chastises Locke for his dismissal of scholasticism:

> "The disputes of the schools." I doubt whether Mr. Locke had ever a clear idea of that term. What does he mean by them in, "O ye schoolmen!" But who are they? all the commentators upon Aristotle in the fifteenth and sixteenth century? Did he read them all? Did he ever read one of them through? I doubt, not. Then he should not rail at he knew not what.[27]

What was it about the schoolmen Wesley thought Locke misunderstood? He does not tell us, but his next critique of Locke attacks him for his dismissal of essences. "A man need only read the first chapter of Genesis, to be convinced that God made every *species* of animals '*after its kind*'; giving a peculiar *essence* to each, whether we know that real essence or no."[28] Note that Wesley defends essences, without claiming to know them separate from existences. This is a profound metaphysical insight.

Along with critiquing Locke for failing to understand essences, Wesley faults him for thinking that Aristotelian logic is the reason we cannot resolve metaphysical issues. Wesley quoted Locke's statement, "Logic has much contributed to the obscurity of language," and then commented:

> The abuse of logic has; but the true use of it is the noblest means under heaven to prevent or cure the obscurity of language. To divide simple terms according to the logical rules of division, and then to define each member of the division according to the three rules of definition, does all that human art can do, in order to our having a clear and distinct idea of

26. See "Remarks upon Mr. Locke's 'Essay on Human Understanding,'" *Works* (Jackson) 13:460 (italics added); this and the following quotes were originally published in *Arminian Magazine* 7 (1784): 254-55.

27. Ibid., 461.

28. Ibid. (Italics added).

every word we use. Had Mr. Locke done this, what abundance of obscurity and confusion would have been prevented![29]

At those points where empiricism most breaks with the metaphysical tradition that came before it, especially that of a metaphysics of participation, Wesley sides with the latter against the former. He refuses Locke's nominalism that reduces all things to the mere name of a simple idea and eschews essences and the logic they entail. In other words, for better or worse, Wesley sides with the medieval metaphysical tradition against Locke's empiricism on these points. But Wesley never thought he had to decide between the two. That is a decision forced on him by those who came after him.

Wesley's criticisms of Locke were not confined to the *Arminian Magazine*. In his sermon "The Case of Reason Impartially Considered," he uses the ancient notion of essential truths to critique Locke. He criticizes those who overvalue and undervalue reason when it comes to faith. In this context he notes that Locke takes a middle way, but charges that it is insufficient. Locke, stated Wesley, "is only remotely applicable to this: he does not come home to the point."[30] Wesley suggests he will supply the defect in Locke, and he does so by arguing that reason is the "foundation of [religion], and the superstructure" in that it gives us access to the oracles of God as well as essential truths.[31] Notice that it is reason and not experience that offers religion its foundation and superstructure. When read within the context of seventeenth- and eighteenth-century debates, this is a significant claim. It suggests an intellectualist reading, against Locke's voluntarism. Wesley then uses an expression by the Cambridge Platonist, Benjamin Whichcote, and encourages his readers to "acknowledge 'the candle of the Lord.'"[32] This expression assumes that the mind is already illumined by its participation in God such that it is no *tabula rasa* awaiting sense impressions. It assumes that the mind participates in the divine ideas (the essences of things), and that is what allows it to know the empirical existence of things. This is a form of aprioristic thinking (although it is not transcendental idealism).

Wesley also equivocates on whether or not there are innate ideas. He wrote in 1784, "It has been a subject of controversy for many years, whether there are any innate principles in the mind of man." He then states, "if there be any practical principles naturally implanted in the soul," then one such principle would be "we ought to honour our parents."[33] He seems ambivalent about innate ideas as late as 1784.

---

29. Ibid., 462. Note also how Wesley pillories Locke for his unwillingness to accept "essences" in ibid., 462-63.
30. Cf. Sermon 70, "The Case of Reason Impartially Considered," §5, *Works* 2:589.
31. Ibid., §I.6, *Works* 2:591-92.
32. Ibid., §II.10, *Works* 2:599.
33. Sermon 96, "On Obedience to Parents," §1, *Works* 3:361.

Wesley was neither an a posteriori empiricist drawing on experience as a source of knowledge nor an a priori Platonist assuming a direct unmediated participation of the soul in reason through eternal ideas, for the positions themselves were not that clearly demarcated.[34] Locke himself could appeal to "the candle of the Lord." In explaining how persons can be saved who never knew Christ, Locke wrote,

> yet God had, by the light of reason, revealed to all mankind, who would make use of that light, that he was good and merciful. The same spark of the divine nature and knowledge in man, which making him a man, shewed him the law he was under as a man; shewed him also the way of atoning the merciful, kind, compassionate Author and Father of him and his being, when he had transgressed that law. He that made use of this candle of the Lord, so far as to find what was his duty, could not miss to find also the way to reconciliation and forgiveness.[35]

How does this fit with Locke's understanding of the mind as a *tabula rasa*? If this candle does not illumine the mind a priori, then how does it work? Why do we need illumination? If empiricism assumes its customary meaning that experience rather than reason is our source of knowledge, then how consistently was Locke himself an empiricist?

Whatever the case with Locke, Wesley never suggested that experience rather than reason could be the source of our knowledge. He identified reason as the foundation and superstructure of religion. As I shall argue later, this is because he followed Malebranche, Cudworth, and Norris in understanding reason in christological and trinitarian terms. He never assumed we had to choose between an a posteriori, empiricist experientialism or an a priori, Platonic intuitionism. He was more like Aquinas in assuming that we know both because our mind participated in the divine

---

34. I don't find persuasive Maddox's assumption that philosophy was "divided into two major camps in the Western intellectual traditions by Wesley's time"—rationalists and empiricists. (See Randy L. Maddox, *Responsible Grace: John Wesley's Practical Theology* [Nashville: Kingswood Books, 1994], 27.) To make Wesley fit into one of these two camps is anachronistic, for it makes him into a modern where these camps can be easily demarcated. I don't think we find this sharp demarcation until pragmatists like William James popularize them in the twentieth century. (See William James, *Pragmatism and The Meaning of Truth* [Cambridge, Mass.: Harvard University Press, 1978], 96.) As we shall see in Wesley's comments on Locke, Wesley adhered to both the Platonic-Augustinian notion that our knowledge was a form of participation in divine ideas and the Aristotelian-Thomistic claim that all our knowledge is mediated through the senses. Wesley's position was not original or unusual. Malebranche's and Norris's epistemology combined these philosophies as did Aquinas himself in the *Summa Theologica, prima pars*, question 15. Maddox does recognize that Wesley could have found a doctrine of the spiritual senses in Malebranche and Norris, but he still works with too sharp a distinction between these two epistemological options— either rationalism or empiricism—as did Runyon before him (Maddox, *Responsible Grace*, 27). For Plato's position see *Phaedo* in *Plato: Complete Works* (ed. John Cooper; Indianapolis: Hackett, 1997), 66-69.

35. Locke, *Reasonableness of Christianity*, 55.

ideas through the Second Person of the Trinity and at the same time that there was nothing in the intellect that was not first in the senses. Both of them developed moral theology as the human creature's renewal into the image of God where the latter assumed the dogmatic context of Trinity and Incarnation.

Wesley's position seems closer to that which we saw in John Norris, which explicitly drew on Thomas Aquinas. The mind is illumined by the mediation of Christ through his church and sacraments, and this is what allows us to know as we should. It is not that the mind only knows from experience qua experience, nor that it naturally participates in eternal ideas. The mind participates in the eternal ideas through its christological mediation. Perhaps this is why Wesley could speak of the law of God as a copy of the eternal mind, a transcript of the divine nature. Our minds can participate in the eternal ideas in God through our participation in the life of Christ by being seized by a vision of him. God's eternity rules out the need to choose between apriorism or aposteriorism.

Locke's epistemology sided with aposteriorism. If Wesley adopted this, then he could not have maintained—as Locke was incapable of maintaining—the central role that the doctrine of the Trinity had in his work as well as his insistence on the coherence between reason and revelation. Locke, like Kant, had difficulties with both these points precisely because he could only view the mind as an empty slate to be furnished with sensible impressions. Locke wrote, "Let us then suppose the Mind to be, as we say, white Paper, void of all Characters, without any *Ideas*."[36] Notice that this assumes the mind does not a priori participate in the divine ideas. The mind is empty, waiting to be furnished from without.

What then furnishes the mind with ideas? Knowledge only comes in from sense perceptions. As Locke puts it, "The senses at first let in particular ideas and furnish the yet empty cabinet."[37] The first aspect of human knowing comes through sensation where objects produce perceptions. The mind then reflects on these sense perceptions from objects, producing ideas. "Reflection," states Locke, is the "source of *Ideas*, every Man has wholly in himself."[38] Notice that he does not argue that we participate in things in the world and this allows us to know them. That is not empiricism. Quite the contrary, we know things only by the resources of reflection we have *wholly* in ourselves. Thus Locke states, "*External Objects furnish the Mind with the* Ideas *of sensible qualities*," and "*the Mind furnishes the Understanding with* Ideas *of its own Operations*."[39] In other words, the mind does not participate in that which it knows.

---

36. John Locke, *Essay concerning Human Understanding* (ed. Peter H. Nidditch; Oxford: Clarendon Press, 1975), 104.

37. Ibid., 55.

38. Ibid., 105.

39. Ibid., 105-6.

This is not Thomistic realism as Fergus Kerr taught us. "Thomas sees no gap between mind and world, thought and things, that needs to be bridged, either by idealist/empiricist representations or . . . by divine intervention."[40] Perhaps Wesley did not as well. Locke like Kant separated mind and world and then had to bring them together. Locke did this when he lost any notion of essence and a metaphysics of participation. Wesley still held to both.

Among the consequences for Locke was the loss of the significance of language. He saw language as something that needed to be overcome through a more secure and certain interior experience. Words constitute empty sounds that function as "signs" of ideas, but they always mislead. And thus religion or morality cannot be based on words. In fact, this is what gets us in trouble because our words are always contingent and therefore misleading. We seldom have a clear and distinct understanding of the words we use. To mitigate against this lack we must look beyond the words to the clear and distinct ideas that the words seek to signify but never do. This is especially the case in biblical interpretation. In Locke's view,

> The volumes of Interpreters, and Commentators on the Old and New Testament, are but too manifest proofs of this [confusion because of language]. Though every thing said in the Text be infallibly true, yet the Reader may be, nay cannot chuse but be very fallible in the understanding of it. Nor is it to be wondred, that the Will of GOD, when cloathed in words, should be liable to that doubt and uncertainty, which unavoidably attends that sort of Conveyance, when even his Son, whilst cloathed in Flesh, was subject to all the Frailties and Inconveniences of humane Nature, Sin excepted. And we ought to magnify his Goodness, that he hath spread before all the World, such legible Characters of his Works and Providence, and given all Mankind so sufficient a light of Reason, that they to whom this written Word never came, could not (when-ever they set themselves to search) either doubt of the Being of a GOD, or of the Obedience due to Him. Since then the Precepts of Natural Religion are plain, and very intelligible to all Mankind, and seldom come to be controverted; and other revealed Truths, which are conveyed to us by Books and Languages, are liable to the common and natural obscurities and difficulties incident to Words, methinks it would become us to be more careful and diligent in observing the former, and less magisterial, positive, and imperious, in imposing our own sense and interpretations of the latter.[41]

The foundation for morality is not found in contingent Christian teachings but in a universal natural religion where God is construed primarily

---

40. Fergus Kerr, *After Aquinas: Versions of Thomism* (Oxford: Blackwell, 2002), 30.

41. Locke, *Essay concerning Human Understanding*, 489-90.

as lawgiver, whose will furnishes us with the necessary laws for moral actions.

Locke was still a metaphysician, but he certainly set in place an empiricism that lent itself toward positivism, which is the assumption that all knowledge is finally about facts that are known through experience and tested by the scientific method. As is well known, this positivism held sway in the nineteenth century. It waged war on metaphysics and theology, and it led to the kind of thinking one finds in the scientism of Carnap's verificationist thesis. This was not Wesley. He could (albeit ambivalently) oppose innate ideas, argue all knowledge first comes through the senses, and cling to the Christianized Platonism of Malebranche, Norris, and Cudworth. For Wesley, as for Aquinas, the eternal ideas are only in God. Truth is the conformity of things to mind, but the mind to which they are conformed is God's. There can be truth in the world independent of human subjectivity, but not of mind. Wesley renders this truth christologically in his discourses on the Sermon on the Mount and makes it the heart of his moral theology. Both Wesley and Aquinas proceed analogically where God and not us is the more excellent term of the analogy (the *via eminentiae*). Thus, as Wesley noted against Locke, there must be essences, even if we do not know what they are. The ideas are not secure in us; it is only as we participate in God that we participate in these essences.

Wesley did not reject Locke's philosophy completely. He found much to affirm in it. But when it challenged the ancient metaphysics of participation, Wesley sided with the ancients. This meant he could not subordinate God to the good as did Locke and Kant. However, Wesley found little to affirm in the moral philosophy of Hobbes and Hume. He rejected their nominalism, arguing that it rendered knowledge of the Triune God impossible and separated love of neighbor from love of God.

THE GOOD WITHOUT GOD (HOBBES AND HUME)

The place for God in Hobbes's moral thought is complex. Some argue that Hobbes thought persons could only obey the ruler of civil society from an obligation to obey "God," whether such an entity existed or not. "God" was a necessary "noble lie" for the sake of obedience to sovereign authority. Others find Hobbes's sense of obligation arising from the motive power of self-interest alone.[42] Hobbes was clearly willing to

---

42. See John Plamenatz's introduction to Thomas Hobbes, *Leviathan* (ed. John Plamenatz; Glasgow: William Collins, 1983), 28-29. (Hereafter referred to as Hobbes, *Leviathan* [Plamenatz].)

appeal to "God" for moral and political authority, but he does so by distinguishing between two cultures of the "seed of religion." One culture nourishes and orders the seed "according to their own intervention," which means through human political sovereignty. The other culture does so "by Gods commandement, and direction."[43] It is the former that is useful for politics because it produces obedience to God's lieutenants. The latter is only useful for the kingdom of God, which has no temporal jurisdiction. The former assists the work of the great Leviathan—"that *Mortall God*, to which wee owe under the *Immortall God*, our peace and defence."[44]

Leviathan is forged out of a covenant based on individual consent. No other covenant can have a temporal claim on individual lives. Hobbes appeals to scripture only in order to insure that revelation has no relation to political life. The purpose of scripture is to show humans the kingdom of God thus "leaving the world, and the Philosophy thereof, to the disputation of men, for the exercising of their naturall Reason."[45] His sharp reason/revelation distinction insures that politics can only be analyzed in terms of philosophy. Revelation, faith, church have no political role. "And whereas some men have pretended for their disobedience to their Soveraign, a new Covenant, made, not with men, but with God; this also is unjust: for there is no Covenant with God, but by mediation of somebody that representeth Gods Person; which none doth but Gods Lieutenant, who hath the Soveraignty under God."[46] And that lieutenant is not the priest, bishop, or any theologian. It is only the temporal political ruler.[47]

For Hobbes, no other voluntary assembly should be permitted if it threatens to take "the Sword out of the hand of the Soveraign."[48] The church can *only* be authorized by this sovereign power. As he put it,

> I define a CHURCH to be, *A company of men professing Christian Religion, united in the person of one Soveraign; at whose command they ought to assemble, and without whose authority they ought not to assemble.* And because in all Common-wealths, that Assembly, which is without warrant from the Civil Soveraign, is unlawful; that Church also, which is assembled, . . . is an unlawfull Assembly.
>
> It followeth also, that there is on Earth, no such universall Church as all Christians are bound to obey; because there is no power on Earth, to which all other Common-wealths are subject.[49]

---

43. Thomas Hobbes, *Leviathan* (ed. C. B. MacPherson; New York: Penguin, 1968), 173. (Hereafter referred to as Hobbes, *Leviathan* [MacPherson].)

44. Ibid., 227.

45. Ibid., 145.

46. Ibid., 230.

47. Cf. Hobbes, *Leviathan* (Plamenatz), 341.

48. Hobbes, *Leviathan* (MacPherson), 287.

49. Ibid., 498.

Does "God" play a role in moral and political thought in Hobbes? Only if the temporal ruler allows it. This is why Hobbes celebrated the latter years of the reign of Henry VIII. He challenged any political jurisdiction of a universal church and strengthened the power of the state against that of any presumptive "catholic" church.[50] The result is a sharp distinction between faith and reason that renders the church and Christianity apolitical and amoral. It casts the teaching received by Moses on Mount Sinai as politically relevant because it gives us useful commands for the common good, while Jesus' teachings on the Mount are seen as mere counsel that individuals can choose only insofar as it does not disturb the public good.[51] Wesley challenged precisely this distinction. For him, like Augustine and Aquinas, the moral life is a synthesis of Moses' received teachings on Mt. Sinai (the law) with Jesus' teaching on the Mount (grace, Beatitudes, gifts). Wesley held together what Hobbes and the liberal tradition that followed him severed.

Whether God exists or not is basically irrelevant in Hobbes's moral and political thought. His turn toward the human body as the basis for moral, political, and religious life could do without God altogether. Yet Hobbes still called upon God in order to explain the good. He wrote,

> Every man, for his own part, calleth that which pleaseth, and is delightful to himself, GOOD; and that EVIL which displeaseth him. Insomuch that while every man differeth from other in constitution, they differ also one from another concerning the common distinction of good and evil. Nor is there any such thing as $\alpha\gamma\alpha\theta o\nu$ $\alpha\pi\lambda\omega\varsigma$, that is to say, simply good. For even the goodness which we attribute to God Almighty is his goodness to us.[52]

"Good" and "evil" name constitutive elements of human bodies. There is no formal essence of the good, no good as a transcendental predicate of being. "Good" merely names a relation we attribute to God in order to account for the pleasure/displeasure produced in the motion of our bodies.

Hobbes explains the good without any substantive reference to God. This is because of his empiricist epistemology and his nominalist account of language.[53] Human understanding begins with sense experience. But

---

50. Cf. Hobbes, *Leviathan* (Plamenatz), 302.

51. See ibid., 239.

52. Thomas Hobbes, *Human Nature and De Corpore Politico* (New York: Oxford University Press, 1994), 44.

53. His nominalism also meant that, unlike Aquinas, he could not fathom such a thing as an unjust law. "To the care of the Sovereign, belongeth the making of Good Lawes. But what is a good Law? By a Good Law, I mean not a Just Law: for no Law can be Unjust. The Law is made by the Sovereign Power, and all that is done by such Power, is warranted, and owned by every one of the people; and that which every man will have so, no man can say is unjust" (Hobbes, *Leviathan* [MacPherson], 387-88).

even when the object of sense is past we can still experience it through imagination. The object produces phantasms that we store in our mind. These phantasms are then ordered internally through discursion. Only after the phantasms are ordered do names, reasoning, and language emerge. Names are nothing but a mark, which is "a sensible object which a man erected voluntarily to himself, to the end to remember thereby somewhat past when the same is objection to his sense again."[54] Understanding is our ability to free names from equivocation, for most of our problems of knowledge arise from a misuse of language. This falsely leads us to believe there are essences. Hobbes plainly states his nominalism: "The universality of one name to many things, hath been the cause that men think that the things themselves are universal . . . deceiving themselves by taking the universal, or general appellation, for the thing it signifieth."[55]

Wesley offers an interesting critique of Hobbes on precisely this point. He writes against him not so much because of his presumed atheism but because of his nominalism. It is Hobbes's account of reasoning and language that Wesley rejects. He finds in these the seeds for a false, extrinsicist (nominalist?) understanding of religion. Hobbes reduced reason to mere externals. When his understanding of language is used for religion, it does the same. Hence, in his sermon "Original Sin," when Wesley argues against mere "outside religion," he says of the latter,

> For an outside religion without any godliness at all would suffice to all rational intents and purposes. It does accordingly suffice, in the judgment of those who deny this corruption of our nature. They make very little more of religion than the famous Mr. Hobbes did of reason. According to him, reason is only "a well-ordered train of words": according to them, religion is only a well-ordered train of words and actions.[56]

Much as Wesley critiqued Locke for failing to attend to essences, he critiques Hobbes for presenting reason as nothing but words that name simple ideas strung together into chains. This could tempt us to think that Wesley was unconcerned with language, actions, and such "external" matters. We could be tempted to contrast his "religion of the heart" to all externalities. But that would be to mistake Wesley's moral theology for Kant's dispositional ethics, where the only good thing is finally a goodwill. Wesley could not have written "The Duty of Constant Communion" if his primary concern were our internal dispositions. What concerns him about Hobbes is that words are mere externals; they do not participate in

---

54. Hobbes, *Human Nature*, 36.
55. Ibid.
56. Sermon 44, "Original Sin," §III.4, *Works* 2:184.

anything other than a bare, positive thing. The result is an inability to understand anything beyond the world of sense objects. Hobbes can only fetishize particular things in the world and not see what sustains them. Wesley says of Hobbes, "None will deny that he had a strong understanding. But did it produce in him a full and satisfactory conviction of an invisible world? Did it open the eyes of his understanding to see

> *Beyond the bounds of this diurnal sphere?*

Oh no! Far from it!"[57] Wesley recognized and critiqued Hobbes for his one-world realism.

Wesley was correct. Hobbes argued that reasoning is "nothing but *Reckoning* (that is, Adding and Substracting) of the Consequences of generall names agreed upon, for the *marking* and *signifying* of our thoughts."[58] Because reasoning has this arithmetical quality it can only occur when it adds things that can be univocally marked and signified. Mixing diversity of names, argued Hobbes, as one does with the expression "*Faith is infused*" is a sign of error.[59] Another source of error is names that signify nothing as with "transubstantiation." If there is no object of sense that can be marked then the term is only erroneous. This is a logical consequence of Hobbes' materialism.[60] Is it not a consequence of a thoroughgoing empiricism as well? Wesley saw this and recognized, as he did with Locke, that without the understanding of an essence we would be locked into Hobbes's nominalist world. But he did not need to discover this alone. Ralph Cudworth had already made the argument in his *Treatise Concerning Eternal and Immutable Morality*, which we will examine below.

Hobbes's nominalism could not countenance the possibility of the will as rational appetite for two reasons. First, the Thomistic position assumes a created order where "good" and "true" are not simply relations to particular individual objects of sense but can also be transcendental predicates of being. Second, Hobbes understood that if such predicates existed, he could not sustain his account of liberty. Thus he explicitly rejected will as rational appetite. Hobbes wrote, "The Definition of the *Will*, given commonly by the Schooles, that it is a *Rationall Appetite*, is not good. For if it were, then could there be no voluntary act against reason. For a voluntary act is that which proceedeth from the will, and no other." Instead, will is

---

57. Sermon 70, "The Case of Reason Impartially Considered," §II.4, *Works* 2:595.
58. Hobbes, *Leviathan* (MacPherson), 111.
59. Ibid., 114.
60. This is why Hobbes cannot adequately think or speak of God. His nominalism polices against a coherent use of theological language, and he thinks this is universally true: "though men may put together words of contradictory signification, as *Spirit*, and *Incorporeall*; yet they can never have the imagination of any thing answering to them" (ibid., 171).

nothing but "the last Appetite, or Aversion, immediately adhaering to the action, or to the omission thereof."[61] It does not seem to be a far step from this point to Hume's claim that reason is a slave to the passions.

Hobbes began his first major work dividing our nature into two parts—reason and passion—and arguing that reason must be put "down for a foundation, as passions not mistrusting may not seek to displace."[62] In other words, reason and not the passions is the foundation for knowledge. In what appears as a complete reversal, Hume will caste reason as a slave to the passions. However, like Kant, Locke, and Hobbes, Hume concedes a complete distinction between faith and reason, so that morality can proceed via reason without any intrusion by faith. "Our most holy religion," Hume states, "is founded on *Faith*, not on reason."[63] By this he insured that faith could not intrude into political or moral life. Even if reason were a slave to the passions, morality proceeded solely from its basis rather than from any theological doctrine.

Hume's work certainly inherited key aspects from Hobbes. For example, his ethics begins with bodies as they are. We find in both thinkers a peculiar feature of the modern world: it fetishizes the body and makes it the foundation for morality, politics, and whatever remains of religion. The assumption that modern philosophers neglected the body is unsustainable. It was all many of them had.

Hume's materialism, constant conjunction, and atheism certainly owe significant debts to Hobbes. As Alasdair MacIntyre notes, Hume "believed himself to be following Hobbes, Shaftesbury, Mandeville, and Hutcheson in giving an account of the constitution of universal human nature and of human society as such" in his efforts to "restore the self to its social identity . . . by means of his account of the complex intentionality and causality of the passions."[64] Like Hobbes, Hume's first major work was "A Treatise on Human Nature." Politics, morality, and religion followed from his understanding of the systematic primacy of the body. For Hume morality is not grounded in reason, it is grounded in passion. But for this reason Hume also gives us a different conception of the will than is found in Hobbes or Locke. Because reason is a slave to the passions, the will cannot be understood in terms of the liberty of indifference. Hume explicitly rejects this option, calling Buridan's ass "a fancied monster."[65]

---

61. Ibid., 127.

62. Thomas Hobbes, *Human Nature and De Corpore Politico* (ed. J. C. A. Gaskin; Oxford World's Classics; London: Oxford University Press, 1994), 19.

63. David Hume, *An Enquiry concerning Human Understanding* (ed. Tom L. Beauchamp; Oxford Philosophical Texts, ed. John Cottingham; Oxford: Oxford University Press, 1999), 186.

64. Alasdair MacIntyre, *Whose Justice? Which Rationality?* (Notre Dame, Ind.: University of Notre Dame Press, 1988), 293.

65. David Hume, *An Enquiry concerning the Principles of Morals* (ed. J. B. Schneewind; Indianapolis: Hackett, 1983), 52.

The passions always come already formed and thus provide a plain foundation of preference.

Hume's principle of morality appears similar to Aquinas's in that "appetite" has a distinct role. However, Hume divides reason from sentiment and fails to consider their connection. This is because the world is not finally reasonable for Hume, unlike what we have seen in Aquinas, Norris, and Wesley. There is no order other than the well-worn path of what is useful or pernicious based on custom. This is all one needs for morality and thus, more so than any other moral philosopher in his day, Hume is willing to develop morality without God. He not only finds God irrelevant to morality, he suggests "God" is positively dangerous.

In his posthumously published *Dialogues concerning Natural Religion*, Hume has Cleanthes state, "Religion, however corrupted, is still better than no religion at all. The doctrine of a future state is so strong and necessary a security to morals, that we never ought to abandon or neglect it." This is a position both Locke and Kant held. Philo responds, surely echoing Hume's own sentiment, "How happens it then . . . if vulgar superstition be so salutary to society, that all history abounds so much with accounts of its pernicious consequences on public affairs? Factions, civil wars, persecutions, subversions of government, oppression, slavery?" In fact, all religion produces is dissimulation and terror.[66] Hume takes away the minor role left to God in eighteenth-century moral philosophy. He shows clearly and convincingly that it is quite possible to think the "good" without any reference to providence or a future state.[67]

This has no deleterious effects on either politics or morality, Hume thought, for he can generate the necessary moral distinction solely from public utility and refuses to see the need to ground it in anything other than that. For morality is primarily a function of convention, of habits deeply engrained in human history that show us where true happiness resides, and this is sufficient to recognize that vice is blamable and virtue rewardable. Mr. Wesley did not find this move to the body satisfactory. He ridiculed it, speaking as a hypothetical sinner:

> "It is true, I often act wrong for want of more understanding. And I frequently *feel* wrong tempers, particularly proneness to anger. But I cannot allow this to be a sin; for it depends on the motion of my blood and spirits, which I cannot help. Therefore it cannot be a sin. Or if it be, the blame must fall, not on *me*, but on him that made me." The very sentiments of pious Lord Kames and modest Mr. Hume![68]

The reader should recognize Wesley's witty use of the term *sentiments*.

---

66. David Hume, *Dialogues concerning Natural Religion* (ed. Martin Bell; London: Penguin, 1990), 131.

67. Hume, *Enquiry concerning Human Understanding*, 189-92.

68. Sermon 128, "The Deceitfulness of the Human Heart," §3, *Works* 4:151.

Hume follows Shaftesbury in developing morality from the practice of everyday life, such as one finds in business and politics, in opposition to what is taught in the philosophical schools and by the theologians. He begins his *Enquiry concerning Human Understanding* by stating, "Moral philosophy, or the science of human nature, may be treated after two different manners; each of which has its peculiar merit, and may contribute to the entertainment, instruction, and reformation of mankind." The first manner of inquiry is to consider "man chiefly as born for action; and as influenced in his measures by taste and sentiment; pursuing one object, and avoiding another, according to the value which these objects seem to possess, and according to the light in which they present themselves." This is an examination of common life. The second species of moral philosophy seeks to "consider man in the light of a reasonable rather than an active being, and endeavour to form his understanding more than cultivate his manners. They regard human nature as a subject of speculation; and with a narrow scrutiny examine it, in order to find those principles, which regulate our understanding, excite our sentiments, and make us approve or blame any particular object, action, or behaviour."[69] Hume was insincerely civil when he stated that both of these manners of inquiry has its peculiar merit, for the latter species of moral philosophy regularly received his wrath.

When Hume develops his account of the origin of morality, he draws on this distinction between morality emerging from common life or from the philosophical schools but posits it as an either-or—either sentiment or reason.[70] His argument for a moral sentiment intrinsic to human bodies is based on the fact that everyone finds professions such as merchandise or manufacture laudable because they procure advantages to society. But the monks and inquisitors become enraged when they discover that their profession is "useless or pernicious to mankind." This is evidence that human beings have a moral sentiment grounded in the approval of public utility or disapproval of a public perniciousness.[71]

Hume assumes and propagates many of the distinctions we have seen common in the eighteenth century, particularly faith versus reason and reason versus sentiment. This sentimental tradition of moral thought, stemming from Shaftesbury and leading to Adam Smith, is a turn away from the priest to the businessman as the model for philosophy. Hume rejects theology, metaphysics, and "school men" philosophy for a morality grounded in everyday life. But everyday life for Hume has nothing to

---

69. Hume, *Enquiry concerning Human Understanding*, 87.

70. Hume, *Enquiry concerning the Principles of Morals*, 13. Hume admits that he received this distinction from Lord Shaftesbury although the latter had only a confused understanding of it.

71. Ibid., 19.

do with church; it is what businessmen do. They never engage in exchanges based on abstract a priori reason; they enter into exchange by valuing public utility. Morality needs no other foundation than this. When philosophers seek for something more, they produce pernicious results.

Two such pernicious results are innate ideas and occasionalism. In his *Essay concerning Human Understanding*, Hume refuses to get dragged into the debate over innate ideas. He argues that the schoolmen misled John Locke when he entered into this debate. Indeed, our language misleads us, for we do not know what is meant by "innate ideas." Hume states, "It is probable, that no more was meant by those, who denied innate ideas, than that all ideas were copies of our impressions; though it must be confessed, that the terms, which they employed, were not chosen with such caution, nor so exactly defined, as to prevent all mistakes about their doctrine."[72] If by *innate* no more is meant than "natural" or "contemporary to our birth" then Hume finds no problem with the term. He recognizes that we have distinct natural impressions of which we cannot know whether they are before, at, or after our birth. Sexual desire is one such impression. Hume thinks Locke did not need to reject innate ideas, for Locke also recognized something like an "innate idea" when it is understood as nothing but a natural impression given to us as bodily creatures. Hume writes, "But admitting these terms, *impressions* and *ideas*, in the sense above explained, and understanding by *innate*, what is original or copied from no precedent perception, then may we assert, that all our impressions are innate, and our ideas not innate."[73] In other words, we cannot be without sensible impressions, even if we have not yet formed ideas about them. They are intrinsic to human bodily existence. But the ideas we have of these impressions are never something other than the constant conjunction of terms that human creatures inhabit through custom and everyday common life.

"Ideas" here are completely severed from essences or any metaphysics of participation and related only to impressions and sense objects. For this reason Hume could also challenge innate ideas when they were used to assume that human society had some a priori blueprint or architectonic rationality to which it was accountable. He wrote, "Have we original, innate ideas or praetors and chancellors and juries? Who sees not, that all these institutions arise merely from the necessities of human society?"[74] There is no "right reason" on which any society is based. There is only the necessity of certain human exchanges that could always be other, for they

---

72. Hume, *Enquiry concerning Human Understanding*, 99n.
73. Ibid., 100.
74. Hume, *Enquiry concerning the Principles of Morals*, 33.

are only based on sentiment and never on reason. Hume notes that Malebranche, Cudworth, and Clarke have all attempted to found everything on reason through their abstract theory of morals at the exclusion of all sentiment. In particular they seek to do this through justice, but Hume finds the latter to be solely based on the interests of society.[75] This is no self-interest. Hume is clear that public utility, not selfishness, is the basis for morality. His understanding of morality, with its rejection of any metaphysics of participation, is based on the conclusions of his inquiry into human understanding, conclusions that (like Hobbes and Locke) remain nominalistic.

Hume's skepticism is based on a division of all objects of human reasoning into two kinds: relations of ideas and matters of fact. The first would be a priori and the second a posteriori. Relations of ideas are intuitively or demonstratively certain and independent of existence. Matters of fact are never independent of actual existences, and because existence itself can always be other, the contrary is possible. To claim that the sun will or will not rise tomorrow can only be a matter of fact. It may very well do so, but I have no a priori assurance that it will or will not.[76] We cannot be assured of the effect simply from the cause. At most all we know is that up until this point this cause and effect were "constantly conjoined with each other."[77] This constant conjunction is not grounded in any a priori reason but emerges from custom alone.

Imagination misleads us to assume that something other than constant conjunction operates in our understanding. The imagination cannot exceed the original stock of ideas furnished by internal/external senses. However "it has unlimited power of mixing, compounding, separating, and dividing these ideas, in all the varieties of fiction and vision."[78] Hume, like Locke, reduces thought to simple ideas. All our thinking is nothing more than a simple idea linked to a copy of our impressions. Everything is singular and particular, but we also have the free play of the imagination to mix and compound simple ideas into complex ones. These complex ideas are abstractions that mislead us. For Hume, unlike Locke, "God" is this kind of an abstraction.

In his *Dialogues concerning Natural Religion*, Hume has Cleanthes challenge the traditional a priori ontological proof for the existence of God. Cleanthes states, "The words, therefore, *necessary existence* have no meaning: or which is the same thing, none that is consistent."[79] This is because nothing in existence can possibly be conceived without its opposite—

---

75. Cf. ibid., 30.
76. Hume, *Enquiry concerning Human Understanding*, 108.
77. Ibid., 109.
78. Ibid., 124.
79. Hume, *Dialogues concerning Natural Religion*, 100.

nonexistence. The term *existence* itself, for Hume, only means that which is, which could have also not been. Thus the term "necessary existence" is unintelligible. As such, if "God" is defined as necessary existence, then it makes as much sense to describe the world itself in the same terms. "But farther; why may not the material universe be the necessarily existent being, according to this pretended explication of necessity?"[80] Why do we get misled into these metaphysical and theological abstractions? We are told that the problem is a problem of language. We unite parts into a whole. This "is performed merely by an arbitrary act of the mind, and has no influence on the nature of things."[81] If we only had clear definitions we could put an end to these verbal disputes that hold us captive to metaphysics and theology, for as Hume through Philo states, "All men of sound reason are disgusted with verbal disputes, which abound so much in philosophical and theological inquiries."[82]

Hume, following Locke, makes something of a "linguistic turn" in metaphysical thinking. As we have already seen, Locke thought the move to universal essences was a mistake of language, where our necessary abstraction from the concrete particular through language misled us into assuming such natures truly existed. Locke still held to real essences, but they were not in the mind of God. They were in the objects of sense and were so minuscule that we would never have access to them.[83] Locke finds our ideas of substance to arise from the combination of simple ideas into complex ideas. The substance "horse," for example, is a collection of those several simple ideas of sensible qualities, which we are accustomed to finding united in the thing called horse. We cannot conceive how these sensible qualities can function separate from a common substance called "horse," so we abstract from these qualities some "common subject; *which Support we denote by the name Substance*, though it be certain, we have no clear, or distinct *Idea* of that *thing* we suppose a *Support*."[84] In other words, there may be some substance called "horse," but if there is, we do not know what it is.

Hume rejected these abstract or general ideas altogether:

> It seems to me not impossible to avoid these absurdities and contradictions, if it be admitted, that there is no such thing as abstract or general ideas, properly speaking; but that all general ideas are, in reality, particular ones, attached to a general term, which recalls, upon occasion, other particular ones, that resemble, in certain circumstances, the idea, present to the mind. Thus when the term *horse*, is pronounced, we immediately

---

80. Ibid.
81. Ibid., 101.
82. Ibid., 128.
83. Cf. Locke, *Essay concerning Human Understanding*, 302.
84. Ibid., 297.

figure to ourselves the idea of a black or a white animal, of a particular size or figure: But as that term is also usually applied to animals of other colours, figures, and sizes, these ideas, though not actually present to the imagination, are easily recalled; and our reasoning and conclusion proceed in the same way, as if they were actually present.[85]

Only the *particular* exists for Hume. Other particulars resemble this particular, and because our imagination can compound simple ideas into universal ones, we mistakenly produce something called "horse" as a substance, essence, or idea. Whereas Locke suggested that such a substance may exist internally to the particular horses, which we can never truly know, Hume denies such a substance altogether. This form of nominalism necessitates a rejection of any intelligible speech about God, especially about a Triune God whose essence is three hypostases.

Because thought is "no more than the faculty of compounding, transposing, augmenting, or diminishing the materials afforded us by the senses and experience," the term *God* only makes sense when we recognize that it "arises from reflecting on the operations of our own mind."[86] What does this mean? Both Aquinas and Malebranche could have made a similar claim. But for them it would mean that we could not think about our own minds well if we did not first think God. Hume reverses this. We are misled into thinking "God" by thinking our own minds as God.

Hume's position becomes clarified in his dialogues concerning natural religion. Three characters make up this dialogue. The first is Demea, who is akin to Malebranche and argues for God based on a priori proof. The second is Philo, who is a thoroughgoing skeptic. He argues that our ideas reach no farther than our experience. The third is Cleanthes, a sober critical philosopher who looks only for proof of God's existence a posteriori. For him, the world is nothing but one great machine.[87] Philo echoes a position similar to Hume's own when he chastises Demea for his argument from design saying, "What peculiar privilege has this little agitation of the brain which we call thought, that we must thus make it the model of the whole universe?"[88] Philo suggests that "god" is nothing but our own mind now imagined to be the foundation for creation. Cleanthes' moderate response to Philo admits the truth of what Philo stated. First he asks Demea, "how do you *mystics*, who maintain the absolute incomprehensibility of the deity, differ from skeptics or atheists, who assert, that the first cause of all is unknown and unintelligible?" Then he takes up the common designation of the "perfect simplicity" of the supreme being and

---

85. Hume, *Enquiry concerning Human Understanding*, 205n.
86. Ibid., 97-98.
87. Hume, *Dialogues concerning Natural Religion*, 51-53.
88. Ibid., 58.

states, "A mind, whose acts and sentiments and ideas are not distinct and successive; one, that is wholly simple, and totally immutable; is a mind, which has no thought, no reason, no will, no sentiment, no love, no hatred; or in a word, is no mind at all."[89] Demea and Philo agree. Thinking of God in terms of the classical attributes like Aquinas will not do. They abstract the pattern of the human mind into a general idea. But this general idea distorts the particular idea of the human mind itself.

The implications of Demea and Philo's argument are significant, but they are implications of Hume's empiricism/materialism. Hume stated earlier than the *Dialogues*, "We have no idea of the Supreme Being but what we learn from reflection on our own faculties."[90] If thought is tied to sensible objects as Hume (and Locke) suggest, then how could we reasonably think God?

One option, which Hume rejects, is Malebranche's "occasionalism." Hume could not, and did not feel the need to, explain why causes and effects were related by constant conjunction. Like Malebranche, he refused to find the connection in some intrinsic nature in the objects themselves. Unlike Malebranche, he refused to find the connection in God. Hume wrote in reference to the Malebranchians:

> They pretend, that those objects, which are commonly denominated *causes*, are in reality nothing but *occasions*; and that the true and direct principle of every effect is not any power or force in nature, but a volition of the Supreme Being, who wills, that such particular objects should, for ever, be conjoined with each other.[91]

Here is where Hume is "Malebranche without God." Hume agrees with Malebranche that we cannot know the relationship of cause and effect by examining the object itself and then discerning a priori what will or will not happen to the object. But once this causal connection is no longer thought valid, how do we understand why causes appear to issue in effects? Malebranche appeals to occasionalism and God's will. Hume attributes the connection to "constant conjunction" and the power of the human will. As he once put it, "It argues surely more power in the Deity to delegate a certain degree of power to inferior creatures, than to produce every thing by its own immediate volition." If we assume it is God's will, then "we are got into fairy land."[92]

Hume did not adopt a liberty of indifference.[93] However, he argued

---

89. Ibid., 69-70.

90. Hume, *Enquiry concerning Human Understanding*, 143.

91. Ibid., 141.

92. Ibid., 142.

93. Cf.: "The prevalence of the doctrine of liberty may be accounted for, from another cause, *viz.* a false sensation or seeming experience which we have, or may have, of liberty or indifference, in many of our actions" (ibid., 158n).

that liberty is essential to morality and that this entails that moral action bears no relationship to God predetermining or foreknowing human actions.[94] He insisted that,

> if human actions can be traced up, by a necessary chain, to the Deity, they can never be criminal; on account of the infinite perfection of that Being, from whom they are derived, and who can intend nothing but what is altogether good and laudable. Or, *secondly*, if they be criminal, we must retract the attribute of perfection, which we ascribe to the Deity, and must acknowledge him to be the ultimate author of guilt and moral turpitude in all his creatures.[95]

Hume considered God's liberty and human liberty to be competitive. If human action were to be moral, it could bear no relationship to the divine will. Likewise, moral human action could bear no relationship to divine reason or wisdom because morality was a matter of taste and sentiment.

Kant and Locke set forth a "moral proof" of God's existence, which became central to eighteenth-century thought. This proof argued that God's existence was necessary to account for human moral concern and freedom. Hume issued a devastating critique of the claim, arguing that belief in providence, a future state, and the need for grace were not necessary to sustain morality; in fact, they destroyed it. Nature itself provided us with a sentiment toward approving and disapproving actions based on their contribution or detriment to public utility. That is all that is needed. The good is more stable without God. Indeed, the good is more stable without any external archetype for it at all. We can now proceed as if all we ever have are ectypes.[96] Demea names correctly the conclusion of Hume's materialism when he states, "To all the purposes of life, the theory of religion becomes altogether useless."[97]

This may or may not have been the consequence Shaftesbury sought when he defended natural affection as the basis for the moral life against Hobbes and Locke's "private interest," but it does seem to be a natural consequence once private friendship and zeal for the public and our country become the basis for the moral life instead of Christian doctrine.[98] To his credit, Wesley saw the consequences of Hume's defense of morality. It severed the second table of commandments from the first and policed God out of all conversations of the good. It was a form of morality that produced atheism.[99]

---

94. Ibid., 161.

95. Ibid., 163.

96. Cf. Philo, arguing as an empiricist, "In all instances which we have ever seen, ideas are copied from real objects, and are ectypal, not archetypal" (Hume, *Dialogues*, 96).

97. Ibid., 80.

98. See Anthony Ashley Cooper, Third Earl of Shaftesbury, *Characteristics of Men, Manners, Opinions, Times* (ed. Lawrence E. Klein; Cambridge Texts in the History of Philosophy, eds. Karl Ameriks and Desmond M. Clarke; Cambridge: Cambridge University Press, 2001), 46-50.

99. Cf. Sermon 120, "The Unity of the Divine Being," §§19-20, *Works* 4:69.

THE GOOD WITH OR WITHOUT GOD, YET DEPENDENT ON OUR "PUBLIC PARENT" (SHAFTESBURY, HUTCHESON, AND ADAM SMITH)

Hume was by far the most significant philosopher from the sentimentalist tradition. This tradition included the third Earl of Shaftesbury (Anthony Ashley Cooper), Francis Hutcheson, and Adam Smith. For some reason, none of the above moral philosophers incurred Wesley's wrath more than Francis Hutcheson. Wesley referred to him as the "smooth-tongued orator of Glasgow."[100] He found Hutcheson's moral theory grounded in disinterested benevolence to be outright atheism. This is surprising and somewhat intriguing. It is surprising in that of all the persons who worked within the sentimentalist tradition none appealed more to God than did Hutcheson. It is intriguing because Wesley recognized that disinterested benevolence produced an other-regarding ethic that required bracketing God out of moral philosophy.

Wesley most likely had not read Adam Smith, and although he seems acquainted with Shaftesbury, he takes Hutcheson as the representative of the "moral sense" tradition. Wesley critiqued him throughout his life. As early as 1746 he stated that the term *conscience* should not be replaced by "moral sense" as some late writers would have it, for conscience, unlike moral sense, is "implanted by God in every soul that comes into the world." This conscience has only one rule, "the Word of God."[101] For Wesley, the conscience is both natural and supernatural at the same time. The moral sense is only natural, and that is why it is problematic. He clearly opposed finding the source of morality in human nature alone.[102] But then he had no conception of humanity as merely humanity. We have a supernatural orientation that conscience itself represented. As late as 1790 Wesley was still going after Hutcheson. He wrote, "But a few years ago a learned man frankly confessed: 'I could never apprehend that God's having created us gave him any title to the government of us. Or that his having created us laid us under any obligation to yield him our obedience.' I believe that Dr. Hutcheson was the first man that ever made any doubt of this."[103] In this 1790 sermon, "The Deceitfulness of the Human Heart," Wesley's argument is that, far from providing the basis for morality as the moral sense theory would have it, the human heart without relation to the divine is the source of deceitfulness. A morality based on mere

---

100. Sermon 106, "On Faith," §II.2, *Works* 3:499.
101. Sermon 12, "The Witness of Our Own Spirit," §§5-6, *Works* 1:302-3.
102. Cf. Outler's introduction, *Works* 1:94.
103. Sermon 128, "The Deceitfulness of the Human Heart," §I.2, *Works* 4:153.

natural moral sense would lead to the severing of the first and second tables of the Law given to Moses. Wesley was correct about the trajectory that moral philosophy was following. But he was somewhat mistaken in suggesting that this began with Hutcheson or that Hutcheson denied divine obligation.

Hutcheson was the first philosopher to use the term "moral sense." He coined the term in developing Shaftesbury's moral philosophy. Hutcheson feared that Shaftesbury's work led to the very thing that Wesley accused him of doing, and it was this concern that prompted Hutcheson to write *An Inquiry into the Original of Our Ideas of Beauty and Virtue*. In this work he sought to distance his moral sense theory from Shaftesbury's prejudice against Christianity—"It is indeed to be wish'd that [Shaftesbury] had abstain'd from mixing with such noble performances, some prejudices he had receiv'd against Christianity; a religion which gives us the truest idea of virtue, and recommends the love of God, and of mankind as the sum of all true religion."[104] Hutcheson's moral philosophy was aesthetic; it related beauty and virtue. For him, this moral sense of beauty comes from God:

> there is a great moral necessity, from God's goodness, that the internal sense of men should be constituted as it is at present so as to make uniformity amidst variety the occasion of pleasure. . . .
> . . . that since the divine goodness, for the reasons above mentioned, has constituted our sense of beauty as it is at present, the same goodness might have determined the Great Architect to adorn this stupendous theatre in a manner agreeable to the spectators.[105]

Hutcheson explains moral goodness as that which "denotes our idea of some quality apprehended in actions, which procures approbation attended with desire of the agent's happiness."[106]

Hutcheson was pivotal in the development of moral philosophy from Shaftesbury to Adam Smith. He was Smith's teacher. Smith's own *Moral Sentiments*, which provided the philosophical basis for his *Wealth of Nations*, owes a tremendous inheritance to Hutcheson. As such, we can be assured that Wesley's criticism of Hutcheson would have carried over to the moral revolution that Adam Smith was about to unleash with his 1776 publication.

Wesley opposed this claim that morality could be grounded in a natural moral sense, universal in all human creatures, especially when this

---

104. Francis Hutcheson, *An Inquiry into the Original of Our Ideas of Beauty and Virtue* (4th ed.; London: D. Midwinter, et al., 1738), xvii.

105. Ibid., 66.

106. Ibid., 69.

universal natural sense is called "benevolence." Note the following interesting critique of Hutcheson by Wesley:

> [Hutcheson] endeavours to prove that virtue and benevolence are one
> and the same thing; that every temper is only so far virtuous as it par-
> takes of the nature of benevolence; and that all our words and actions are
> then only virtuous when they spring from the same principle. "But does
> he not suppose gratitude or the love of God to be the foundation of this
> benevolence?" . . . Nay, he supposes just the contrary; he does not make
> the least scruple to aver that if any temper or action be produced by any
> regard to God, or any view to a reward from him, it is not virtuous at all;
> and that if any action spring partly from benevolence and partly from a
> view to God, the more there is in it of a view to God, the less there is of
> virtue.[107]

Wesley read Hutcheson sufficiently to know that he presents "love of
God" as the foundation of benevolence, so in the middle of his critique he
quotes an assumed interlocutor who is surprised that Wesley accuses
Hutcheson of atheism. Wesley's concern is that Hutcheson's "disinterested benevolence" finds moral action to be good insofar as it promotes
public utility alone. It cannot be referred to God. This destroys the teleology of moral theology. One must expect happiness to be found in God in
order to act well in the world. Wesley rightly worries that Hutcheson's
disinterested ethic grounded in public utility threatens this moral theology. It is insufficient to appeal to God as the author of our moral sense and
then not envision God as the end of our actions, the one who alone can
make us happy. Wesley's critique of Hutcheson shows us he is not a simple pietist who is willing to accept any appeal to God in order to ground
the good.

Wesley's critique of Hutcheson calls into question the whole sentimental tradition, beginning with Shaftesbury. Hutcheson received the notions
of disinterestedness and public utility from Shaftesbury and passed them
on to Hume. Shaftesbury produced something of a revolution in moral
philosophy. He was tutored by John Locke, and, like Locke and Hobbes,
he located the foundation for morality in the human body. However,
unlike Locke and Hobbes (in fact explicitly against them), he rejected the
thesis that self-interest could generate morality. That is, he rejected "philosophical egoism." Rather than the individual body providing the foundation for morality, Shaftesbury founded it in the social body of persons
engaging freely in exchange—especially in the freedom of "wit and
raillery."

Shaftesbury found neither Locke nor Hobbes persuasive. He saw them
as thoroughgoing nominalists who failed to recognize the priority of

---

107. Sermon 90, "An Israelite Indeed," §90, *Works* 3:279.

human sociability to any state of nature or pursuit of self-interest. As Lawrence Klein notes, "Shaftesbury read Hobbes unsympathetically, but not inaccurately, as a thorough nominalist: because, for Hobbes, human signs and their referents were entirely conventional, moral injunctions derived from custom or fiat."[108] Locke was also read as a nominalist because he relied on the commands of God to ground ethical principles. Morality was grounded in the will of God that rewarded or punished based on obedience to divine commands. Thus it was grounded in self-interest.

Shaftesbury sided with the Cambridge Platonists against the liberal tradition. His first published work was an edited volume of Benjamin Whichcote's sermons. Cudworth's *True Intellectual System of the Universe* had also influenced him.[109] Shaftesbury was no atheist. He could appeal to God as a support for human sociability that was prior to even nature, but the god to which he appealed was not the Triune God of Cudworth. He needed only the same stoic god that Hutcheson and Adam Smith appealed to in their moral philosophy, a god who creates a world ruled by disinterested benevolence. For this reason, any account of a future judgment was a threat to virtue. Virtue was its own reward.

Shaftesbury stated that Christian theologians "made virtue so mercenary a thing and have talked so much of its rewards that one can hardly tell what there is in it, after all, which can be worth rewarding. . . . If the love of doing good be not of itself a good and right inclination, I know not how there can possibly be such a thing as goodness or virtue."[110] Shaftesbury was ambiguous on the relationship between religion and virtue. He had little time for atheism, but he also had little time for clerics. In his "Inquiry Concerning Virtue" he wrote, "Religion and virtue appear in many respects so nearly related that they are generally presumed inseparable companions" and we think "well of their union." However no clear connection between them exists. Thus, he concludes, "It may however be questioned whether the practice of the world in this respect be answerable to our speculation." Religious zeal is often combined with a want of "common affections of humanity." And atheists are "observed to practise the rules of morality."[111] What role then has a deity in the practice of morality? The deity provides a sense of right and wrong. Yet actual teachings about God matter little. It does not matter whether someone finally holds doctrines consistent with theism, atheism, polytheism, or demonism. This sense of right and wrong is "as natural to us as natural affection itself" such that "there is no speculative opinion,

---

108. Shaftesbury, *Characteristics*, xxviii.
109. Ibid., xxix.
110. Ibid., 46.
111. Ibid., 163.

persuasion or belief which is capable immediately or directly to exclude or destroy it."[112]

False belief can destroy our natural affection, and it does so for Shaftesbury when our beliefs yield obedience simply to power, as if the moral life is primarily a matter of accruing disadvantage or benefit.[113] Shaftesbury thought Hobbes's and Locke's nominalism assumed this kind of relationship between God and morality. In opposition to it, he argued that anyone who thinks God is good "must suppose that there is independently such a thing as justice and injustice, truth and falsehood, right and wrong, according to which he pronounces that God is just, righteous and true."[114] This Platonic theme will also be found in Wesley and the Cambridge Platonists—with one essential difference. The "just, righteous and true" is not an independent source. It is incorporated into the doctrine of the Trinity; it is the Second Person.

Another significant difference between Shaftesbury, the sentimental tradition, and Wesley is the role of disinterestedness in the moral life. For Shaftesbury, like Hutcheson, true virtue requires disinterestedness.[115] Christianity was judged lacking in this regard, due to its concern with the next life. In particular, he charged that "private friendship and zeal for the public and our country are virtues purely voluntary in a Christian. They are no essential parts of his charity . . . [because the Christian's] conversation is in heaven."[116] The doctrine of heaven prohibits the public spirit that alone can give rise to true virtue. It can come only from a social feeling or sense of partnership with humankind. Virtue and the public spirit emerge only from a love and devotion to one's "public parent," that is, one's own nation. This public parent does not emerge from a state of nature where each individual wars with another. The public parent is the most natural of all inclinations, just as herding is as natural as eating and drinking.[117] One loves the public parent not for the benefits accrued, but simply because it is worthy of one's disinterested affection. One gives one's life for it.

Wesley was aware of Shaftesbury's work. He cited it on occasion. Some similarities existed between them. Both allowed for an ethics grounded in a common life with its everyday exchanges. For Wesley this common life was found in Christian community; for Shaftesbury it was found in the nation and its business transactions. Both wrote in a popular style for ordinary readers. Both could make space for a moderate form of enthusiasm

112. Ibid., 179.
113. Ibid., 183.
114. Ibid., 181.
115. Ibid., 46.
116. Ibid., 46-47.
117. Ibid., 50-51.

because passion was not to be feared. Both also feared a more radical form of enthusiasm. Neither person developed an elaborate system within which to present moral life. (Shaftesbury wrote, "The most ingenious way of becoming foolish is by a system.")[118] Both rejected the nominalism present in Hobbes, and both insisted that the moral life required sociability. In fact, Wesley's statement, "Christianity is essentially a social religion," takes on a richer significance when read against the critiques of Christianity as asocial found in Shaftesbury.[119] Whether or not this statement was an intentional response to Shaftesbury's denial that Christianity promotes sociability, Wesley sets forth the moral significance of Christianity as social in the heart of his own moral theology, which answers Shaftesbury's charge. In one sense, the entirety of the Methodist movement witnessed against Shaftesbury that human sociability was as much, and even more, a part of the Christian moral life as it was that of the "men of the world," whom Shaftesbury defended.

Wesley also rejected key elements in the sentimental tradition. He explicitly critiqued tying the "moral sense" to the public good in his sermon "On Conscience." Hutcheson, Wesley states, says

> every man . . . has a "moral sense," whereby he approves of benevolence and disapproves of cruelty. Yea, he is uneasy when he himself has done a cruel action, and pleased when he has done a generous one.
>
> All this is in some sense undoubtedly true. But it is not true that either the "public" or the "moral sense" (both of which are included in the term conscience) is now *natural* to man. Whatever may have been the case at first, while man was in a state of innocence, both the one and the other is now a branch of that supernatural gift of God which we usually style "preventing grace." But the professor does not at all agree with this. He sets God wholly out of the question. God has nothing to do with his scheme of virtue from the beginning to the end. So that to say the truth, his scheme of virtue is atheism all over. This is refinement indeed! Many have excluded God out of the world: he excludes him even out of religion![120]

Wesley does not reject the claim that human creatures have a moral sense, nor does he reject that it serves a public good. He rejects that this moral sense and public good can be founded in human nature as it is. It only comes as a supernatural gift that must then be mediated to us. To forgo this gift and mediation is to render God superfluous not only to the moral life but to religion itself. Although Wesley is well aware that Hutcheson appeals to God for this moral sense, his stoic disinterestedness prohibits God from being the object of desire. He destroys the heart of the

---

118. Ibid., 130.
119. Cf. Sermon 24, "Sermon on the Mount, IV," §I.1, *Works* 1:533.
120. Sermon 105, "On Conscience," §§I.8-9, *Works* 3:483-84.

Christian moral life: God as the end of our desires whose service makes us both happy and holy.

Hutcheson's aesthetic morality assumed our desire for the good and beautiful did not arise from a supernatural gift but was found in the natural powers we already securely possessed. He stated, "There is a natural power of perception or sense of beauty in objects, antecedent to all custom, education, or example."[121] Like Shaftesbury and Hume, the key to this moral goodness is that it promotes the public good. How does it do so? Not by the threat of reward/punishment, but instead "a wise and good God must determine us to approve . . . actions useful to the publick."[122] Something more than God's will makes things good, just, and holy. Otherwise, states Hutcheson, we would have an insignificant tautology: God's will is good, and the good is nothing but what God wills.[123] It is not God's will that determines the good. Instead, "there is something in actions which is apprehended absolutely good, and this is benevolence or desire of the publick natural happiness of rational agents, and our moral sense perceives this excellence."[124] God, like us, is moral because of his disinterested, universal benevolence.

Wesley is not far wrong when he charges the sentimentalist tradition with subtly excluding God from morality and religion. If virtue is linked only to benevolence, which is the disinterested pursuit of the public good, then the body of the public parent has usurped God as the basis for the moral life. Ethics serves the interest of the nation. Wesley correctly warns the Methodists against this understanding of morality. Our actions should not be disinterested before God solely in service to the nation. We should expect reward in another city, the city of God. Our actions should be done with recognition that our holiness and happiness are linked in this life and the next. But this is not a species of philosophical egoism as found in Hobbes and Locke, because Wesley was no nominalist. The Christian moral life was not mere obedience to commands. Such obedience was a necessary but insufficient basis for the Christian life. It was at most a "religion of the world" or the "religion of the Pharisees," as we shall see in the next chapter. Law was no end in itself. Its purpose was to form in us those supernatural gifts, beatitudes, and holy tempers that alone can make us happy and restore us to the "natural" image of God within which we were created. Wesley did not need to choose between the sentimentalist or the liberal, empiricist tradition. He could recognize the truth and falsity in both of these seventeenth- and eighteenth-century traditions of thought, for he had an alternative to them in his moral theology.

---

121. Hutcheson, *Inquiry into Original*, 56.
122. Ibid., 174.
123. Ibid., 175. We see here, as with Shaftesbury, the influence of Plato's *Euthyphro* on the sentimentalist tradition.
124. Ibid.

Where Adam Smith fits within the sentimentalist tradition is not easily deciphered. On the one hand he does not seem to posit a relationship between benevolence (public good) and virtue. In his famous statement of economic exchanges published in the 1776 *Wealth of Nations* he states, "It is not from the benevolence of the butcher, the brewer, or the baker, that we expect our dinner, but from their regard to their own interest. We address ourselves not to their humanity but to their self-love, and never talk to them of our own necessities but of their advantages."[125] Smith seems less concerned for human sociability as the foundation for morality than did Shaftesbury and Hutcheson. However, like Hutcheson, Smith finds no competition between self-interest and the public good. In a sense, he combines Hobbes and Shaftesbury, and he does so through his stoic doctrine of god. This is evident in the one reference to the "invisible hand" in the *Wealth of Nations* where Smith states that a person engaged in trade "intends only his own gain, and he is in this, as in many other cases, led by an invisible hand to promote an end which was no part of his intention. Nor is it always the worse for the society that it was no part of it. By pursuing his own interest he frequently promotes that of the society more effectually than when he really intends to promote it."[126] Smith does not reject making the public good the heart of the moral life. He follows Shaftesbury and Hutcheson in locating the emergence of morality in terms of this body. God is not necessary for the good, but god can be useful. And the god that is useful is the stoic god whose disinterested universal benevolence insures the best possible outcome. This is Smith's doctrine of unintended consequences. He wrote,

> The ancient stoics were of opinion, that as the world was governed by the all-ruling providence of a wise, powerful, and good God, every single event ought to be regarded as making a necessary part of the plan of the universe, and as tending to promote the general order and happiness of the whole: that the vices and follies of mankind, therefore, made as necessary a part of this plan as their wisdom or their virtue; and by that eternal art which educes good from ill, were made to tend equally to the prosperity and perfection of the great system of nature.[127]

Because Wesley critiqued Hutcheson's more mild sentimentalism where benevolence and virtue were identified, had he been acquainted with Smith's stoicism where benevolence, virtue, and vice appear linked together, we would expect him to have been even more harsh.

---

125. Adam Smith, *The Wealth of Nations* (ed. Edwin Cannan; New York: The Modern Library, 1965), 14.
126. Ibid., 423.
127. Adam Smith, *The Theory of Moral Sentiments* (Indianapolis: Liberty Fund, 1976), 90.

GOD AND THE GOOD COMBINED—
THE CHRISTIAN PLATONISTS
(MALEBRANCHE AND CUDWORTH)

Wesley never read Kant. He was familiar with Hobbes and Locke, rejecting Hobbes's nominalist account of language and Locke's unwillingness to regard essences as anything more than mistakes of language. He associated Hume with Voltaire and other well-known atheists. He wrote little about Shaftesbury, although he was familiar with his work and made references to it. He was as harsh on Hutcheson as he was on Hume or Hobbes, perhaps because he thought as much was to be feared from Hutcheson's use of God as from Hobbes's or Hume's uselessness for God. Overall I think it safe to say that Wesley's moral theology was less influenced by the significant philosophical transitions of the eighteenth century than it was by the philosophy of the seventeenth.

As previously noted, Wesley urged clergy to be able to read Henry More's works, Malebranche's *Search after Truth*, and Dr. Clarke's *Demonstration of the Being and Attributes of God*. More published his *Enchiridion Ethicum* in 1677. Malebranche was born the year after Descartes published his *Discourse on Method* in 1637. He died in 1715. Cudworth, another influential Christian Platonist whose work Wesley knew, lived from 1617 to 1688. Hobbes published *Leviathan* in 1651, and Locke issued *Essay on Human Understanding* in 1689. The latter would have tremendous influence in the eighteenth century, for it was an age of science and empiricism, giving way to positivism. More, Malebranche, and Cudworth grew less influential as their peculiar mix of unorthodox Cartesianism, Christian doctrine, and Platonism gave way to scientism. Yet their work makes more sense of Wesley's moral theology than does Locke's empiricism, for they were able to combine Christian doctrine and the moral life in a way that few theologians and philosophers have done since them.

Nearly every central philosophical and theological theme found in Wesley's published work can be found in Malebranche, who was influential on Wesley. He was read by the Holy Club in the 1730s, part of the curriculum of the Kingswood school and recommended reading by Wesley as late as 1774.[128] Preventing grace, divine illumination, spiritual reaction, the end of the Christian life as happiness and holiness, salvation as renewal of the defaced image of God, the significance and listing of God's perfections, a spiritual sensorium, the rejection of innate ideas in favor of a metaphysics of participation, the importance of sanctification beginning

---

128. See Albert Outler's description of Wesley's use of Malebranche in *Works* 1:59, n. 17.

with the "circumcision of the heart," opposition to nominalism, an emphasis on perfection, a privileging of Christian antiquity, and the Thomistic doctrine that grace perfects but does not contradict nature are all present in Malebranche.[129]

These similarities between Malebranche and Wesley depend on a much more foundational similarity, which is that Jesus Christ renders nature intelligible. This is the essential element in Wesley's moral theology. It cannot be emphasized enough. It is also the heart of Malebranche's position, which can be found in his statement, "I believe that God had Jesus Christ so much in view in the formation of the universe, that what is perhaps most wonderful in providence is the relation it constantly establishes between the natural and the supernatural, between what occurs in the world and what happens to the church of Jesus Christ."[130] Jesus provides the hermeneutic key to understanding creation. He appeared to be only a human, sensible object. But this appearance would be misleading, for he is also divine. A human observer could not look at his body and sense from it exactly who he is. Such a version of empiricism would lead to a false understanding. We would not see well who Jesus is. In fact, we cannot see anything well through mere observation.

For this reason, Malebranche argues that there is a natural revelation that all persons must tacitly share to be able to see anything well. But this natural revelation is no longer intrinsic to human being. It can only come as a gift even for the philosophers who do not understand it.

> God's essence is His own absolute being, and minds do not see the divine substance taken absolutely but only as relative to creatures and to the degree that they can participate in it . . . for God is all being, since He is infinite and comprehends everything; but He is no being in particular. Yet what we see is but one or more particular beings, and we do not understand this perfect simplicity of God, which includes all beings. . . .
> . . . It is God Himself who enlightens philosophers in the knowledge that ungrateful men call natural though they receive it only from heaven. . . . In a word, He is the true light that illumines everyone who comes into the world."[131]

Here Malebranche brings together his rejection of innate ideas with a metaphysics of participation and doctrine of illumination. What connects them together is Christology.

---

129. See Appendix A.

130. Nicolas Malebranche, *Dialogues on Metaphysics and on Religion* (ed. Nicholas Jolley; trans. David Scott; Cambridge Texts in the History of Philosophy, ed. Karl Ameriks and Desmond M. Clarke; Cambridge: Cambridge University Press, 1997), 213.

131. Nicolas Malebranche, *The Search after Truth* (ed. Thomas M. Lennon and Paul J. Olscamp; Cambridge Texts in the History of Philosophy, ed. Karl Ameriks and Desmond M. Clarke; Cambridge: Cambridge University Press, 1997), 231.

Wesley's discussion of "natural conscience" bears a striking resemblance to these key themes in Malebranche. He states, "though in one sense it may be termed 'natural,' because it is found in all men, yet properly speaking it is not *natural*; but a supernatural gift of God, above all his natural endowments. No, it is not nature but the Son of God that is 'the true light, which enlighteneth every man which cometh into the world.' So that we may say to every human creature, 'He,' not nature, 'hath shown thee, O man, what is good.'"[132] "Natural conscience" receives a christological orientation and requires illumination. This is why Wesley condemns Hutcheson's scheme of virtue, which relies on the public sense and the moral sense, as "atheism all over."[133] What Wesley suggests about natural conscience, he also suggests about all our human understanding.

Malebranche explicitly set forth the relationship between the Incarnation and human understanding in his introduction to book 3, "The Understanding, Or Pure Mind," of *Search after Truth*. He writes, "Let us carefully reject all the confused ideas we have as a result of our dependence upon our bodies, and only admit the clear and evident ideas the mind receives through the union it necessarily has with the divine Word, or with eternal truth and wisdom, as we shall explain in the following book, concerning the understanding or the pure mind."[134] For Malebranche, it is not an ability to know the pure givenness of things that allows us to understand the world. It is because of our own *enhypostatic* existence that we can know anything. Only because our being is not secure in itself, but participates in the divine Word, can we see the world rightly. This is why we need illumination. Malebranche states, "The first man's sin has so weakened our mind's union with God that it can be felt only by those whose heart is purified and whose mind is enlightened, for this union appears imaginary to all those who blindly follow the judgments of the senses and the impulses of the passions."[135] This allows for a holy form of skepticism. We should be skeptical about the report our senses make about all the bodies surrounding us. This skepticism arises from revelation itself; "This is one of the truths that the eternal Wisdom apparently wised to teach us by His Incarnation. . . . Whatever of Christ is perceptible deserves our reverence only because of its union with the Word, which cannot be the object of anything but the mind alone."[136]

This emphasis on mind did have negative consequences in Malebranche. At times, despite his protest, he seems to posit a univocal relationship between our mind and God's mind that gives us a direct

---

132. Sermon 105, "On Conscience," §I.5, *Works* 3:482.
133. Ibid., §I.9, p. 484.
134. Malebranche, *Search after Truth*, 195.
135. Ibid., xxxiv.
136. Ibid., xxxviii.

intuition of God simply because we have a mind, which also defines God's being.[137] As we have seen, Hume rightly critiqued him for this univocal conception of mind. Wesley could also be read as setting forth a direct intuition of God's essence that eschewed all mediation, which of course would conflict with his basic Thomistic insight that there is nothing in the intellect that is not first in the senses.[138] But we should not forget that Aquinas himself combined this insight with the *intellectus*, an intellectual virtue in human creatures where through illumination they were capable of directly intuiting first principles. Yet Malebranche so emphasized mind that he thought animals did not truly suffer, and we should not be taken in by their cries. And he did not give proper significance to the role of Christ's human body for our redemption. Malebranche explained why God unites mind and body through a Christology that annihilates the body as the way to redemption:

> Apparently God desired to give to us, as He gave to His Son, a victim we could offer to Him. He desired to have us merit the possession of eternal goods, through a kind of sacrifice and annihilation of ourselves. . . . It is through [the body], as occasional cause, that we receive from God thousands and thousands of different sensations which constitute the stuff of our merit through the grace of Jesus Christ.[139]

This emphasis led to Malebranche's occasionalism. Occasionalism assumes that no secondary causality truly operates, but everything is a direct cause of God's will. Malebranche's occasionalism opposed the scholastic form/matter distinction. He argued that material objects do not transmit species resembling them and that it is inconceivable that the mind receive anything from the body and become more enlightened by turning toward it. He opposed without qualification the Thomistic assumption that knowledge occurred *"per conversionem ad phantasmata."*[140] For Malebranche, the body is a mere "occasion" by which God acts directly. Wesley did not adopt Malebranche's occasionalism, nor does he explicitly endorse the secondary causality of Aquinas. However he does adopt Aquinas's position that there is nothing in the intellect that is not first in the senses. Along with his insistence on an Aristotelian logic against Locke, this would imply more of a Thomistic notion of secondary causality than occasionalism. But Malebranche did not deny the

---

137. For an example of the protest, consider: "We should not jump to conclude, then, that the word *mind*, which we use to express what God is and what we are, is a univocal term signifying the same or quite similar things. God is a mind or spirit, He thinks, He wills; but let us not humanize Him—He does not think or will as we do" (ibid., 251). Contrast this claim with Locke, et al. who argue that to think God is to think something in ourselves.

138. Sermon 62, "The End of Christ's Coming," §III.1, *Works* 2:481.

139. Malebranche, *Dialogues on Metaphysics*, 60.

140. Malebranche, *Search after Truth*, 220, also 102.

significance of the senses altogether. He also stated, "The occasional causes of what must happen to the soul can be found only in what happens to the body, since it is the soul and the body which God willed to unite together. Thus, God can determine to act in our soul in a particular way only by the various changes that occur in our body."[141] Malebranche's work was both familiar to and had some influence on early Methodists.[142]

For Malebranche, human understanding is to be thought according to the doctrine of the Incarnation. He considers the mind or soul to be composed of two faculties: the will and the understanding. The mind—not the body or matter—is where truth is discovered. The mind must be illumined by its participation in the divine life in order to understand body or matter properly. Like Malebranche, Wesley finds illumination necessary for both knowledge per se and moral knowledge in particular. For Malebranche, the good cannot be thought without God, and God cannot be thought without the good. But the good does not move us without God's love for God's self. This is the source of the good and our natural inclination toward it.[143] God can only create us to love God's self and the good, because God can only create consistent with God's own perfections. Following Aquinas, Malebranche identifies three natural inclinations. The first is for the good in general. The second is self-preservation or self-love. The third is toward other creatures who are useful either to us or to those whom we love.[144] Unlike Hutcheson there is no disinterestedness in Malebranche's moral thought. Self-love and the love of others who are useful to us are natural inclinations, necessary for moral action. The difficulty is that we reverse the order and allow the second and third natural inclinations to order our actions without the first. Malebranche insists that we cannot make self-preservation and self-love an end in itself, and both "faith and reason teach us that only God is the sovereign good." But "without grace, we always love Him imperfectly and through self-love."[145]

When we love God only as God is for us, we love only through our second and third natural inclinations. A different kind of love is possible, one that loves God because God is worthy of love, because God is perfect. But this is not a disinterested love, nor is it one that refuses pleasure. Malebranche rejects this position and the popularity of the disinterested

---

141. Malebranche, *Dialogues on Metaphysics*, 222. He also stated, "For you always forget that it is God Himself who produces in our soul all those various sensations by which it is affected on the occasion of the changes that happen to our body" (ibid., 94).

142. See John Clayton's letters to John Wesley (August 1, 1732), *Works* 25:331 and (August 2, 1734), *Works* 25:391.

143. See Malebranche, *Search after Truth*, 266.

144. Ibid., 267-68.

145. Ibid., 287.

stoicism that was on the rise during his era. He states, "We must speak to men as Jesus Christ did and not as the Stoics." This means that "pleasure is always a good, and pain always an evil; but it is not always advantageous to enjoy pleasure, and it is sometimes advantageous to suffer pain."[146] True pleasure should arise from the "prevenient delight" of loving God and not from self-love alone or the love of useful, sensible objects. "Hence sensible objects are not good, they are not worthy of love."[147] The love of good, like the search for truth, can only be satisfying for Malebranche, and Wesley, when we see the world as it is, which can only occur when we see all things "in Him, who contains them in an intelligible manner."[148] Without this vision, which is grace, we cannot distinguish the truth of things from their utility.[149] The *pragmata*—the useful things—distract us from the truth because we only see them, failing to see that in which they exist and are sustained. But this discussion comes only after Malebranche has already stated that this third natural inclination toward pleasure is good—it just cannot exist without the first and second natural inclinations. Thus Malebranche states that "in order to be virtuous and happy, it is absolutely necessary to love God above all things and in all things." This is "the foundation of the whole Christian morality."[150] Wesley said something similar:

> The love of Christ constrains us, not only to be harmless, to do no ill to our neighbour, but to be useful, to be "zealous of good works," "as we have time to do good unto all men," and be patterns to all of true genuine morality, of justice, mercy, and truth. This is religion, and this is happiness, the happiness for which we were made. This begins when we begin to know God, by the teaching of his own Spirit. As soon as the Father of spirits reveals his Son in our hearts, and the Son reveals his Father, the love of God is shed abroad in our hearts; then, and not till then, we are happy.[151]

We have natural inclinations toward the good and the true that draw the will, but not infallibly. For Malebranche, the will is a blind power, which can proceed only toward things the understanding represents to it. This places limits on our will. For instance, it is not in the power of our will not to wish to be happy. The will is the *"impression or natural impulse that carries us toward general and indeterminate good."*[152] The understanding is the power to search for truth. It depends on the will's impulse toward

---

146. Ibid., 310, 307.
147. Ibid., 310.
148. Ibid., 313.
149. Ibid., 314.
150. Ibid., 271.
151. Sermon 120, "The Unity of the Divine Being," §17, *Works* 4:67.
152. Malebranche, *Search after Truth*, 5.

the good as the will depends on the understanding's vision of truth. Both mislead each other. *"The power that the mind has of turning this impression toward objects that please us so that our natural inclinations are made to settle upon some particular object"* misleads the understanding, just as

> the will, being led only to things that the mind has some knowledge of, must be led to what has the appearance of truth and goodness. But because what has the appearance of truth and goodness is not always what it seems, it is obvious that if the will were not free and if it were infallibly and necessarily led to everything having the appearance of truth and goodness, it would almost always be deceived.[153]

Although at many places in his work Malebranche argues that only the grace of Christ mediated by the church redeems our dilemma, he also resolves this dilemma by positing a freedom for the will that contradicts what he has just stated. The result is that our search for truth can occur by adhering to two general rules. The first rule states, *"never give complete consent except to propositions which seem so evidently true that we cannot refuse it of them without feeling an inward pain and the secret reproaches of reason."* The second is *"we should never absolutely love some good if we can without remorse refuse to love it."*[154] This suspension of judgment is not as thorough as will occur in the tradition of liberalism. It is not a suspension of judgment that ends in tolerance and openness for its own sake. Instead, a good use of our freedom is to "refrain from consenting" in judgments of truth and goodness "until forced to do so by the powerful voice of the Author of Nature."[155] Nevertheless, Malebranche's position points in the direction of a liberty of indifference. Wesley could have easily developed it from him as from Locke.

Wesley also knew the work of Cudworth who developed the intellectualist school in opposition to the voluntarist and nominalist school. He included an extract of Cudworth's sermon *The Life of Christ* in his *Christian Library*.[156] The stated goal of this sermon was to "stir Christians up to the real establishment of the righteousness of God in their hearts, and the participation of the divine nature, which the Apostle speaketh of."[157] The passage 2 Peter 1:4 referred to here is at the heart of Wesley's moral theology (as it is for Aquinas). In one of his most speculative sermons, "On Eternity," Wesley drew on Cudworth's work, *The True Intellectual System*

---

153. Ibid., 10.
154. Ibid.
155. Ibid., 11.
156. John Wesley, *Christian Library* (Bristol: Farley, 1749–1755), 17:5-50.
157. Ralph Cudworth (1617–1688), *The Life of Christ, The Pith and Kernel of all Religion; a sermon preached before the Honourable House of Commons, at Westminster, March 31, 1647* (Cambridge: Roger Daniel, 1647), 3.

of the Universe. As previously noted, Wesley refused to adhere to the ancient principle that matter was as eternal as God. He adhered without exception to *creatio ex nihilo.* There is no preexistent matter that the deity fashions into creation. However, he also thought it possible to consider matter as eternal, not *a parte ante* but *a parte post.* "The substance may remain one and the same, though under innumerable forms."[158] Exactly what he means by this is confusing, especially because he insists on creation out of nothing. I take it that he uses this idea as did Cudworth to reject the idea that good and evil, the true and false, or the just and unjust were mere conventions.

Cudworth insisted that the good and true could not be considered simply as "made by law and men." Nor could they simply be a consequence of the divine will. They were part of an "eternal and immutable morality" that depended upon an incorporeal substance. They were not merely volitional but natural.[159] Wesley follows Cudworth in insisting on an incorporeal substance, which does not rival God, "for it is impossible there should be two Gods, or two Eternals."[160] He is willing to call it eternal in a qualified sense. It is eternal only in that it is contained in the mind of God and God is not arbitrary. He does not exercise uncontrollable power to undo what he has done. God's power is not the nominalist power of being able to do anything that does not involve a logical contradiction. God's power is to act consistent with God's essence, which is itself true, good, and just. This is part of God's immutability, which is why God, unlike us, does not repent.[161] For Wesley the incorporeal substance is primarily the soul. Souls will not be annihilated at death. But is it also, as with Cudworth, the good?

Wesley addresses this important question that Cudworth and others raised in the seventeenth century, a question that had its antecedent in Plato's *Euthyphro* and *Philebus.* Wesley asks, "But is the will of God the cause of his law? Is his will the original of right and wrong? Is a thing therefore right because God wills it? Or does he will it because it is right?" He answers,

> I fear this celebrated question is more curious than useful. And perhaps in the manner it is usually treated of it does not so well consist with the regard that is due from a creature to the Creator and Governor of all things. 'Tis hardly decent for man to call the supreme God to give an account to him! Nevertheless, with awe and reverence we may speak a little. The Lord pardon us if we speak amiss!

---

158. Sermon 54, "On Eternity," §7, *Works* 2:362.

159. See Ralph Cudworth, *A Treatise concerning Eternal and Immutable Morality* (ed. Sarah Hutton; Cambridge Texts in the History of Philosophy, ed. Karl Ameriks and Desmond M. Clarke; Cambridge: Cambridge University Press, 1996), 3, 10.

160. Sermon 54, "On Eternity," §7, *Works* 2:361-62.

161. Ibid.

It seems, then, that the whole difficulty arises from considering God's will as distinct from God. Otherwise it vanishes away. For none can doubt but God is the cause of the law of God. But the will of God is God himself. It is God considered as willing thus or thus. Consequently, to say that the will of God, or that God himself, is the cause of the law, is one and the same thing.

Again: if the law, the immutable rule of right and wrong, depends on the nature and fitnesses of things, and on their essential relations to each other (I do not say their eternal relations; because the eternal relations of things existing in time is little less than a contradiction); if, I say, this depends on the nature and relations of things, then it must depend on God, or the will of God. . . .

And yet it may be granted (which is probably all that a considerate person would contend for) that in every particular case God wills this or that (suppose that men should honour their parents) because it is right, agreeable to the fitness of things, to the relation wherein they stand.

The law then is right and just concerning all things. And it is *good* as well as *just*. This we may easily infer from the fountain whence it flowed. For what was this but the goodness of God?[162]

It is no mere coincidence that John Wesley uses "immutable," "eternal," "nature," and "will" in this discussion of God and the good. Cudworth rejected the nominalist thesis that the good is merely what God wills. Thus he also rejected the thesis that morality is primarily the fulfillment of duty—simply doing what is commanded, that is, what is just. Wesley defends the thesis that God wills what is right or just in every particular case, but this alone does not make it just. For the law is good as well as just, and the reason it is good is because it is not only God's will but at the same time it is "agreeable to the fitness of things."

Wesley appears to be engaging issues Cudworth raised. For instance, in his *True Intellectual System of the Universe*, Cudworth noted that some theologians conclude

the perfection of the Deity not at all to consist in goodness, but in power and arbitrary will only. As if to have a will determined by a rule or reason of good, were the virtue of weak, impotent, and obnoxious beings only, or of such as have a superior over them to give law to them, that is, of creatures; but the prerogative of a being irresistible powerful, to have a will absolutely indifferent to all things, and undetermined by any thing but itself, or to will nothing because it is good, but to make its own arbitrary or contingent and fortuitous determination the sole reason of all its actions, nay, the very rule or measure of goodness, justice, and wisdom itself. And this is supposed by them to be the liberty, sovereignty, and dominion of the Deity.[163]

---

162. Sermon 34, "The Original, Nature, Properties, and Use of the Law," §§III.6-10, *Works* 2:12-13.

163. Ralph Cudworth, *The True Intellectual System of the Universe* (London: Thomas Tegg, 1845), 3:461.

In opposition to these "theists," Cudworth argues that God is not "bound or obliged to do the best, in any way of servility, (as men fondly imagine this to be contrary to his liberty) much less by the law and command of any superior (which is a contradiction) but only by the perfection of its own nature, which it cannot possibly deviate from, no more than ungod itself."[164]

Wesley understood the issues between the nominalists and intellectualists. Without denying the significance of God's will as the cause for all that is, he also affirmed its goodness, its fittingness in relating things in the world. The moral life then was not simple obedience to commands. It was the reception and cultivation of those holy tempers that would order one's life with what is fitting in the world. Pagan virtues could imperfectly point one in such a direction, but only the vision of Christ could perfectly order one's life to its true end, for Christ defines what is most fitting in creation. It is in him, through him, and toward him that creation is.

WESLEY AND THE SEVENTEENTH- AND EIGHTEENTH-CENTURY CONVERSATION ON MORAL PHILOSOPHY/THEOLOGY

Phenomenalism, idealism, empiricism, realism, nominalism, occasionalism, skepticism, materialism, and immaterialism were all philosophical positions being forged or solidified in Wesley's day. Each of them related God, morality, mind, world, language, and thought in some kind of systematic coherence. Wesley did not adopt any of these positions. We cannot say he was an empiricist, Cambridge Platonist, or occasionalist. Instead he continued the Anglo-Catholic tradition that developed morality primarily based on Christian doctrine. Wesley's moral theology assumes Jesus as archetype (against Hume's ectype). This necessitated an apriorism. What something is cannot be determined solely from its brute givenness; it is intelligible against the background of the archetype. But this does not dissolve the world into essences and ideas that have no real existence. The pattern for reason is the hypostatic union where humanity and divinity are brought together such that a particular individual discloses to us the fullness of divinity.

This entails that Wesley rejected materialism. We can say with certainty that Wesley was no materialist, nor was he a logical positivist. The former was an option for him that he rejected. The latter was not an option for him except as it developed out of materialism. Wesley rejected Hobbes's

---

164. Ibid., 3:464.

nominalist account of language. He clearly adopted key themes found in Malebranche, Norris, and Cudworth, especially their doctrine of illumination and a metaphysics of participation. He embraced Christian Platonism and did not see an irremediable conflict with what he found in it and key aspects of Locke's thought. I will argue below that this is less because he was an empiricist than that his moral theology was more like the Thomism that came before him than the empiricism that came after him.

Wesley's insistence on the divine perfections as well as his correlation between God's will and God's goodness approaches Cudworth's position more so than any we have examined to this point. I am not arguing that Cudworth was *the* influence on Wesley, there is no such single cause of Wesley's work. He was born into the middle of a conversation in British moral philosophy and theology as all of us are born into the middle of some such conversation. He did not have God's vantage point on this conversation, allowing him to see everything clearly and distinctly. He never thought he had to choose between positions like empiricism or intuitionism as his later interpreters would ask of him. Nevertheless we Methodists would do well to take Cudworth's work as our compass, for although Wesley affirmed in a confused way Locke's liberty as prior even to will, he also taught us that Locke should only be read with a "judicious Tutor."[165] Cudworth can be that tutor, allowing us to read Locke from the vantage point of the doctrine of illumination that Wesley also affirmed. But Wesley's insistence on the freedom of the will could lead to the very nominalistic liberty of indifference Cudworth rightly feared. For he saw where modern theology was headed. The "herd of modern philosophers and theologers," Cudworth stated, make it "an indifferent and blind will fortuitously determining itself, to be both the first mover, and the hegemonic or ruling principle in the soul too." But this is absurd for it is "a will that is nothing else but will, mere impetus force and activity without any thing of light or understanding."[166] The will needs the light of understanding for it to be something other than a mere will to power.

Wesley did not reduce morality to moral *noema* as did More. He was unwilling to mathematize morality, grounding it in self-evident first principles anyone could intuit. Nor was he willing to countenance a *natural*

---

165. Wesley stated,

> From a careful consideration of [Locke's Essay], I conclude that, together with several mistakes, (but none of them of any great importance,) it contains many excellent truths, proposed in a clear and strong manner, by a great master both of reasoning and language. It might, therefore, be of admirable use to young students, if read with a judicious Tutor, who could confirm and enlarge upon what is right, and guard them against what is wrong, in it. They might then make their full use of all the just remarks made by this excellent writer, and yet without that immoderate attachment to him which is so common among his readers.

See "Remarks upon Mr. Locke's 'Essay on Human Understanding,'" *Works* (Jackson) 13:464.

166. Cudworth, *Treatise concerning Eternal and Immutable Morality*, 176-77.

moral sense or reduce morality to benevolence or a public ethic, for such reductions failed to incorporate the center of the moral life for him, which was Christology and Trinity. A public or communal ethic without Christology is Shaftesbury or Hutcheson. Wesley opposed this. It may be better than Hobbes's self-interested ethic, but for Wesley it is still atheism. A public or communal ethic with Christology is Wesley's moral theology, and it makes ecclesiology central. It requires a movement of persons gathering together to seek perfection because Christianity is *essentially a social religion*.

In his sermon "The End of Christ's Coming," written in 1781, Wesley critiqued the reduction of religion to morality in what he refers to as "this enlightened age." In response to the question, what is real religion? Wesley insists that it is the restoration of the image of God in us, "implying not barely deliverance from sin but the being filled with the fullness of God." And then he bemoans the present lack of knowledge of this.

> How little is it understood in the Christian world! Yea, or this enlightened age, wherein it is taken for granted, the world is wiser than ever it was from the beginning of the world. Among all our discoveries, who has discovered this? How few either among the learned or the unlearned? . . . Beware of taking anything else, or anything less than this for religion. Not anything else: do not imagine an *outward form*, a round of duties, both in public and private, is religion. Do not suppose that honesty, justice, and whatever is called "morality" (though excellent in its place) is religion.[167]

Wesley recognized the temptation in the Enlightenment to reduce religion to morality. Even though he defended the importance of morality— "excellent in its place"—he also insisted that it was less than religion. He denounced Hume as "the most insolent despiser of truth and virtue that ever appeared in the world."[168] Although he valued Locke's work, he also expressed dissatisfaction with him, especially as he related reason and revelation. If reason is valued above revelation then religion is reduced to morality. The result is Enlightenment thinkers like Hume. If revelation is valued without reason then the result is enthusiasm, a mere willfulness that refuses knowledge altogether.[169] Wesley sought, as did Malebranche,

---

167. Sermon 62, "The End of Christ's Coming," §III.5, *Works* 2:482-83.

168. May 5, 1772, *Works* 22:321; see also Outler's introduction to Sermon 67, "On Divine Providence," *Works* 2:534.

169. Wesley asked, "Is there then no medium between these extremes, undervaluing and overvaluing reason? Certainly there is. But who is there to point it out? To mark down the middle way? That great master of reason, Mr. Locke, has done something of the kind, something applicable to it. . . . But it is only remotely applicable to this: he does not come home to the point." The "overvaluers of reason" were the modern Enlightenment philosophers such as Hume who thought they could deny Christian revelation. The "undervaluers of reason" were the enthusiasts who thought they could deny reason. Sermon 70, "The Case of Reason Impartially Considered," §5, *Works* 2:588-89.

Norris, and Cudworth, to bring reason and revelation together. But this means that reason and Christian doctrine cannot be separated.

Wesley explains "true religion" in his important sermon "The Unity of the Divine Being":

> It is in consequence of our knowing God loves us that we love him, and love our neighbour as ourselves. Gratitude toward our Creator cannot but produce benevolence to our fellow-creatures. The love of Christ constrains us, not only to be harmless, to do no ill to our neighbour, but to be useful, to be "zealous of good works," "as we have time to do good unto all men," and be patterns to all of true genuine morality, of justice, mercy, and truth. This is religion, and this is happiness, the happiness for which we were made. This begins when we begin to know God, by the teaching of his own Spirit. As soon as the Father of spirits reveals his Son in our hearts, and the Son reveals his Father, the love of God is shed abroad in our hearts; then, and not till then, we are happy. We are happy, first, in the consciousness of his favour, which indeed is better than the life itself; next in the constant communion with the Father, and with his Son, Jesus Christ; then in all the heavenly tempers which he hath wrought in us by his Spirit.[170]

Benevolence, morality, happiness, friendship (or constant communion with God), and the Trinity are inseparable. Wesley consistently related our knowledge of the Trinity with morality. He did not relate some generic reason with revelation. It was a specific account of reason that concerned him. If we do not know God as Triune, we cannot receive the holy tempers for the moral life that will make us happy.

In fact, for Wesley, the moral life is only possible christologically. It is within the context of the question, "Do not all men, however uneducated or barbarous, allow it is right to do to others as we would have them do to us? And are not all who know this condemned in their own mind when they do anything contrary thereto?" that Wesley answers, "No, it is not nature but the Son of God that is 'the true light, which enlighteneth every man which cometh into the world.' So that we may say to every human creature, 'He,' not nature, 'hath shown thee, O man, what is good.'"[171] If we know the good, we know Christ. If we know Christ, we know the good. For better or worse, that is the heart of Wesley's moral theology.

Wesley tied theology and ethics together at a time when in England and on the continent they were coming apart. Even to say that Wesley "tied them together" does not state well his understanding of theology and ethics, for they had not yet been unraveled. He did not work with a distinction between them even when he recognized that in England and elsewhere they were coming apart. This makes his work more like

---

170. Sermon 120, "The Unity of the Divine Being," §17, *Works* 4:67.
171. Sermon 105, "On Conscience," §§I.4-5, *Works* 3:482.

Cudworth and Norris than Locke or Kant. For it is the latter who decisively separated God and the good—cleaving them apart by the intrusion of the will and its absolute freedom (both God and ours). Wesley used the language of Locke in explaining his moral psychology, but fortunately it never did much work for him. Lessons he learned from Henry More and Gerard Langbaine remained more decisive. And those lessons hark back to an older tradition of moral theology that refuses the cleavage modern ethics executes.

But this does pose a difficulty for us, and perhaps this difficulty is the reason moral theology such as Wesley's waned in influence. A reasonable critique of Wesley, Cudworth, and Malebranche's moral theology is the life of Hume. None of them could have thought he was truly happy. But, as his biographer, Boswell, suggested, he appeared to die happy without God. If this is possible, a moral theology that ties happiness and holiness together appears to be called into question. This is an accentuated version of the theological question, how do we make sense of vicious Christians and virtuous pagans? Hume's life accentuates this question, for he suggests that theological doctrine is positively dangerous to morality. Happiness results from its exclusion. One response is to deny that Hume was happy; he may have been heroic, but he could not have been happy if happiness entails knowledge of God. Pagan virtue without God cannot make one truly happy. But that is a difficult position to sustain. Another possibility is to disregard happiness altogether and make morality a matter of duty alone. That is Kant's position; it is not Wesley's. An ethics of duty suggests that obedience to commands may or may not bring happiness, but that does not matter. Fulfilling one's obligation alone counts. Morality is reduced to justice. Such a position destroys virtue, for it assumes a world where goodness and truth compel the will and intellect to search for them and when they are found one's being finds happiness. Any disinterested ethic destroys the teleological ordering of the good and true.

What then of virtuous pagans? Unlike Luther's severe Augustinianism where pagan virtues were splendid vices, Wesley had a place for pagan virtues. They were not to be destroyed by grace, even though they could not be perfected without a vision of Christ. Pagan virtues set one out on a journey to avoid harm and do the good. This ancient quest was itself the lure of grace, a preventing "delight" as Malebranche put it, or "prevenient grace" in Wesley's words. This journey was to be celebrated, and all who were on it could find something in common. However, this journey to avoid evil and achieve the good could not satisfy, for it had no end until Christ was its true end. When the end is known the journey becomes more intelligible. For this reason, Wesley could adopt general rules for the Methodist movement, tell people they were necessary to follow, and then tell them that even if they followed them they had still accomplished nothing. They were preparatory for the reception of grace that would then make living the rules possible out of joy and delight rather than mere obligation. This seems similar to the medieval concept of *potentia obedientialis*, understood as our nature given supernaturally and never in terms of pure nature.

What then of vicious Christians? If the moral life were a supernatural gift given in part through knowledge of God in Christ, how do we account for the fact that the gift does not seem to accomplish its purpose? We cannot. It is absurd—something we cannot account for theoretically. Instead it is taken into account practically through a movement of persons whose distinct charism is to be so formed by that supernatural gift that in their social life together perfection itself may be evidenced. Perhaps the Wesleyan movement itself was to be an answer to this question. This is a kind of pragmatism, but one that is inextricably linked to the truth of Christian doctrine and does not begin to find truth only in the utility of everyday life.

Given Runyon's proper insistence that Wesley sought a mediated Christianity and thus rejected innate ideas, it does make sense to believe he had a bit of the empiricist in him. For after all, would not Lockean empiricism lead us to believe that knowledge of God is finally mediated through our senses? Yes it is, but Malebranche, Norris, and Cudworth could also affirm this while at the same time insisting on the Christian doctrine of the Trinity as that which allows us access to the ideas in the mind of God by which our senses give us knowledge. While Locke appears sympathetic to a mediated Christianity, he finally rejects it in favor of natural religion, the very thing Wesley railed against. However, the Christian Platonists can be read as losing the external world, collapsing it into ideas. For Wesley, neither ideas nor senses finally allow us to see what we need to see. If he has an epistemology, and I would argue that he did not because he was not yet a modern, Wesley's epistemology was grounded in the gift of faith.

Wesley's sermon "Walking by Sight and Walking by Faith" takes as its text 2 Corinthians 5:7, "We walk by faith, not by sight."[172] This is the closest thing to a statement on epistemology that he has. He begins, "All the children of men that are not born of God 'walk by sight,' having no higher principle. By *sight*, that is, by *sense*; a part being put for the whole" (§3). Sight as "sense" signifies knowledge of the visible world. But this puts us in a quandary, for Wesley argues, "All our external senses are evidently adapted to this external, visible world. They are designed to serve us only while we sojourn here, while we dwell in these houses of clay. They have

---

172. Sermon 119, "Walking by Sight and Walking by Faith," *Works* 4:49-59.

nothing to do with the invisible world: they are not adapted to it" (§6). Precisely because Wesley admits the Thomistic principle *"nihil est in intellectu quod non fuit prius in sensu"* (§7), he affirms how deep our difficulty is. Those who "walk by sight," that is, those who only live by their sense, who find experience alone to provide them with knowledge cannot "see" the invisible and eternal. Wesley asks, "But is there no help? Must they remain in total darkness concerning the invisible and the eternal world? We cannot affirm this: even the heathens did not all remain in total darkness concerning them" (§8). For some light reached even them. But only when "the Father revealed the Son" in their hearts, and "the Son revealed the Father" (§11) could anyone be properly illumined. Wesley states, "It is where the sense can be of no farther use that faith comes into our help. It is the grand *desideratum*: it does what none of the senses can; no, not with all the helps that art hath invented" (§12). Only through the supernatural gift of faith can we understand our true nature. Wesley relates this to morality. "They that *live* by faith, 'walk by faith.' But what is implied in this? They regulate all their judgments concerning good and evil, not with reference to visible and temporal things, but to things invisible and eternal" (§14). Wesley then asks the Methodists if they value things by the visible or the invisible. He does so by asking them a practical question, "which do you judge best, that your son should be a pious cobbler or a profane lord? Which appears to you most eligible, that your daughter should be a child of God, and walk on foot, or a child of the devil, and ride in a coach and six?" (§15). Here is Wesley's moral theology. It is neither empiricist nor intuitionist. It is theological, based on a doctrine of illumination—something we do not have by nature, but receive as gift. And it is also a matter of practical reason.

CHAPTER 4

WESLEY'S MORAL THEOLOGY

From a twenty-first-century vantage point, we see clearly what Wesley only saw emerging in the eighteenth century. God would not be excluded from moral and political matters on the basis of some anti-moral sentiment. It was instead precisely an understanding of religion as identical with morality that rendered "God" a useless and irrelevant category. "God," like all other "values," became a private preference and thus devalued. The highest values indeed devalued themselves, but not without some help from the philosophers and theologians. The human body itself, either as an individual thing or as a collective corporate body, would provide the foundation for morality and politics. Once this occurred, "God" was useful only insofar as this term rendered those bodies secure. But we are now in a posthumanist era. This ethical foundation is quickly becoming as antiquated and quaint as Wesley's moral theology.[1]

---

1. Michel Foucault argued that "man" arises only with the loss of classical discourse at the end of the eighteenth century. Once the transcendentals of "labor, life, and language" emerge as the conditions for the possibility of thought, then "man appears in his ambiguous position as an object of knowledge and as a subject that knows." This in turn produces the invention of "man" and the "human sciences" that study his ambiguous and double position. It also leads to the dominance of the "unthought" and the "unconscious" as the key that will allow us to understand him. But Foucault argues that "man" is coming to an end. "Man is an invention of recent date. And one perhaps nearing its end." See Michel Foucault, *The Order of Things: An Archaeology of the Human Sciences* (New York: Vintage Books, 1973), 387. To say we are in a posthumanist era is to agree with Foucault that the assumption of "humanity" as a secure and certain subject and object of knowledge is now unraveling. It no longer provides the center it once did.

125

Ethics grounded in the human body no longer holds the dogmatic certainty it did from the later-eighteenth through the mid-twentieth centuries. It can no longer claim a foundation in universal reason. Faith in humanity and its progress requires at least as much, if not more, of an intellectual sacrifice than faith in the Triune God. Will "ethics" disappear without this humanist foundation? Will Nietzsche be proved correct as we move "beyond good and evil"? Or will it be the case that contending communal ethics will now shape our lives, where every question of the good is always dismissed with the response, "that may be your good; it is not mine (or ours)"? Such questions are better left for prophets or our posterity to answer.

Like Wesley, we are living through significant transitions in moral theory and practice. We also are in the midst of a conversation whose contours do not come clearly to view. How shall we go on? We can no more *return* to Wesley than we can to Aquinas or to the Bible, as if there were some previous space and time that exists to which we have unmediated access. Time machines remain illusions of science fiction. However, we can *pick up* on conversations that we neglected or were thought to be behind us. I do not think we can, or should, restore Wesley's moral theology. I do think the conversation of which he was a part was able to hear and engage the witness of past centuries of practical wisdom in a manner that became unnecessarily problematic for us. The purpose of this chapter and the next is to pick up where that conversation left off.

In the last chapter I positioned Wesley's moral theology within the shifts that occurred in moral philosophy in the eighteenth century. I did not argue that Wesley knew all these authors or their significance. Nor did I argue that he understood these shifts, for he worked in the middle of them. In his best moments, Wesley recognized that God was being policed out of morality, and religion, by the very arguments philosophers and theologians used to defend God. Wesley's own understanding of the moral life inherited ancient theological and philosophical themes. Because he did not find these themes wanting, he made no effort to be novel and modernize the moral life. Aristotle, Plato, Augustine, and Aquinas provided many of these themes. Of course, above all, the Scripture was his primary source, along with the ancient creeds, and the teaching of the Anglican Church.

Consistent with orthodox teaching itself, Wesley argued that a "bare orthodoxy" would not suffice, for, after all, the demons themselves believe and tremble. Nor was the mere observance of God's commandments adequate. The Pharisees accomplished this, and although observance of the commands was necessary, like a bare orthodoxy, it was insufficient. Ritual observance would not suffice either. Even though we are under divine obligation to attend to the Means of Grace as often as we have opportunity, the observance itself could not substitute for a holy life. All of these resources for the Christian moral life—orthodox doctrines, laws and commandments, and ritual observance—occupied the same position in Wesley's moral theology. They were all necessary but insufficient. We will misunderstand Wesley if we think these ecclesial practices of doctrine, law, and sacrament are dispensable—as if we could have Methodism without the discipline these practices provide. Yet even though they are necessary, more is required. The more is faith, hope, and, above all, charity. Wesley explains this more in his sermon "The Important Question." This question is, "What is religion?" Wesley answers,

> It is easy to answer if we consult the oracles of God. According to these it lies in one single point: it is neither more nor less than love—it is love which "is the fulfilling of the law," "the end of the commandment." Religion is the love of God and our neighbour—that is, every man under heaven. This love, ruling the whole life, animating all our tempers and passions, directing all our thoughts, words, and actions, is "pure religion and undefiled."[2]

Of course this is nothing new in Christian teaching. It is an Augustinian theme. No Christian theologian could deny this, and I cannot think of one who has. It is, as Wesley noted, the scriptural witness. The tradition of moral theology recognized this, albeit with significant variations in explaining how charity is the "more." Augustine taught that charity is the form of all the virtues. Aquinas stated that the Christian life "consists chiefly in charity whereby the soul is united to God."[3] Wesley's claim is nothing new.

Yet Wesley also notes that love is the "end" of the commandment that animates all tempers and passions. While this too is a biblical theme, Wesley's use and development of this central biblical theme bears a striking resemblance to the tradition articulated so well in Thomas Aquinas. This tradition teaches that law directs human acts to virtuous ends where the final end is charity. It is an infused virtue in the human soul as well as the characteristic of the Triune life. Without violating the distinction between the Uncreated and the created, Aquinas argued that the life of God (grace, which is the presence of the Holy Spirit) animates the soul to accomplish its supernatural end: participation in the divine life. This participation sanctifies the soul, allowing a person to live by the new law of

---

2. Sermon 84, "The Important Question," §III.2, *Works* 3:189.

3. *Summa Theologica* II-II.184.1, ad. 2. See also Serge-Thomas Bonino's "Charisms, Form, and States of Life," in *The Ethics of Aquinas* (trans. Mary Thomas Noble; ed. Stephen Pope; Moral Traditions Series, ed. James F. Keenan; Washington, D.C.: Georgetown University Press, 2002), 347.

the gospel. This new law renders intelligible the old law by fulfilling it. In other words, the law, whose basic principle is do good and avoid evil, is a means and never an end in itself. One could keep the law and never do a harmful action against a neighbor (never kill, steal, bear false witness, and so on) and still miss the law's true end if the infused gift of charity did not animate these actions. One might accomplish this out of fear of reprisal or because one is an ethicist or clergy member and it is necessary for advancement in one's career. One might accomplish this simply out of a stoic disinterestedness; one lacks the passions that might lead to retaliation. While the end result is still good—neighbors are not harmed—the law is not fulfilled.

Although one cannot fulfill the law through its mere observance, nor can one claim to fulfill it through neglect, it is better for the law to be kept through moral heroism or fear of reprisal than not kept at all. Wesley's criticism of bare orthodoxy, observance of commandments, and ritual formality could mislead interpreters to think that he teaches a dispositional ethic where all that matters is "the religion of the heart." But if by that term a dispositional ethic is meant, then Wesley's moral theology has been traded for Kant's ethics. While the observance of the law cannot guarantee its fulfillment, its neglect guarantees that it remains unfulfilled. This helps us understand the important role of the General Rules for Wesley. A rule such as the Methodist rule that members shall not own slaves or traffic in slave-made goods could not be abrogated on the basis of some internal disposition no one but the individual knew. There was no private space where "love" permitted disobedience. Nor could one plead the merits of Christ and neglect the rules. Observance of the rules bore an intentionality within them, which functioned at least negatively. While the observance itself did not guarantee one was tending toward the proper end of charity, neglect of the rules proved the agent lacked the proper intention. Neither an appeal to a charitable disposition nor even the merits of Christ could justify an abrogation of the law and render it innocuous. Forgiveness was available, but that forgiveness would issue in the fruits of a sanctified life. For this reason, when publishing his *Works* edition of his sermons in 1771, Wesley placed the crucial individual sermon "The Lord Our Righteousness" before his series of discourses on the Sermon on the Mount. This sermon, following upon "The Great Privilege of Those that are Born of God" and leading into the discourses on the Sermon on the Mount, provides an intriguing shape to Wesley's moral theology. This shape is underscored by the placement of three sermons on law after the Sermon on the Mount series: "The Original, Nature, Properties, and Use of the Law," and "The Law Established through Faith, I and II." This set of sermons reveals some of the key themes in moral theology that Wesley inherited.

One theme is indicated by the fact that Wesley's discussion of the law comes after he articulates the virtues, gifts, and Beatitudes that Jesus taught, and gave, to his disciples. As we shall see, the law (including the General Rules) makes no sense without the virtues, gifts, and Beatitudes. But these in turn make no sense apart from their placement in Christian orthodoxy. If we do not know who Jesus is, his teaching on the Mount loses its spiritual depth. The first thing Wesley establishes in his discourses on the Lord's Sermon, and the point he returns to in the sermons on the law, is that Jesus himself is the Eternal Law, the Second Person of the Trinity, now made flesh. The teaching of the Sermon on the Mount can only have its full force when we recognize the Chalcedonian grammar that the one who speaks it is truly God and truly human and yet one person. This vision alone directs our gaze to its proper end, ordering our tempers and passions as they should be ordered naturally and supernaturally at the same time.

Perhaps the central theme throughout these sermons is Wesley's exegesis of the significance of the expression "the Lord our righteousness." He opens with this theme and returns to it in the concluding second discourse on "The Law Established through Faith."[4] The law of love is itself the foundation for creaturely being. Adam saw this naturally, but this sight is lost through sin. We cannot see it, and thus the law can no longer be established by sight alone. That poses a problem for us because Wesley follows Thomas Aquinas in stating that there is nothing in the intellect that is not first in the senses. If our natural powers were capable of seeing what is most essential to be seen, then the law would be established by sight, and all would be well with our soul. But it is not. A supernatural gift restores us to our natural state. This comes through infusion by the Holy Spirit in a sacramental action. Thus Wesley defines faith as "the grand means of restoring that holy love wherein man was originally created."[5]

The infused virtue of faith is never an end in itself. Wesley orders the theological virtues hierarchically. Faith is the "handmaid of love."[6] Faith ordered toward love perfects its work. It does so by completing all goodness, righteousness, and truth. What does this look like? To answer that question takes us into the specifics of the Christian moral life, which Wesley develops in his thirteen discourses on the Sermon on the Mount. These specifics are predicated upon three themes, which Wesley assumes and uses throughout his sermons. The first is that law directs human acts to a virtuous end, which is both natural and supernatural. The infused theological virtues—faith, love, and hope—give shape to all other virtues,

---

4. Sermon 36, §I.6, "The Law Established through Faith, II," *Works* 2:37.
5. Ibid., §II.6, *Works* 2:40.
6. Ibid., §II.1, *Works* 2:38.

tempers, and passions. Pagan virtue has a place in Wesley's moral theology, yet it needs perfecting by these infused virtues. The second essential theme is that grace perfects, not destroys, nature. This is a clear Thomistic inheritance mediated through persons such as Malebranche, Norris, and Cudworth. It depends on their intellectualist ontology. Although our nature is totally depraved for Wesley, it has tempers and passions that naturally yearn for what is good, right, and true. Left to its own empirical reality, human nature cannot discover what satisfies these natural cravings. Only faith achieves that by ordering our affections toward the love of God. Such an ordered life will entail holiness and happiness. Without these two the expression "the Lord our righteousness" establishes nothing but self-deception. The third assumed theme is that the Christian moral life is a life of virtue, gifts, and beatitude that assumes a particular sociality where doctrine, laws, and sacraments are crucial means, but never ends, for the cultivation and reception of these gifts. The importance of this sociality should not be lost on the reader as I develop the content of Wesley's moral theology. It only works within the context of a community of Christians seeking holiness through practices such as pursuing works of mercy through a common discipline.

THE LORD OUR RIGHTEOUSNESS

I will begin presenting Wesley's moral theology with his sermon "The Great Privilege of those that are Born of God" in *Sermons on Several Occasions*. This is a rather arbitrary beginning point. I could have begun with the first sermon in this collection, for what he develops in his discourses on the Sermon on the Mount and in the establishment of the law builds on the theological themes that came before and after these important sermons. However, "The Great Privilege of Those that are Born of God" explicates 1 John 3:9, which, along with 2 Peter 1:4, is at the heart of Wesley's moral teaching. First John 3:9 states "Whosoever is born of God doth not commit sin." Wesley makes explicit reference to moral teaching in this sermon, noting that by faith and the return to God through "spiritual respiration" one is "capable of 'discerning' spiritual 'good and evil.'"[7] The moral life is a recovery of the spiritual discernment of good and evil. The new birth is depicted in active, moral terms. It is a "vast inward change" which requires us to "live in quite another manner than we did before; we are, as it were, in another world."[8] It is a work of the Holy Spirit, who provides a spiritual sensorium. That is to say, we are given "spiritual senses capable of discerning spiritual objects."[9]

---

7. Sermon 19, "The Great Privilege of Those that are Born of God," §I.8, *Works* 1:434-35.
8. Ibid., §I.1, *Works* 1:432.
9. Ibid., §I.6, *Works* 1:434.

Wesley explains what it means to be born of God by assuming an *exitus-reditus* schema. Through creation one "subsists" in God. Thus in one sense all creation is born of God. But this subsistence in God is defined primarily by a sensible life, which he refers to consistently as "sight." We are misled into thinking that the sensible objects before us constitute our being. We see only what is before us, missing its depth. However, to be born of God is to return and be restored to the image of God, who is Jesus Christ. This occurs through faith. It is the virtue by which the newborn soul receives the animating life of the Spirit. And the life of faith, which is God's presence in the soul, is returned to God by love, prayer, praise, and thanksgiving. This constitutes Wesley's theme of action/reaction. God infuses life into the soul, and the person then cooperates by returning that life to God through specific acts. This is why Wesley would say that this gift of faith "implies not barely the being baptized."[10]

One could easily misunderstand Wesley here, as I fear some of the churches in the Wesleyan communion have, by separating church membership from baptism. But that would be to overlook the relationship between the internal and external working of faith. Wesley is not arguing that the external work of baptism bears no relation to the infused virtue of faith. That interpretation would conflict with what he already established in the sermon "The Means of Grace."

The influence of Malebranche's law of the union of soul and body helps us understand why Wesley insists that senses are misled by mere external objects like the water of baptism. For instance, in "The Means of Grace" Wesley wrote, "*before* you use any means let it be deeply impressed on your soul: There is no *power* in this. It is in itself a poor, dead, empty thing: separate from God, it is a dry leaf, a shadow."[11] The sacrament as an empirical object of the senses alone is nothing but a "shadow," an interesting term for Wesley to use. To see the empirical object and fail to see what sustains it is to fail to see reality and see only its illusions. This is Malebranche's law of the union of the soul and body. To see the body without realizing that we can only see it in the context of the invisible world that sustains it is to be in error. But this does not mean that we then can dispense with the body and claim some immediate intuition without its mediation through the bodily senses.

We need the externals; we cannot be nor understand without them. Insofar as the Wesleyan communions have interpreted Wesley as saying that baptism does not matter but only faith, they miss the point. The matter of the sacrament—water, bread, wine—like proper Christian doctrine and General Rules, are necessary but insufficient external realities. To

---

10. Ibid., §I.1, *Works* 1:432.
11. Sermon 16, "The Means of Grace," §V.4, *Works* 1:396.

fetishize them as objects of the senses and treat them as if they were the reality is to miss reality itself. This is why the third General Rule insists that we attend upon the ordinances of God, and yet Wesley also stresses that we must not trust in their sensible, bodily reality alone.

Faith as an infused gift lets us see what our physical sight alone cannot see. This gift of faith is a participation in the "candle of the Lord" that illumines the eternal, invisible reality that shows sensible objects to be what they are: mere shadows. The bread we eat, the wine we drink, and the water we pour is here only a fleeting moment. Despite all appearances it has no substance in itself. Even though all created reality subsists in the divine Word, without illumination we will be tempted to see it subsisting in itself, and that would mean it subsists in nothing. Does this mean that we can do without these sensible objects and gain some unmediated, intuitive access to God? When he is consistent, this does not appear to be Wesley's position. For he never backs away from his claim that there is nothing in the intellect that is not first in the senses.

Wesley appeals to "spiritual senses being now awakened,"[12] clearly recognizing that placing *spiritual* and *sense* together is a surprising conjunction of terms. It is a metaphor. Senses are by definition not spiritual. They are the material means by which objects are perceived. In order to place these terms together Wesley must make allusion to the doctrines of illumination and participation in the divine nature. He makes reference to both doctrines, drawing on 2 Peter 1:4 and 2 Corinthians 4:6 in explaining how a believer comes to sense what is beyond sensibility:

> He clearly perceives both the pardoning love of God and all his "exceeding great and precious promises." "God, who commanded the light to shine out of the darkness, hath shined" and doth shine "in his heart, to enlighten him with the knowledge of the glory of God in the face of Jesus Christ." All the darkness is now passed away, and he abides in the light of God's countenance.
>
> . . . Thus the veil being removed which before interrupted the light and voice, the knowledge and love of God, he who is born of the Spirit, "dwelling in love, dwelleth in God and God in him."[13]

Only when illumined by Christ can we see what is there to see. This occurs only as we receive the "exceeding great and precious promises," which are nothing less than partaking in the divine nature itself.

Much as Thomas Aquinas correlated the seven sacraments to seven natural ordinary activities of daily living, Wesley correlated spiritual illumination to the everyday sensibility of human living. Taste, touch, hearing, smell, and vision in themselves can only mislead. If experience

---

12. Sermon 19, "The Great Privilege of those that are Born of God," §I.10, *Works* 1:435.
13. Ibid.

depends only on these material sources, then our knowledge of reality will be no better than that of Hobbes. But through illumination by the glory of God in the face of Jesus Christ, these senses can provide access to something more. Here is a concrete example of Wesley's use of the teaching that "grace perfects nature." Nature itself, with its sensibility, is necessary for knowledge even of God, but only when this nature is illumined by the glory that proceeds from the face of Jesus Christ.

Illumination does not occur without this vision of Jesus who unveils God's face. Wesley's doctrine of illumination does not assume some transcendent mystical experience distinct from the mediation of God's glory in Jesus. This is where his moral theology begins, and this is why his work can best be explained by the term moral *theology*. It is now commonly argued that the tradition of moral theology lost its theological moorings through the manualist tradition in Counter-Reformation Catholic theology. Vatican Council II sought to recover the theological context for the moral life, particularly by drawing—as did Aquinas—more fully on Scripture and patristic resources. Even though he had a distinct place for law, practical reasoning, and a kind of casuistry, Wesley's moral theology never veered from its christological and sacramental context. The language of the ancient creeds and the Chalcedonian definition renders his moral theology intelligible. It will make little sense if that language is not presupposed. In the material, fleshly body of Jesus Christ we find the glory of God. This occurs without human nature becoming something other than human nature, or divinity becoming something other than divinity. Both maintain their distinction from each other. At the same time both become one through the hypostatic union such that what we say about Christ's humanity must also be said about his divinity and vice versa. This leads us to make statements such as "Mary gave birth to God," even though we know that divinity is not derived from human activity. It is this noncompetitive nature of the divine and human in Jesus Christ that gives us knowledge of God's glory. Only from this foundation in the Incarnation can we dare to consider that the glory of God can be mediated through vision, smell, hearing, touch, and taste—not as they are in themselves, but as they become illumined and participable as something other than themselves in Christ's Incarnation, Life, Crucifixion, Resurrection, and Ascension. This is the "great privilege" of those who are "born of God."

Wesley precedes his discourses on the Christian moral life with a discussion of this great privilege. He distinguishes justification from the new birth. Although they are inseparable in time, they each have their own distinct nature. Justification implies a relative change, where "God . . . does something *for* us." The new birth is a real change, where God does something *in* us. "The one restores us to the favour, the other to the image of God."[14] The moral life is a restoration of the image of God through sanctifying grace.[15] It begins with faith and as long as faith reigns it will direct us to love. The result is that sin is impossible. Wesley does not argue that believers do not sin. He argues that as long as faith reigns in the believer's soul, sin is impossible. The presence of sin reveals that faith does not reign.

In "The Great Privilege" Wesley offers a theological analysis of sanctifying human action and its participation in God's infused action. He provides a nine-step schematic of human action, infused virtues, and the fall into sin.[16] He begins with a term he will use throughout his moral theology: the "divine seed" of faith makes it possible for us to participate in God's life. Because this is a participation in God's life, it will entail the possibility of perfection. We will look at each of the nine steps in turn.

"The divine seed of loving, conquering faith remains in him that is 'born of God.'"

Christian moral action begins by the participation of God in our soul. The "exceeding great promise" given to us is this participation. As long as we participate in this reality, sin is not possible. However, to live by faith and not by sight is not easily accomplished.

"A temptation arises, whether from the world, the flesh, or the devil, it matters not."

Temptation emerges when the materiality of the world appears to be an end in itself. The flesh is nothing but flesh; it is pleasing to the eye, taste, and touch. Wesley returns throughout his sermons to Augustine's *triplex concupiscentia*—lust of the eye, desire of the flesh, desire to be made wise—where the temptation account in Genesis 3 is read in terms of John's first Epistle urging believers not to be conformed to this world with its temptations of touch, taste, and sight.

"The Spirit of God gives him warning that sin is near, and bids him more abundantly watch unto prayer."

---

14. Ibid., §2, *Works* 1:431-32.

15. Randy Maddox rightly notes that the restoration of the image of God in humanity as a form of renewed participation in the life of God is at the heart of Wesley's theology and anthropology. However, Maddox primarily reads this as an Eastern influence on Wesley and misses how pervasive it was in the Western sources Wesley knew. Maddox is too indebted to Zizioulas's sharp distinction between the East and the West and fails to see how Western theological sources were as committed to these doctrines as was the East. See Randy L. Maddox *Responsible Grace: John Wesley's Political Theology* (Nashville: Kingswood Books, 1994), 68 and 287 n. 19. Sarah Coakley's *Re-Thinking Gregory of Nyssa* (Oxford: Blackwell, 2003); David Hart's *The Beauty of the Infinite* (Grand Rapids, Mich.: Eerdmans, 2004); and A. N. Williams's *The Ground of Union: Deification in Aquinas and Palamas* (Oxford: Oxford University Press, 1999) should put an end to the sharp distinction between East and West that has misled interpreters of Wesley since Albert Outler first interpreted him in those terms.

16. See "The Great Priviledge of Those that Are Born of God," §II.9, *Works* 1:440.

Having been infused by grace, which is the life of the Spirit animating the soul of the believer, the believer should walk by faith and not by sight. Although one cannot walk by faith without sight, one can walk by sight without faith. Prayer is the prophylactic that avoids the hindrance of walking by sight alone.

"He gives way in some degree to the temptation, which now begins to grow pleasing to him."

Pleasure is not an evil for Wesley. He opposed any disinterested account of the moral life. It entails happiness along with holiness. But pleasure only in the sensible without the eternal orders our life toward a baseness that, for Wesley, could not bring true happiness. The will is not determined. It remains free to pursue an apparent good that tempts it away from God.

"The Holy Spirit is grieved; his faith is weakened, and his love of God grows cold."

Faith and love are always related in Wesley's work. Faith, which is a kind of knowledge, lets us know who God is and what God has done for us. This entails love of God and neighbor. The relationship between these two infused virtues is similar to the relationship between justification and the new birth. The intellect and will are inextricably connected. We can only love what we know, and we can only know what we love. If faith weakens, love grows cold. If love grows cold, faith weakens.

"The Spirit reproves him more sharply, and saith, 'This is the way; walk thou in it.'"

The pneumatological aspect of the Christian moral life remains central throughout Wesley's moral theology. The Spirit is the witness that witnesses to our spirit without the latter being usurped by the former. Both act concurrently. The Spirit acts first, but we remain at liberty to cooperate with the Spirit's witness. This assumes a noncompetitive dual causality in human action patterned on the Incarnation.

"He turns away from the painful voice of God and listens to the pleasing voice of the tempter."

The Christian moral life depends on turning, it is a function of that to which one is ordered. This shows the teleological character of Wesley's moral theology. What is our end? Will it be God's voice, which appears painful? Or will it be the pleasing voice of the tempter?

"Evil desire begins and spreads in his soul, till faith and love vanish away."

Although the infused virtues of faith and love are gifts, they must at the same time be cultivated. They cannot be acquired, but the Christian must cooperate in them or the gifts vanish.

"He is then capable of committing outward sin, the power of the Lord being departed from him."

What is the power of the Lord but the ability to actualize the potentiality of the infused virtues of faith and love? This "divine seed" becomes ours in the process of sanctification. When our will no longer cooperates with this power, then sin is possible.

In "The Great Privilege," Wesley begins with a positive construal of human action as faithful participating in the life of God. He then moves to a discussion of failed human action. This analysis of sinful human action is Wesley's commentary on Genesis 3, which he uses as the archetype of failed human action. His entrance into the discussion of the Christian moral life focuses on sin as a violation of a known law of God. One context for his discussion of the moral life is that God has given us commands that we are to obey. Sin is a voluntary transgression of those commands.

This could easily degenerate into the casuistic practical divinity of both Puritanism and Counter-Reformation Catholic moral theology, such as can be found among the Jesuits and Redemptorists.[17] Methodist moral theology can easily degenerate into a legalistic ethics of obligation. However, there is a context prior to the context of command and obligation even in this sermon. Christian moral life is a life restored into the image of God. It is a reciprocal, although by no means mutual, exchange. Wesley stresses that the

> life of God in the soul of a believer is . . . the continual inspiration of God's Holy Spirit: God's breathing into the soul, and the soul's breathing back what it first receives from God; a continual action of God upon the soul, the re-action of the soul upon God; an unceasing presence of God, the loving, pardoning God, manifested to the heart, and perceived by faith; and an unceasing return of love, praise, and prayer, offering up all the thoughts of our hearts, all the words of our tongues, all the works of our hands, all our body, soul, and spirit, to be an holy sacrifice, acceptable unto God in Christ Jesus.[18]

All our bodily senses, along with our soul and spirit, are to respond to the inspiration and illumination of the Holy Spirit. We are kept in the perpetual cycle where God gives, we respond, God gives yet more, we respond still more, then failed human action becomes unthinkable, a theological absurdity. Its reality in the life of believers is not something to be excused but forgiven. It is only as we participate in God's Being through this reaction of gift-reception-return that it is possible for us not to commit sin. Thus the moral possibility here is inseparable from God and human participation in the life of each other. This is why it is inseparable

---

17. See Raphael Gallagher, "Interpreting Thomas Aquinas: Aspects of the Redemptorist and Jesuit Schools in the Twentieth Century," in Pope, *Ethics of Aquinas*, 374-84.

18. Sermon 19, "The Great Privilege of Those that Are Born of God," §III.2, *Works* 1:442.

from the creedal affirmations on the Trinity and Christology. While Wesley does not explicate the christological basis of the moral life in "The Great Privilege," it is evident implicitly. He articulated this basis clearly in his 1765 published sermon "The Lord Our Righteousness."

THE LORD *OUR* RIGHTEOUSNESS

In the 1748 edition of *Sermons on Several Occasions* Wesley followed up "The Great Privilege" with his thirteen discourses on the Sermon on the Mount. But when publishing his collected *Works* in 1771 he placed "The Lord Our Righteousness" between "The Great Privilege" and the thirteen discourses. Why? Albert Outler notes that this placement resulted from the ongoing debates between Wesley and the Calvinists over whether Christ's obedience was the "formal" or "meritorious" cause of salvation. If Christ's atoning death was the formal cause of justification, then it allowed for little significant human participation (other than that of Christ) in our redemption. This position was consistent with predestination and irresistible grace. But if Christ's atoning death was the meritorious cause, then while still evangelical, it also allowed for prevenience, free will, and universal redemption.[19] The former emphasized imputed righteousness at justification, the latter, inherent righteousness. The Calvinist James Hervey argued that Wesley's position turned Christ's atoning work into a "meritorious cause" that failed to take into account that Christ alone is our righteousness. He saw Wesley's position as similar to that of Cardinal Bellarmine. Hervey stated that Wesley "is pleased to associate with the Papists in ascribing our salvation partly to inherent, partly to imputed, righteousness."[20] "The Lord Our Righteousness" was Wesley's response to Hervey's claims.

Wesley began by reaffirming his commitment to the Protestant emphasis that Christ alone is our righteousness. He cites Luther's *"articulus stantis vel cadentis ecclesiae"* to demonstrate his Protestant credentials: the church stands or falls by its fidelity to the claim that Christ alone is our righteousness. But he then makes reference to the Athanasian creed to support his argument. This shows that the emphasis is not only Protestant but also a traditional Catholic argument as well. Wesley states, "[the Lord our righteousness] is certainly the pillar and ground of that faith of which alone cometh salvation—of that *catholic* or universal faith which is found in all the children of God, and which 'unless a man keep whole and undefiled, without doubt he shall perish everlastingly.'"[21] That Christ alone is

19. See Outler's introduction to Sermon 20, "The Lord Our Righteousness," *Works* 1:444-46.
20. Quoted in ibid., 446.
21. Ibid., §4, *Works* 1:451.

our righteousness is for Wesley an essential theme of the catholic faith that determines one's status in the church diachronically and synchronically.

Wesley is somewhat romantic about the ability for Protestants and Catholics to agree on the meaning of the theme "the Lord our righteousness." He suggests that if we just had a clearer definition of the terms involved we would be able to have a common meaning that Christians everywhere could find compelling. His sermon attempts to offer such a clarification. What he offers is a traditional Chalcedonian reading of Christ's righteousness, presenting this as essential for the Christian moral life. It forms the basis for his subsequent development of moral theology from Jesus' Sermon on the Mount.

What is Christ's righteousness? It is both divine and human, as Jesus himself is both fully divine and fully human. Righteousness describes both natures working together in perfect harmony. As divine, Christ is "ὁ ὤν." He is Being itself. Wesley simply repeats the common Christian confession, drawing on Exodus 3, that God's most literal and proper name is "Being" or "the one who is." For Wesley in this sermon, God's Being is God's perfections. Here the fullness of Being is associated with divine righteousness; God's nature and God's righteousness are identical. This assumes the classical notion of God's simplicity and that God's essence equals God's existence.

Wesley uses these terms not only to establish the Triune relationship between God and Jesus but also to understand what it is Christians mean when they say "the Lord our righteousness." He writes,

> His divine righteousness belongs to his divine nature, as he is ὁ ὤν, "He that existeth, over all, God, blessed for ever": the supreme, the eternal, "equal with the Father as touching his godhead, though inferior to the Father as touching his manhood." Now this is his eternal, essential, immutable holiness; his infinite justice, mercy, and truth.[22]

This righteousness, which is nothing less than the divine nature itself, is not what is imputed to us. Otherwise we would become God. Although we become participants of the divine nature, Wesley insists that we do not become identical to the divine nature itself. He always maintains the distinction between creation and the Uncreated. Our status as creatures continues even into eternity, for it is precisely in and through our creaturely status that God redeems us. However, Christ's human righteousness is imputed to us, and through this imputation we participate in the divine

---

22. Ibid., §I.1, *Works* 1:452. This language is consistent with Wesley's first response to what someone must believe if "their heart is as his heart." Here is another explication of God's "being and perfections."

nature. The essential Chalcedonian language is maintained throughout Wesley's moral theology. It cannot work without it.

Wesley presents Christ's human righteousness as both "external" and "internal."[23] His external human righteousness bears both a negative and positive meaning. Negatively, Christ refrained from sin; he avoided evil. This is necessary but not sufficient for his righteousness. Positively, "He did all things well." In other words, he did the good fully. He was fully obedient to the will of God on earth, as angels are in heaven. His was a perfect performance of human righteousness. He fulfilled the law. These two aspects of Christ's human righteousness are the first precept of the natural law as well as the first two General Rules for the Methodist people. Christ's negative human righteousness avoided evil; his positive human righteousness fulfilled the good. Wesley gave these classical themes in moral theology a christological determination.

Broadening this point, Wesley explained that Christ fulfilled the law through *both* his active and passive righteousness. His active righteousness was determined by his positive actions in the world. As Wesley puts it, "The whole and every part of his obedience was complete."[24] It is this active obedience that leads to his passive righteousness, which is "suffering the whole will of God from the time he came into the world till 'he bore our sins in his own body upon the tree.'"[25] Christ's sufferings were not ends in themselves. He did not seek suffering and death, they are the consequence of his active righteousness. He willingly, but passively, endured them. They are only indirectly willed because of the directly willed active righteousness he performed. In other words, in a world of sin where failed human action reigns, an infallible performance of God's will can only be perceived as a threat. Suffering, persecution, and death are the result. This is the eighth beatitude, which is the consequence of a life that embodies the first seven beatitudes, the life Christ himself lived.

Suffering and death do not have the last word. Christ's external human righteousness, along with his active and passive obedience, produces an internal righteousness. It is the "image of God stamped on every power and faculty of his soul. It is a copy of his divine righteousness, as far as it can be imparted to a human spirit. It is a transcript of the divine purity, the divine justice, mercy, and truth."[26] Christ's human performance mirrors the divine performance that relates God and Jesus. His human performance is a "transcript" of that original Triune relationship. Once again we see the influence of Christian Platonism on Wesley's thinking. Who Christ is in his Triune relationship is copied in his human relationship.

---

23. Ibid., §I.2, *Works* 1:452.
24. Ibid., §I.3, *Works* 1:453.
25. Ibid., §I.4, *Works* 1:453.
26. Ibid., §I.2, *Works* 1:452.

The hypostasis of the Second Person of the Trinity is Christ's original righteousness. The hypostatic union relating the divine and human in Jesus mirrors that original hypostasis in human terms. It is this human righteousness that can be imputed to all other human beings. This righteousness "includes love, reverence, resignation to his Father; humility, meekness, gentleness; love to lost mankind, and every other holy and heavenly temper: and all these in the highest degree, without any defect, or mixture of unholiness."[27]

These virtues will be repeated with variations in a number of different lists throughout Wesley's work as the essence of the Christian moral life.[28] They are what Wesley means by "the religion of the heart." What must be emphasized at this point is their trinitarian form. Love, reverence, and resignation to God describe the relationship between the First and Second Persons. Through Christ's human righteousness, we are invited into this same relationship. The Spirit draws us into it, for these virtues are not only what is imputed, but this imputation becomes inherent in human nature. This possibility emerges from the Incarnation. It results from Jesus' *human* performance in both its active and passive righteousness. Jesus is both fully divine and fully human without mixture, but in one Person. His human performance is a copy or transcript of the divine righteousness, which not only is imputed to us but can inhere in us. It is a divine righteousness that can become creaturely without ceasing to be divine.

The expression "the Lord our righteousness" is much more than simply a forensic justification of sinful humanity in Wesley's work. Wesley recognizes this is a Protestant theme. He states unequivocally that "all believers are forgiven and accepted, not for the sake of anything in them, or of anything that ever was, that is, or ever can be done by them, but wholly and solely for the sake of what Christ hath done and suffered for them."[29] But this is only the beginning of the Christian life. Christ's work is not simply to justify but also to sanctify. So a Calvinist like Hervey would ask, "But do not you believe *inherent* righteousness?" Wesley responded, "Yes, in its proper place; not as the *ground* of our acceptance with God, but as the *fruit* of it; not in the place of *imputed* righteousness, but as consequent upon it. That is, I believe God *implants* righteousness in every one to whom he has *imputed* it."[30] Note the similarity between what Wesley argued in the earlier sermon "The Great Privilege" where he spoke of the "divine seed" and his use of the verb *implants* in "The Lord Our Righteousness." Does this imply something like created grace in

---

27. Ibid., *Works* 1:452-53.
28. See Appendix B.
29. Sermon 20, "The Lord Our Righteousness," §II.5, *Works* 1:455.
30. Ibid., §II.12, *Works* 1:458.

Wesley's thought? The righteousness of God becomes ours, while maintaining the distinction between the Uncreated and creation.

Wesley insists that he no more denies Christ's righteousness than Christ's Godhead, and in fact to deny one is to deny the other.[31] He is not arguing that we merit justification or sanctification through our own efforts. He is arguing that Christ's righteousness is not only a formal but also a meritorious cause in that his life makes possible a new way of life for us. He fears that if we only use the expression "the Lord our righteousness" as a formal cause of salvation, it will be used to legitimate our unrighteousness. So he writes,

> In the meantime what we are afraid of is this: lest any should use the phrase, "the righteousness of Christ," or, "the righteousness of Christ is 'imputed to me,'" as a cover for his unrighteousness. . . . though a man be as far from the practice as from the tempers of a Christian, though he neither has the mind which was in Christ nor in any respect walks as he walked, yet he has armour of proof against all conviction in what he calls the "righteousness of Christ." . . . O warn them that if they remain unrighteous, the righteousness of Christ will profit them nothing.[32]

Christ's righteousness does not provide some secure internal form of salvation despite all evidence of practices and tempers. Here again we see Wesley's denial of a dispositional ethic. Wesley could never use the expression that we must not judge because no one knows what is really in someone's heart. He admonishes the Methodists to warn others that if no external evidences are present in tempers and practices, persons cannot appeal to "the Lord our righteousness" and think themselves redeemed. While these external evidences themselves are no guarantee, their absence requires rebuke.

THE LORD OUR *RIGHTEOUSNESS*: BEATITUDE AS TRUE RELIGION

Only after Wesley has explained Christ's righteousness by explicit references to the doctrine of the Trinity and the Incarnation, and after explaining how this righteousness is not simply imputed to us but also inherent in us, can he then show us the shape of this righteousness. In classical fashion he does so by way of commentary on Christ's Sermon on the Mount. Jesus' life and teaching are the shape of righteousness.

---

31. Ibid., §II.14, *Works* 1:459.
32. Ibid., §§II.19-20, *Works* 1:462-63.

Wesley states in an open letter the purpose of his thirteen discourses on the Sermon on the Mount. They "assert and prove every branch of *gospel obedience* as indispensably necessary to eternal salvation."[33] Christ's active human righteousness is to become our righteousness. The shape of this righteousness will be found in the first seven beatitudes. If we embody this righteousness, then we should expect to embody also his passive righteousness, found in the eighth beatitude: blessedness in persecution.

Wesley begins his commentary on the Sermon by establishing whom it is that speaks on the Mount. "Let us observe who it is that is here speaking, that we may 'take heed how we hear.'" He tells us that the one speaking is "the eternal Wisdom of the Father . . . who knows how we stand related to God, to one another, to every creature which God hath made."[34] As the "Wisdom of the Father," Christ is the Eternal Law upon which every creature is called into being. To know him is to know the relations of all things. Wesley also states, "It speaks the Creator of all—a God, a God appears! Yea, ὁ ὤν, the being of beings, Jehovah, the self-existent, the supreme, the God who is over all, blessed for ever!"[35] The Sermon on the Mount is divine discourse intended for all believers, offering us the shape of that righteousness that Jesus is, and which he makes to be ours. Wesley understands it as a repetition of the ten words given to Moses on Mount Sinai, with "a wide difference." The wide difference is that here God himself appears.[36]

Wesley then outlines the Sermon on the Mount. He divides it into three parts based on the three chapters of Matthew 5–7. The fifth chapter shows us "the sum of all true religion . . . laid down in eight particulars." Wesley treats them in his first five discourses. He refers to the first six beatitudes—poverty of spirit and mournfulness (both treated under "humility"), meekness, righteousness, mercy, and purity of heart—as "the religion of the heart."[37] These tell us what Christians are supposed to be. The seventh beatitude, "peacemakers," tells us what Christians are supposed to do. It is the outward conversation that issues from the inward holiness of the first six beatitudes.[38] The eighth beatitude shows what the person who has this religion of the heart should expect.[39] Here are those

---

33. Cited by Outler in his introduction to sermons 21-33, *Works* 1:466.

34. Sermon 21, "Upon Our Lord's Sermon on the Mount, I," §2, *Works* 1:470. Wesley offers seven descriptions as to who Jesus is as he speaks on the Mount. He is "Lord of heaven and earth," "the Creator," "the Lord our Governor," "the great Lawgiver," "the eternal Wisdom of the Father," "The God of love, who, having emptied himself of his eternal glory, is come forth from his Father to declare his will to the children of men," and "the great Prophet of the Lord."

35. Ibid., §9, *Works* 1:474.

36. See ibid., §7, *Works* 1:473-74.

37. Sermon 23, "Upon Our Lord's Sermon on the Mount, III," §II.1, *Works* 1:517.

38. See ibid.

39. Ibid., §III.1, *Works* 1:520.

holy tempers that are the ends toward which doctrine, General Rules, and sacraments tend. If orthodoxy, observance of commandments, and the means of grace do not produce this religion of the heart in eight particulars, then they are for naught; they are bare.

The sixth chapter offers "rules for that right intention which we are to preserve in all our outward actions, unmixed with worldly desires, or anxious cares for even the necessaries of life."[40] Wesley explains this in discourses six through ten, which set forth a holy intentionality. He asserts that the second part of the Sermon shows how actions "indifferent in their own nature, may be made holy and good and acceptable to God, by a pure and holy intention."[41] This occurs through works of mercy and works of piety. But this is also where he examines the actions of common life. Here is his social ethics; although that is a very inappropriate term, for Wesley does not divide personal and social or internal and external. The seventh chapter of the Sermon on the Mount issues warnings as to what should be avoided in order to attain the religion of the heart that will issue in external and social fruits. The seventh chapter, which Wesley discusses in discourses ten through thirteen, is presented as offering cautions against the main hindrances of religion. These are primarily improper judging, casting pearls before swine, and neglecting ritual observances such as prayer.[42] These three parts to the Sermon correlate to the three General Rules of the Methodist societies. The third part shows us how to avoid evil, the second how to do good, and the first how to attend to the ordinances of God.

In his first five discourses Wesley exegetes the eight Beatitudes as the sum of all true religion in eight particulars. The Christian moral life begins in humility, which defines the first two beatitudes: poverty in spirit and mournfulness. But humility itself is no virtue. One must never take pride in humility. It is nothing but emptiness, a receptivity to be filled by God's infused beatitudes. For Wesley the first two beatitudes are evidence of our total depravity. Who is the one who is poor in spirit and who mourns, he asks? Such a person is convinced of sin and has a "deep sense of the loathsome leprosy of sin, which he brought with him from his mother's womb, which overspreads his whole soul, and totally corrupts every power and faculty thereof."[43] Notice his language here: every power and faculty is totally corrupted.

That the moral life begins with this kind of total depravity places Wesley in the tradition of Calvin and Augustine. This tradition contrasts with Aquinas where the first principles of the moral law are not

---

40. Sermon 21, "Upon Our Lord's Sermon on the Mount, I," §10, *Works* 1:474-75.
41. Sermon 26, "Upon Our Lord's Sermon on the Mount, VI," §1, *Works* 1:573.
42. Sermon 30, "Upon Our Lord's Sermon on the Mount, X," §§8-18, *Works* 1:654-59.
43. Sermon 21, "Upon Our Lord's Sermon on the Mount, I," §I.4, *Works* 1:477.

corrupted. For Aquinas, the beginning of human action was unaffected by sin. The first practical principle of the natural moral order is do good and avoid evil. Every human creature intuits this formal practical principle just as every human creature intuits "being" as the first principle of all knowledge. Such intuition occurs through the virtue of *intellectus*. But it is a formal principle that only sets one out on a journey of desiring both goodness and being. This natural desire cannot be naturally satisfied. For Aquinas, however, if the basic principle to achieve good and avoid evil were corrupted, then we would be less than human; we would be reduced to brutes, for we would not then be on a quest toward goodness. Yet even for Aquinas, our inclinations toward the natural end of virtue are diminished, and our knowledge and desire for the end is corrupted such that our natural inclination to achieve the good and avoid the evil cannot occur without the aid of supernatural grace.[44]

Wesley appears to begin the Christian moral life in a very different place than Aquinas. He begins with a total corruption of every faculty and power. Nevertheless, when he explains the Beatitudes, Wesley insists that God has implanted passions in us that are good. They cannot be completely corrupted by our disordered will and intellect because these passions come from God. For instance, the meek "are exceeding 'zealous for the Lord of hosts'; but their zeal is always guided by knowledge, and tempered in every thought and word and work with the love of man as well as the love of God. They do not desire to extinguish any of the passions which God has for wise ends implanted in their nature."[45]

A preoccupation with the passions was commonplace in the seventeenth and early eighteenth centuries. Malebranche, Norris, and More all wrote on the passions, following Aristotle and Aquinas. Aquinas taught that there were passions in the soul, which was surprising in that the soul is "simple" rather than composite; it does not include form and matter. Passions were primarily understood as things suffered in the body because it had potentiality. Because the person is composed of both soul and body, it would be reasonable to think passions are only in the body. But Aquinas argued passions are found in the soul. The soul receives something through feeling and understanding. But the soul also loses something. This loss can be negative and produce sorrow. It can be positive and produce joy. All three forms of passion are found in the soul.[46] They are in themselves neither good nor evil. They are not to be exterminated, but properly ordered. They are also inextricably linked to the

---

44. See Eileen Sweeney, "Vice and Sin," in Pope, *Ethics of Aquinas*, 158.
45. Sermon 22, "Upon Our Lord's Sermon on the Mount, II," §I.5, *Works* 1:490.
46. *Summa Theologica*, I-II.22.1.

virtues. As Aquinas put it, "Virtue overcomes inordinate passion; it produces ordinate passion."[47]

These passions are primarily found in the "sensitive appetite" rather than the intellectual appetite, which is the will. Passions are concupiscible or irascible. The concupiscible passions take as their object good and evil simply, which produce pleasure and pain. The irascible passions are similar except that their object is not simply good or evil, but good or evil as arduous. Concupiscible passions are joy, sorrow, love, and hatred. They flow through us without struggle. Irascible passions are daring, fear, hope. God implants them in us for good reasons. They allow us to be moved to God. Thus the movement of the sensitive appetite is both spiritual and natural.[48] This movement makes possible natural inclinations. They will be ordered toward some good, but the good may only be apparent. Most of us do not naturally know that God is the good to which our passions should be ordered. And even if we could discover this, we would not know who this God is. For Aquinas, as for Wesley, sin diminishes this natural movement, and thus our natural inclinations alone cannot be trusted. At most it gives us a formal orientation toward the good and away from evil.

Aquinas's affirmation of natural inclinations moving us toward God and the good is often contrasted with Calvin's doctrine of total depravity. However, Calvin himself wrote, "There is within the human mind, and indeed by natural instinct, an awareness of divinity."[49] Still these natural passions did have a more positive role in Aquinas's work than in Calvin's. How does Wesley's appeal to passions fit with his beginning point in total depravity? If meekness is a beatitude that preserves natural passions, then Wesley's theology would seem to be more nuanced in the direction of Aquinas than of Calvin—not all our powers and faculties are completely depraved. We have "natural" inclinations that are diminished, but not extirpated. They cannot be trusted without grace. But with grace they are rightly preserved. These natural inclinations are not some original blessing. There is no argument here that a seemingly natural orientation is itself sufficient for the Christian moral life. Aquinas, Calvin, and Wesley would agree on that point. In fact, even the difference among them on our state of total depravity is slight and should not be exaggerated. For Aquinas and Wesley "grace perfects nature," which is precisely a claim that what is natural is not in itself sufficient—even without the ravages of sin.

47. Ibid., I-II.59.5, ad. 1.
48. Ibid., I-II.23.3.
49. *Institutes*, bk. 1, ch. 3.

Wesley begins with total depravity because he believes that the Christian moral life begins in repentance. Humility is the doorway to the virtues; it is never itself virtuous. Yet it always accompanies the virtues, for it reminds us that our natural powers themselves are insufficient. If humility were a virtue then it would teach us "to be proud of knowing we deserve damnation."[50] Rather than humility as a virtue that casts us back on ourselves, it should direct us to our "strong helper," who is Jesus Christ the righteous.[51] Poverty of spirit points in the direction of faith and love. It issues the call "dare to believe!" where we receive "true, genuine, Christian humility, which flows from a sense of the love of God, reconciled to us in Christ Jesus."[52] For Wesley, this is the only starting point for the moral life.

Because he was familiar with the ancient virtue tradition, Wesley knew that humility was not something Aristotle or Plato recognized as virtuous. Because the Christian moral life begins in humility and repentance, Wesley opposes it to heathen morality. "Christianity begins just where heathen morality ends: 'poverty of spirit,' 'conviction of sin,' the 'renouncing ourselves.' "[53] There was no place, or even a name, for humility in antiquity.

Wesley does to the ancient virtue tradition precisely what Aquinas himself did when he made infused virtue the essence of the moral life. Virtue is no longer a human achievement, an *aretê* or heroic power.[54] Neither Achilles nor Socrates is the paradigm of virtue. Little room remains for Aristotle's "great-souled man," who remains untouched by the passions of those beneath him. Instead, virtue is now a gift, not something we can acquire through our own powers. For this reason Wesley develops it primarily in terms of Jesus' teaching in the Sermon on the Mount. The virtues receive a new context: that of Christ pronouncing blessedness on forms of life that were not countenanced in pagan morality. Wesley did not construct this new context, it was already well-established in the Christian tradition. He inherited it and, like all good accounts of tradition, advanced it by infusing it with life.

Matthew 5: The Religion of the Heart and Doing Good

Wesley's account of the first beatitude, poverty of spirit, builds on biblical ideas he had already used in both "The Great Privilege" and "The

---

50. Sermon 21, "Upon Our Lord's Sermon on the Mount, I," §I.7, *Works* 1:479.
51. Ibid., §I.8, *Works* 1:480.
52. Ibid., §I.13, *Works* 1:482.
53. Ibid., §I.9, *Works* 1:480.
54. See R. E. Houser's essay, "The Virtue of Courage" in Pope, *Ethics of Aquinas*, 304. He shows how the virtue of courage arose from considerations of Achilles' actions. *Aretê* was sometimes linked to Ares, the god of war.

Lord Our Righteousness." It also plays on the notion of the passions, especially joy and sorrow, with which Wesley was well acquainted from the virtue tradition. This beatitude, writes Wesley, "begins where a sense of guilt and of the wrath of God ends."[55] The Beatitudes are not judgments; they are states of blessedness. They do not begin in wrath but in promise; even though a sense of God's wrath is necessary for the requisite humility to enter into the state of blessedness. Poverty of spirit "is a continual sense of our total dependence on him for every good thought or word or work; of our utter inability to all good unless he 'water us every moment': and an abhorrence of the praise of men, knowing that all praise is due unto God only."[56] This is the virtue of resignation, which was associated with true piety. Poverty of spirit is not determined by a lack but by God's presence. The divine seed noted in "The Great Privilege" and alluded to in "The Lord Our Righteousness" is here watered so that it can bear fruit. Poverty of spirit defines the condition of openness to this process of cultivation, the spiritual action/reaction Wesley set forth in the earlier sermons.

The whole process of poverty of spirit and mourning is also an eschatological process tending toward hope. Wesley writes, "mourning for an absent God and recovering the joy of his countenance" is a repetition of the evening before Christ's Passion where he says, "'ye shall weep and lament' . . . when ye do not see me" (John 16:19-22). Yet Jesus also tells his disciples, "'But I will see you again; and your heart shall rejoice' with calm, inward joy 'and your joy no man taketh from you.'"[57] This joy produces hope and expectation, but it is a satisfied joy; for those who mourn Christ's absence are satisfied in the presence of the Comforter. "But although this mourning is at an end, is lost in holy joy, by the return of the Comforter, yet is there another, and a blessed mourning it is, which abides in the children of God. They still mourn for the sins and miseries of mankind: they 'weep with them that weep.'"[58] Here natural concupiscible passions, joy and sorrow, find their true ends.

Wesley's second discourse on meekness, righteousness, and mercy takes up where the first discourse ends, in an eschatological vision. When the time of mourning is past, and "at the brightness of his presence the clouds disperse," then we shall see that the life of true beatitude is found in meekness.[59] But what is meekness? Wesley's discussion of meekness reveals most clearly his indebtedness to the virtue tradition. Meekness is a mean between two extremes. "It keeps clear of every extreme, whether

---

55. Sermon 21, "Upon Our Lord's Sermon on the Mount, I," §I.13, *Works* 1:482.
56. Ibid.
57. Ibid., §II.5, *Works* 1:486.
58. Ibid., §II.6, *Works* 1:486.
59. Sermon 22, "Upon Our Lord's Sermon on the Mount, II," §I.1, *Works* 1:488.

in excess or defect. It does not destroy but balance the affections, which the God of nature never designed should be rooted out by grace, but only brought and kept under due regulations."[60] As we saw with Malebranche, Wesley finds stoic apathy to be the extreme deficiency that threatens meekness. Surely this is why he found Hutcheson to be such a threat to the moral life. Passion has its proper place; disinterestedness and lack of passion or zeal are as much a threat to the beatitude of meekness as would be its excess in enthusiasm. Meekness is not ignorance, insensibility, apathy, or lack of zeal for God. It is the virtue Wesley calls "resignation," which defines Jesus' relation to God the Father. Wesley states,

> When this due composure of mind has reference to God it is usually termed resignation—a calm acquiescence in whatsover is his will concerning us, even though it may not be pleasing to nature, saying continually, "It is the Lord; let him do what seemeth him good." When we consider it more strictly with regard to ourselves we style it patience or contentedness. When it is exerted toward other men then it is mildness to the good and gentleness to the evil.[61]

This makes clear Wesley's approach to moral theology. It begins with the eschatological vision of the life of blessedness. This state of happiness is the end toward which our life is ordered. Such a life makes possible beatitudes, in this case that of meekness. Wesley calls them "divine tempers." They are gifts that properly order our passions in their relationship to God (which is the virtue of resignation), to ourselves (which is the virtue of patience or contentedness), and to others (which is the virtue of mildness or gentleness). We are to cultivate these divine tempers, even though they are not an achievement. God provides occasions for such cultivation, and one of them has to do with the irascible passion of anger. Anger is permissible only when it is directed at sin. Wesley writes, "In this sense our Lord himself is once recorded to have been angry."[62] But anger directed toward others is impermissible since Christ's giving of the new law on the Mount.

Wesley provides an excursus on the three beatitudes of poverty of spirit, mournfulness, and meekness. He explains the deficiency each removes. Poverty of spirit produces humility that removes pride. Mourning removes levity and thoughtlessness. Meekness removes the inordinate passions of anger, impatience, and discontentedness.[63] Wesley does not leave the discourses on the other beatitudes behind as he moves through them. Each assumes the other such that the development of the

60. Ibid., §I.3, *Works* 1:489.
61. Ibid., §I.4, *Works* 1:489-90.
62. Ibid., §I.8, *Works* 1:491-92.
63. Ibid., §II.1, *Works* 1:495.

Christian life gains texture as it unfolds throughout the sermon. This richness comes to a climax in Wesley's discussion of righteousness.

Poverty of spirit, mournfulness, and meekness are gifts that remove the hindrances that prevent a proper ordering of our passions. Once the false cravings of pride, thoughtlessness, and the inordinate passions of anger, impatience, and discontentedness are removed, a person's true hunger can begin to be seen for what it is: a desire for the righteousness of Christ. This vision renews us into the image of God. Righteousness "is the image of God, the mind which was in Christ Jesus. It is every holy and heavenly temper in one; springing from as well as terminating in the love of God as our Father and Redeemer, and the love of all men for his sake."[64] Only the righteousness of Christ satisfies; for it is only in him that we can participate in the life of God and be restored in God's image. The hunger and thirst for righteousness is a hunger and thirst after the image of God.

But even here there is danger. This hunger and thirst for righteousness is the strongest of all our spiritual appetites, a passion of the soul. But like all such passions, it will require an external reality in order to satisfy a spiritual passion. Because it is so strong it can tempt us to "the religion of the world," which Wesley characterizes by three things: "First, the doing no harm, . . . secondly, the doing good, . . . thirdly, the using the means of grace."[65] The first two things implied in the religion of the world is what Aquinas called the first principle of practical reason: do good and avoid evil. Wesley plays on this basic theme of the natural law, but he sees it as a temptation. Our hunger and thirst for righteousness could wrongly stop at this basic precept of natural reason, and we would miss the importance of the *new law* of the gospel altogether. Of course we are not to violate this basic precept by ignoring it; we are to fulfill it by something more.

This religion of the world is also referred to as "the righteousness of the Pharisee" in Wesley's fifth discourse on the Sermon on the Mount.[66] As both the "religion of the world" and the "righteousness of a Pharisee," the first principle of the practical reason is not something to be removed. Wesley does not insist that the Methodist people flee from doing good and avoiding evil. He makes it essential to the movement; it is a condition for membership. The General Rules that are binding on all the Methodist people (supposedly even to this day) assume a threefold pattern. The first is do no harm. The second is do good. And the third is attend upon all the ordinances of God. These are also the works of mercy and piety that define the Christian moral life. They are to be done out of obligation, even if one is not disposed to do them. That Wesley makes "the religion of the

---

64. Ibid., §II.2, *Works* 1:495.
65. Ibid., §II.4, *Works* 1:496.
66. Sermon 25, "Upon Our Lord's Sermon on the Mount, V," §§IV.7-9, *Works* 1:565-67.

world" and "the righteousness of a Pharisee" into the General Rules as conditions for membership in the Methodist movement is telling and intriguing. This cannot be understood without recognizing what he is doing in his discourses on the Sermon on the Mount and its dependence on the principle that grace perfects nature. The spiritual passions cannot be satisfied without the external means of commands, doctrines, and sacraments. However, these external means satisfy spiritual passions, which are more than mere externals. Therefore, the externals are necessary but insufficient. They must be attended to, but they must not be that in which faith is placed. That would be a species of the very materialism Wesley found problematic in Hobbes. What is to be trusted is Christ's righteousness. It alone satisfies, even though it is ordinarily only mediated through these external means.

This worldly religion, which is necessary, will not satisfy, and one should not be content with it. "This is only the outside of that religion which he insatiably hungers after. . . . God shall satisfy them with the blessings of his goodness, with the felicity of his chosen."[67] One cannot get to the inside without this outside, but to stop at the outside would be failed human action, a bare materialism that fails to see eternity. "Let nothing satisfy thee but the power of godliness, but a religion that is spirit and life; the dwelling in God and God in thee, the being an inhabitant of eternity."[68]

Once Christ's righteousness inheres in us through participation in the life of God, then the next gift received will be the beatitude of mercy. It is a more tender love for those who are still "without God in the world."[69] Here we see clearly how Wesley's reading of the Beatitudes depends on the human righteousness of Christ discussed in "The Lord Our Righteousness." That righteousness was defined as "love, reverence, resignation to his Father; humility, meekness, gentleness; love to lost mankind, and every other holy and heavenly temper: and all these in the highest degree, without any defect, or mixture of unholiness."[70] This righteousness is the basis for the Beatitudes. Wesley's discourses on the Sermon on the Mount are an extended commentary on Christ's human righteousness and how we can participate in what he has accomplished.

The two beatitudes of the righteousness of Christ and mercy function similar to the two tables of the Law in Moses. The first orders our passions toward God, which will entail immediately an orientation toward our neighbor, characterized by mercy. Mercy has a special role to fulfill in that it orders our passions toward the proper love of neighbor. Wesley defines

---

67. Sermon 22, "Upon Our Lord's Sermon on the Mount, II," §§II.4-5, *Works* 1:497.
68. Ibid., §II.6, *Works* 1:498.
69. Ibid., §III.1, *Works* 1:499.
70. Sermon 20, "The Lord Our Righteousness," §I.2, *Works* 1:452-53.

"the merciful" as they who love their neighbors as themselves. He then provides an extended excursus on 1 Corinthians 13 showing how this merciful love avoids envy, presumption, falsehood, and evil speech.[71] Mercy is a virtue of sociability. It is necessary for any good community. This is intriguing in that it rejects Hobbes's politics and answers Shaftesbury's criticisms of Christianity. The state of nature is not a state of the war of all against all. Politics does not emerge through the containment of an original violence. The political life is grounded in mercy, without it human sociality degenerates into a state of war. Good political relations require forgiveness and truth. Wesley writes,

> only a man of love . . . weeps over either the sin or folly of his enemy, takes no pleasure in hearing or in repeating it, but rather desires that it may be forgotten forever.
> But he "rejoiceth in the truth," wheresoever it is found . . . bringing forth its proper fruit, holiness of heart and holiness of conversation. . . . As a citizen of the world he claims a share in the happiness of all the inhabitants of it.[72]

This juxtaposition of avoiding evil communication and rejoicing in the truth requires practical wisdom, which is the political virtue of prudence. Evil speaking tears at the bonds of communal life by spreading in secret what destroys those bonds without any public accountability. It is better for such evil not to be spread at all. However, genuine evil should not always be given the privilege of the cult of secrecy. Thus, Wesley allows an exception to evil speech, which is not so much an exception in that evil speech thrives by secrecy. "Sometimes," Wesley writes, a person "is convinced that it is for the glory of God or (which comes to the same) the good of his neighbour that an evil should not be covered."[73] Wesley offers five rules to the person compelled to make evil known publicly. First, superior love must constrain him. Second, there must be no confusion about the good end to be achieved through making the evil public. Third, there must be no other way to achieve the good end. Fourth, such public exposure must only be done reluctantly to expel poison. Fifth, it should be done sparingly.

The reason for the reluctance in speaking evil of neighbors is because it destroys both the bonds of community and the witness of the faithful. Wesley ends his discussion of the beatitude of mercy with a poignant witness to failed human action on behalf of Christians through war, greed, and domestic strife.

---

71. Sermon 22, "Upon Our Lord's Sermon on the Mount, II," §§III.5-13, *Works* 1:500-505.
72. Ibid., §§III.12-13, *Works* 1:504.
73. Ibid., §III.14, *Works* 1:505.

You may pour out your soul, and bemoan the loss of true genuine love in the earth. Lost indeed! You may well say (but not in the ancient sense), "See how *these* Christians love one another!" These Christian kingdoms that are tearing out each other's bowels, desolating one another with fire and sword! These Christian armies that are sending each other by thousands, by ten thousands, quick into hell! These Christian nations that are all on fire with intestine broils, party against party, faction against faction! These Christian cities where deceit and fraud, oppression and wrong, yea, robbery and murder, go not out of their streets! These Christian families, torn asunder with envy, jealousy, anger, domestic jars—without number, without end! Yea, what is most dreadful, most to be lamented of all, these Christian churches! –churches ("Tell it not in Gath"; but alas, how can we hide it, either from Jews, Turks, or pagans?) that bear the name of Christ, "the Prince of Peace," and wage continual war with each other! . . . O God! How long? Shall thy promise fail? Fear it not, ye little flock. Against hope believe in hope. It is your Father's good pleasure yet to renew the face of the earth. Surely all these things shall come to an end, and the inhabitants of the earth shall learn righteousness. "Nation shall not lift up sword against nation, neither shall they know war any more." . . . They shall all be without spot or blemish, loving one another, even as Christ hath loved us. Be thou part of the first-fruits, if the harvest is not yet. Do thou love thy neighbour as thyself. The Lord God fill thy heart with such a love to every soul that thou mayst be ready to lay down thy life for his sake! May thy soul continually overflow with love, swallowing up every unkind and unholy temper, till he calleth thee up into the region of love, there to reign with him for ever and ever.[74]

Wesley concludes his second discourse as he did his first, and as he began the second, with an eschatological vision. This is the context for the Sermon on the Mount, Christ pronouncing a blessed judgment. This judgment has not yet come to pass, even in so-called Christian nations, but it will. Wesley calls the Methodist people to be "firstfruits" of that which is coming.

Purity in heart is the beatitude of perfection. It is "'perfect holiness in the' loving 'fear of God.'" Purity in heart occurs through the combination of the five previous beatitudes. Wesley states,

"The pure in heart" are they whose hearts God hath "purified even as he is pure"; who are purified through faith in the blood of Jesus from every unholy affection; who, being "cleansed from all filthiness of flesh and spirit, perfect holiness in the" loving "fear of God." They are, through the power of his grace, purified from pride by the deepest poverty of spirit; from anger, from every unkind or turbulent passion, by meekness and gentleness; from every desire but to please and enjoy God, to know and love him more and more, by that hunger and thirst after righteousness which now engrosses their whole soul: so that now they love the Lord their God with all their heart, and with all their soul, and mind, and strength.[75]

---

74. Ibid., §III.18, *Works* 1:507-9.
75. Sermon 23, "Upon Our Lord's Sermon on the Mount, III," §I.2, *Works* 1:510-11.

Purity in heart is the virtue emanating from divine illumination, for the pure in heart are blessed "with the clearest communications of his Spirit" such that they see "all things full of God."[76]

Hindrances to the vision of God can come from something as noble as family and marriage. They keep one from a pure heart by exciting unholy desire. As Jesus taught, the remedy is drastic: pluck out your eye. Wesley does not hesitate to tell the Methodists that on occasion they must forcibly separate from such persons, even if they are family members. But before making this drastic step he suggests two prior ones: prayer and fasting, and seek counsel from the one who "watcheth over thy soul."[77]

Purity in heart characterizes the religion of the heart, which entails all of the first six beatitudes. This is the blessed Christian life. Wesley states that with these first six beatitudes, our Lord has shown what Christians are to be. But now beginning with the seventh beatitude, peacemaking: "He proceeds to show what they are to do also: how inward holiness is to exert itself in our outward conversation."[78] As the virtue tradition taught, "being" precedes "doing."

The "doing" that proceeds from "being," which is the religion of the heart, is characterized in its entirety by Jesus' blessing the peacemakers. For Wesley, "peacemaking" is what Christians do. The term has both a literal and a general meaning. "In its literal meaning it implies those lovers of God and man who utterly detest and abhor all strife and debate, all variance and contention; and accordingly labour with all their might either to prevent this fire of hell from being kindled, or when it is kindled from breaking out, or when it is broke out from spreading any farther."[79] The general meaning, or the full extent of the word, is that

> a "peacemaker" is one that as he hath opportunity "doth good unto all men"; one that being filled with the love of God and of all mankind cannot confine the expressions of it to his own family, or friends, or acquaintance, or party; or to those of his own opinions; no, nor those who are partakers of like precious faith; but steps over all these narrow bounds that he may do good to every man; that he may some way or other manifest his love to neighbours and strangers, friends and enemies.[80]

In other words, peacemaking is keeping the law. The first six beatitudes produce a faith that loves God and neighbor. This issues, of necessity, in the seventh beatitude—keeping the moral law inviolate—whose basic precept is "do good." Wesley's moral theology takes as its basic shape a

76. Ibid., §I.6, *Works* 1:513.
77. Ibid., §I.4, *Works* 1:512.
78. Ibid., §II.1, *Works* 1:517.
79. Ibid., §II.3, *Works* 1:517-18.
80. Ibid., §II.4, *Works* 1:518.

faith that loves through keeping the law, bringing joy and happiness, culminating in hope.

When peacemaking occurs, persecution follows, for "the spirit which is in the world is directly opposite to the Spirit which is of God."[81] The first seven beatitudes are a participation in the active human righteousness of Christ. If we participate in them fully, we should also expect to participate in his passive human righteousness, which the eighth beatitude names. This brings to a close Wesley's first three discourses on the Sermon on the Mount. Each beatitude has been outlined and its relations noted. Discourses four and five bring out those relations more fully under the category of "the beauty of holiness." The heart of the matter for Wesley is that our being must be properly ordered by faith, love, and hope before it can issue in the doing of good to God and our neighbors. Being precedes doing, but doing forms our being. There is interplay between the internal and external where we must do certain externals such as assent to creedal Christianity, observe the General Rules, and attend the sacraments. But this doing is never an end. It is a means of waiting on the gifts of the Beatitudes and Spirit-infused virtues, which order our lives to God. These gifts only come as we know God in Jesus Christ, as we walk by faith and not by sight. Knowledge of God is essential, and thus the gifts, beatitudes, and virtues we need cannot be had without doctrine, proper Christian teaching. The simplest meaning of faith for Wesley is "assent to knowledge." But that is nothing but a bare external if it does not issue forth in a holy life of joyful obedience, loving God and neighbor. The external presupposes the internal, but the internal cannot be had without the external.

Wesley consistently warned those who trusted only in the means of grace, the creeds, and the General Rules that they should beware that they do not cultivate a mere "outside religion" at the expense of "heart-religion." But Wesley also warned those that claimed heart religion that they beware unless they begin to trust in some internal disposition that refuses any outward demonstration such as keeping the law, confessing the faith, and attending the sacraments. This is a consistent theme throughout Wesley's work. He articulated it well in his 1746 preface to *Sermons on Several Occasions*.

> And herein it is more especially my desire, first, to guard those who are just setting their faces toward heaven (and who, having little acquaintance with the things of God, are the more liable to be turned out of the way) from formality, from mere outside religion, which has almost driven heart-religion out of the world; and secondly, to warn those who know the religion of the heart, the faith which worketh by love, lest at

---

81. Ibid., §III.4, *Works* 1:523.

any time they make void the law through faith, and so fall back into the
snare of the devil.[82]

Two warnings are issued. First, Wesley warns those who trust in a mere
formality, in outward religion. This would be those who use the sacraments as an end and have not received the gifts of the first six beatitudes,
which constitute the religion of the heart. Second, Wesley warns those
who have faith that they not use it to negate working the law. The first six
beatitudes must issue in the seventh, peacemaking or doing good, which
is keeping the law. In his fourth and fifth discourses, Wesley articulated
this complex relationship between the internal and external as he developed his account of the moral law.

In his fourth discourse, Wesley notes the importance of the "beauty of
holiness." It characterizes those who are renewed after the image of God.
They are ornamented with a meek, humble loving spirit. This spirit itself
witnesses to God's goodness. Wesley makes it clear that a beautiful holiness is a moral matter; it "will at least excite the approbation of all those
who are capable in any degree of discerning spiritual good and evil."[83] He
returns to Christology to explain this renewed image of God. It is
"χαρακτὴρ τῆς ὑποστάσεως αὐτοῦ," which is the character of his person
or hypostasis.[84] In the Sermon on the Mount, Jesus' words impart a
share in his own hypostasis with those who hear and are changed. The
result is twofold. First, Wesley argues, "I shall endeavour to show, first,
that Christianity is essentially a social religion, and that to turn it into
a solitary one is to destroy it; secondly, that to conceal this religion is
impossible."[85]

What does Wesley mean when he says that Christianity is a social religion that cannot be concealed? If we recall that Wesley was aware of the
kinds of arguments Shaftesbury and others were making, then this claim
takes on a rich significance. Shaftesbury argued that Christianity was a
religion that was worried more about the individual's soul in the next life.
It did not have an adequate account of ordinary, everyday conviviality.
It did not produce the virtues necessary for social life. In his fourth
discourse, Wesley argues that Christianity must be social. He develops
a variation on themes already present in the first three discourses by
exemplifying the social character of the Beatitudes. Meekness, he argues,
"as it implies . . . mildness, gentleness, and long-suffering, it cannot possibly have a being . . . without an intercourse with other men. So that to
attempt turning this into a solitary virtue is to destroy it from the face of

---

82. Preface, *Sermons on Several Occasions* (1746), §6, *Works* 1:106.
83. Sermon 24, "Upon Our Lord's Sermon on the Mount, IV," §1, *Works* 1:531.
84. Ibid. The Greek Wesley cites is Hebrews 1:3.
85. Ibid., §5, *Works* 1:533.

the earth."[86] And he offers similar arguments with respect to peacemaking, mercifulness, purity of heart, or any other branch of Christ's institution.

> For will any man affirm that a solitary Christian (so called, though it is little less than a contradiction in terms) can be a merciful man—that is, one that takes every opportunity of doing all good to all men? What can be more plain than that this fundamental branch of the religion of Jesus Christ cannot possibly subsist without society, without our living and conversing with other men?[87]

Anyone who read only the first three discourses might be confused at this point. Wesley has been emphasizing the religion of the heart. Does this not assume an individualism? a solitary religion? Wesley himself raises this objection in an imagined interlocutor's voice: "religion does not lie in outward things but in the heart, the inmost soul." And he responds to this objection. "I answer, it is most true that the root of religion lies in the heart, in the inmost soul. . . . But if this root be really in the heart it cannot but put forth branches. And these are the several instances of outward obedience, which partake of the same nature with the root, and consequently are not only marks or signs, but substantial parts of religion."[88] Here we see this interplay between the internal and external. The externals are not to be discarded; they are substantial parts of religion as marks or signs that prevent Christianity from being turned into an individual, solitary dispositional matter.

This leads nicely into Wesley's important fifth discourse. More than any other of his thirteen discourses, the fifth discourse explains his moral theology, the substance of which is that Jesus does not take away the moral law but fulfills it. He explicitly rejects any supersessionist theology where the morality of the Jewish holiness codes are done away with in order for the gospel to emerge. He states, "there is no contrariety at all between the law and the gospel; that there is no need for the law to pass away in order to the establishing of the gospel. Indeed neither of them supersedes the other, but they agree perfectly well together."[89] To explain this Wesley exegetes Jesus' statement that our righteousness must exceed the righteousness of a Pharisee. He does not turn this into an easy teaching by making the Pharisees the worst hypocrites that ever existed so that sincerity alone exceeds the Pharisees' righteousness. Quite the contrary, Wesley interprets the Pharisees somewhat positively. He states that the Pharisee did no harm to others, and in externals he was singularly good. The Pharisee also used all the means of grace.[90] Since the basic meaning

---

86. Ibid., §I.3, *Works* 1:534.
87. Ibid., §I.4, *Works* 1:535.
88. Ibid., §III.1, *Works* 1:541-42.
89. Sermon 25, "Upon Our Lord's Sermon on the Mount, V," §II.2, *Works* 1:554.
90. Ibid., §§IV.7-8, *Works* 1:565-66.

of *justice* is the combination of doing no harm and doing good, the Pharisees were just. They also fulfilled the obligations of piety. They attended to the means of grace, fasted, and tithed.

All of these externals are good and necessary. Wesley uses the righteousness of a Pharisee to chide the Methodists asking them if their righteousness even equaled the Pharisees? The obvious answer is no. Then Wesley tells the Methodists that even if it equaled theirs, it would profit them nothing, for Jesus taught that it must exceed theirs. How does it exceed theirs? It does so by participating in Christ's righteousness in the Beatitudes given on the Sermon on the Mount. "Thus to do no harm, to do good, to attend the ordinances of God (the righteousness of a Pharisee) are all external; whereas, on the contrary, poverty of spirit, mourning, meekness, hunger and thirst after righteouensness, the love of our neighbour, and purity of heart (the righteousness of a Christian) are all internal."[91] Once again Wesley's second warning in the 1746 preface to *Sermons on Several Occasions* must be heeded at this point. That Christ's righteousness is internal and thus exceeds that of the Pharisees does not imply that "to do no harm, to do good, [and] to attend the ordinances of God" are negated. Methodists would have known that these three injunctions, which are the righteousness of a Pharisee, are the three General Rules binding all the Methodist people together. They were to be observed. But our observance of them means little if by them we do not discover ourselves participating in Christ's righteousness and receiving his beatitudes, his blessed eschatological judgments. Such reception entails the sociality of the Christian life.

Matthew 6: A Holy Intentionality through Attending to the Ordinances of God

Wesley does not leave the beauty of holiness or the righteousness of a Pharisee behind as he moves from Matthew chapter 5 to chapter 6. Discourses six through nine move from Matthew 5 where "the Lord has described inward religion in its various branches . . . those dispositions of soul which constitute real Christianity: the inward tempers contained in that holiness 'without which no man shall see the Lord'" to chapter 6 with its concern that "all our actions likewise, even those that are indifferent to their own nature, may be made holy and good and acceptable to God, by a pure and holy intention."[92] He told us in his fifth discourse that the Beatitudes, even though they are internal, are also always social. They are directed outward toward God and neighbor at the same time. Discourses

---

91. Ibid., §IV.11, *Works* 1:568.
92. Sermon 26, "Upon Our Lord's Sermon on the Mount, VI," §1, *Works* 1:572-73.

six through nine develop this social orientation by setting forth the same activities that Wesley claimed the Pharisees themselves accomplished. He looks at almsgiving, prayer, fasting, what is prohibited and encouraged in the actions of common life, and how Christians should use their money.

Wesley's sixth discourse is a discourse on holy intention. It makes even indifferent actions a matter of obedient love. In order to explain "holy intention," Wesley examines works: the works of charity or mercy and works of piety. Works of mercy include all the activities of Matthew 25, "feeding the hungry, the clothing the naked, the entertaining or assisting the stranger, the visiting those that are sick or in prison" and then more such as "the comforting the afflicted, . . . the reproving the wicked, the exhorting and encouraging the well-doer."[93]

Wesley's work on holy intention is suggestive but somewhat disappointing. As often occurs in his sermons, he does not actually do what he tells the reader he intends to do. He does not explicitly develop what constitutes a holy intention. Instead he tells us that it emerges from "purity of heart," and gives practical counsel on how we should do works of charity and piety, particularly how we should give alms and pray. Yet the work is suggestive in that the works of mercy are to make our intentions holy. Intentionality almost functions retroactively. We do not do works of mercy because we have a holy intention; we do works of mercy in hopes that our intentions will be made holy. We see this also in his command for Methodists to fast.

In his seventh discourse Wesley discusses fasting. He begins, as he did his 1746 preface to *Sermons on Several Occasions*, with his dual warning as one more reminder to the reader that he or she should not fall into the temptation on the one side that all that matters is some internal disposition nor on the other side that he or she trust mere, external actions. He writes, "It has been the endeavour of Satan from the beginning of the world to put asunder what God had joined together; to separate inward from outward religion."[94] The convergence of both inward and outward in Wesley's work crystalizes nicely in the practice of fasting. Fasting is for Wesley "a way which God hath ordained wherein we wait for his *unmerited* mercy; and wherein, without any desert of ours, he hath promised *freely* to give us his blessing."[95] This does not mean that one dispenses with it once the blessing is received any more than one would then dispense with the sacraments, General Rules, or Christian orthodoxy. One fasts in patience waiting on the gift of godly sorrow or mourning. It is the beatitude that renders the activity of fasting intelligible. But the gift of mourning will not then put an end to fasting. It will continue as a sign of this gift.

---

93. Ibid., §I.1, *Works* 1:573.
94. Sermon 27, "Upon Our Lord's Sermon on the Mount, VII," §1, *Works* 1:592.
95. Ibid., §IV.2, *Works* 1:609.

In the sixth and seventh discourses Wesley explains how the works of piety, particularly almsgiving, prayer, and fasting, wait upon and make habitual the Beatitudes already elucidated in the first five discourses. In the eighth discourse he moves from works of piety or "religious actions" to works of mercy or the actions of "common life."

These actions refer to everyday activities such as working, raising a family, feeding and clothing one's self and others. Wesley discusses these in terms of what is and is not forbidden. These are those actions that assist one in being a peacemaker, that is, avoiding harm and doing good. He notes four things that are not forbidden: (1) "to 'provide things honest in the sight of all men' [and] to 'owe no man anything'"; (2) to provide "for ourselves such things as are needful for the body"; (3) "to provide for our children and those of our own household"; and (4) "to lay up from time to time what is needful for the carrying on our worldly business" in order to accomplish the first three points.[96]

What is forbidden, he states, "is the designedly procuring more of this world's goods than will answer the foregoing purposes."[97] Anything that is beyond the four points enumerated above is "robbing the poor." Much like the Catholic tradition, Wesley recognizes that all our possessions are trusts to be used for a universal destination. Our wealth is for the purposes of sustaining all God's creatures. If we are wealthy and others are poor it ipso facto points out that our intention is not holy. As Wesley states it, "whosoever . . . being already in these circumstances [points 1-4 above], seeks a still larger portion on earth— he lives in an open habitual denial of the Lord that bought him."[98] Here is a concrete external work that conveys our intention. If the situation prevails where we have more of the earth's goods than what the above permits, then we cannot claim, "the Lord is my righteousness" and think that alone suffices. Holy intention is demonstrated in concrete externals, even though concrete externals cannot infallibly verify holy intention.

John Wesley concluded the eighth discourse with the exhortation,

> We exhort *you* in the name of the Lord Jesus Christ to be "willing to communicate," κοινωνικούς εἶναι; to be of the same spirit (though not in the same outward state) with those believers of ancient times, who "remained steadfast" ἐν τῇ κοινωνίᾳ, in that blessed and holy "fellowship" wherein "none said that anything was his own, but they had all things common."[99]

---

96. Sermon 28, "Upon Our Lord's Sermon on the Mount, VIII," §11, *Works* 1:618-19.
97. Ibid., §12, *Works* 1:619.
98. Ibid., *Works* 1:620.
99. Ibid., §28, *Works* 1:630.

This is a reference to the early Pentecostal communities in Acts 2 and 4 where believers had all things in common. In explaining the rise of the Methodists in 1735 at Oxford forty years after the fact, Wesley used these passages as the pattern for the Methodist movement. He presented a socialist vision grounded in Christian orthodoxy with a common life, order, and discipline. He explained what brought the early Methodists together:

> They were all precisely of one judgment as well as of one soul. All tenacious of order to the last degree, and observant, for conscience' sake, of every rule of the church. . . . They were all orthodox in every point; firmly believing not only the three creeds, but whatsoever they judged to be the doctrine of the Church of England, as contained in her Articles and Homilies. As to that practice of the apostolic church (which continued till the time of Tertullian, at least in many churches) the "having of all things in common," they had no rule, nor any formed design concerning it. But it was so, in effect, and it could not be otherwise; for none could want anything that another could spare.[100]

Here at the end of his life, Wesley articulates the importance of the "common life" for the Methodists. They had a common order, doctrine, and economic life. He sees the Methodists as embodying the Pentecostal miracle of Acts 2 and 4. Of course, Wesley would also say that these were externals that one could not finally trust in if they did not produce the religion of the heart, while at the same time stating that the religion of the heart would produce these externals.

This vision of Methodism raises some central questions. When did the Methodists ever live into this vision? It did not work even in Wesley's day, which he recognized at the end of his life. Who of us lives out this vision today? If this common life is the sign of a holy intention without which we deny Christ, do not most of us deny Christ most of the time? One is tempted here to appeal to forensic notions of justification and say, "I have no righteousness of my own, the Lord is my righteousness." But Wesley's moral theology takes that option away from us. What then is to be done?

That the normative vision of Methodism is seldom lived does not entail that we then change the normative vision to the pragmatic realities of our lives through compromise and accommodation. The tension between the normative vision and our lives cannot be resolved by an appeal to "practical"; rather, the Wesleyan movement is an effort to hold forth the vision of sanctification, even perfection, as a possibility in this life. To lose this is to lose the charism of the Methodist movement. We can point to persons who have embodied this form of life. Their lives are to be the rule and not those of us who do not yet find ourselves embodying it. For instance, in

---

100. Sermon 112, "On Laying the Foundation of the New Chapel," §I.3, *Works* 3:581-82.

the twentieth century the Catholic Worker movement, started by Dorothy Day, embodied the Wesleyan movement better than did any of the churches that bore the name Methodist or Wesleyan. I find it unsurprising that in explaining the religious influences in her adolescence, Day writes, "I remember coming across a volume of John Wesley's sermons when I was thirteen and being strongly attracted to his evangelical piety."[101]

What do those of us do who are not yet living such a sanctified life? We wait as we should, observing the General Rules, confessing the ancient creeds, attending the sacraments, performing the works of mercy and piety. At the same time, we refuse to trust in these alone for the One on whom we wait cannot be contained by any of these external, sensible realities. When he visits us, and our lives participate in his, then we will perform these works out of joyful obedience. But we cannot claim a holy intention without attending to these works.

Matthew 7: Avoiding Evil

In discourses ten through thirteen Wesley examines the third part of the Sermon on the Mount, Matthew 7. He begins the tenth discourse reminding us once again of the overall structure to his moral theology. Matthew 5 is the "sum of true religion." It is an analysis of "those dispositions of soul which constitute real Christianity; the tempers contained in that holiness 'without which no man shall see the Lord'; the affections which, when flowing from their proper fountain, from a living faith in God through Christ Jesus, are intrinsically and essentially good, and acceptable to God." The second part of his discourses "laid down rules touching that right intention." In chapter 7, Jesus "proceeds to point out the main hindrances of this religion, and concludes all with a suitable application."[102]

Three main hindrances are noted: judging, casting pearls before swine, and neglecting prayer. Wesley recognizes the inevitability of judgment. He is not so self-deceived as to repeat the modern mantra "thou shalt not judge" as he wags his finger at us.[103] Wesley suggests the judging that

---

101. Dorothy Day, *The Long Loneliness* (New York: Harper & Brothers, 1952), 29. For a more nuanced view of the Wesleyan movements relation to property and poverty see the introduction and Richard P. Heitzenrater's "Poor and the People Called Methodists," in *The Poor and the People Called Methodists* (ed. Richard P. Heitzenrater; Nashville: Kingswood Books, 2002), 9-38. As Heitzenrater notes, Wesley thought he "could do away with destitution" by emulating "the model solution in the New Testament—in the sharing community in Acts, which was bound not by secular laws but by the law of love" (p. 37).

102. Sermon 30, "Upon Our Lord's Sermon on the Mount, X," §1, *Works* 1:650-51.

103. For an illuminating analysis of how the last moral judgment in the modern era is "thou shalt not make moral judgments," see Mary Midgley, *Can't We Make Moral Judgments?* (New York: St. Martins, 1991).

Jesus condemns is of a threefold nature. It is first "judging the innocent," which is thinking another to blame when he is not. It is second "condemning the guilty in a higher degree than he deserves," which is an offense against justice as well as mercy. And finally, "condemning any person at all where there is not sufficient evidence."[104] To avoid this improper judging, Wesley calls on the Methodists to practice Matthew 18 to resolve their disputes.[105]

Given that the first hindrance is judging, it comes as something of a surprise that the second hindrance is casting pearls before swine. If persons utterly reject the truth of the gospel, Wesley states, "Tell not them of the 'exceeding great and precious promises' which God hath given us in the Son of his love. What conception can they have of being made 'partakers of the divine nature' who do not even desire to 'escape the corruption that is in the world through lust.'"[106] But this is not a counsel of despair, for this is not abandoning these persons. Instead, one turns to prayer. "The neglect of this is a third grand hindrance of holiness."[107]

Wesley takes us through a three-stage process in offering the necessary practical judgments holiness requires. He first insists that judgment be carried out proportionately and according to Matthew 18. But he also recognizes that some will refuse to hear the truth or be attracted to holiness. Such persons should not be told of the promise of participation in divine life because they will not be able to receive it. Dialogue with them should come to an end. But this is not to despair; it is to turn to prayer in order that they and we might receive the moral life as the gift it is. Wesley concludes the tenth discourse with an explicit reference to morality. He says, "This is pure and genuine morality." What is it? It is to live a common life by walking according to the "same rule." Wesley summarizes his moral teaching. "Let us love and honour all men. Let justice, mercy, and truth govern all our minds and actions. Let our superfluities give way to our neighbour's conveniencies (and who then will have any superfluities left?); our conveniencies to our neighbour's necessities; our necessities to his extremities."[108] Then Wesley stipulates the relationship between this moral teaching and theology:

> But then be it observed, none can walk by this rule (nor ever did from the beginning of the world), none can love his neighbour as himself, unless he first love God. And none can love God unless he believe in Christ, unless he have redemption through his blood, and the Spirit of God bearing witness with his spirit that he is a child of God. Faith therefore is still the root of all, of present as well as future salvation.[109]

---

104. Sermon 30, "Upon Our Lord's Sermon on the Mount, X," §§8-12, *Works* 1:654-55.
105. Ibid., §14, *Works* 1:656.
106. Ibid., §17, *Works* 1:658.
107. Ibid., §18, *Works* 1:659.
108. Ibid., §26, *Works* 1:662.
109. Ibid., §27, *Works* 1:662.

Wesley connects theology and morality, God and the good, so intimately that he can speak of morality and salvation synonymously. This does not reduce theology to ethics, but insists that morality is finally not possible without faith in the Triune God. That poses difficulties for many persons who live in the twenty-first century and believe that morality is a more universal category than theology. Wesley did not share that belief.

Wesley's eleventh and twelfth discourses present his demonology. The world, the flesh, and the devil present grave hindrances to morality. They set forth a "broad way" where riches, power, an improper courage, and other supposed virtues are permitted for the Christian. Interestingly, one of Wesley's few references to courage, one of the four cardinal virtues in ancient morality, appears in this sermon as part of the hindrance to morality. Even though Wesley could affirm many natural passions and ancient virtues, the fact that he had little to no place for one of the four cardinal virtues is telling. This shows that he was less open to pagan morality than was Aquinas. The reason for this is that Wesley worries how narrow the way to salvation is. Virtues that cannot be made perfect through beatitude can only be hindrances. "The way to hell has nothing singular in it; but the way to heaven is singularity all over." The only way forward is to be saved "from all our sins."[110] Without perfection, there is no salvation.

The final hindrance in the eleventh discourse is when "the watchmen themselves fall into the snare against which they should warn others." This is a warning against the clergy who are "false prophets." Wesley says that they will appear "in the most mild, inoffensive manner," with an appearance of usefulness, religion, and love.[111] Should the Methodists refuse to hear them and leave their churches? Wesley uses Jesus' words about the Pharisees to encourage the Methodists not to leave or refuse the services of the false clergy. "'Then spake Jesus unto the multitude, and to his disciples, saying, The scribes and the Pharisees sit in Moses' seat,' are the ordinary, stated teachers in your church: 'All therefore whatsoever they bid you observe, that observe and do. But do not ye after their works; for they say and do not.'"[112] Wesley reaffirms that the "validity of the ordinance doth not depend on the goodness of him that administers, but on the faithfulness of him that ordained it."[113] His commitment to the sacramental practices of the church recognized that they did not depend on the goodness of the clergy but on the faithfulness of God. They were to be attended even if the clergy were "false prophets."

Wesley's final discourse concludes in hope based on faith. It both recapitulates what was said before and emphasizes that all is worthless

---

110. Sermon 31, "Upon Our Lord's Sermon on the Mount, XI," §III.4, *Works* 1:672-73.
111. Sermon 32, "Upon Our Lord's Sermon on the Mount, XII," §§I.1-II.5, *Works* 1:676-79.
112. Ibid., §III.6, *Works* 1:682.
113. Ibid., §III.8, *Works* 1:682-83.

without faith in Jesus; it alone makes possible the theological virtue of hope. As Wesley did in his first sermon, he begins this concluding sermon by reminding us who it is that gives us this sermon. "Our divine Teacher" has declared "the whole counsel of God with regard to the way of salvation, and observed the chief hindrance of those who desire to walk therein."[114] Wesley ends his discourses as he began them, with a Chalcedonian grammar; the fullness of divinity is present in the humanity of Jesus. The righteousness of Christ is the beginning and ending of his thirteen discourses. In Christ we see that God held nothing back; all the counsel or wisdom of God is present in Jesus, in himself, his words, and his actions. But God also reminds us that simply knowing that Jesus is fully divine and fully human and the Lord of all is necessary but insufficient. For Jesus concludes the sermon with the haunting words, "Not everyone that saith unto me, Lord, Lord, shall enter into the kingdom of heaven; but he that doeth the will of my Father which is in heaven."[115]

Drawing out the implications of Jesus' statement that those who do his will build on rock while those who do not build on sand, Wesley returns again to the external practices Methodists should observe. He asks, "What is the foundation of *my* hope?" Is it "orthodoxy," "doing no harm," "attending all the ordinances of God," which includes partaking of the Lord's Supper, using public and private prayers, fasting often, and hearing and searching Scripture? Is the foundation doing "good to all"? Wesley responds, "These things likewise ought you to have done, from the time you first set your face towards heaven. Yet these things also are nothing, being alone. They are nothing without the weightier matters of the law. And those you have forgotten. At least you experience them not: faith, mercy, and love of God; holiness of heart; heaven opened in the soul."[116] Orthodoxy, sacraments, General Rules, and the basic precepts of morality all hold the same place in Wesley's moral theology. They are the external works we are to perform without trusting in them. If they do not produce the religion of the heart or the "sum of true religion" found in Jesus' pronouncement of beatitudes, they will be nothing. But if they do produce this, then they will not be discarded. They will lead us to the righteousness of Christ, which is the fulfillment of the law. Note that Wesley concludes this final discourse by a reference to the "weightier matters of the law." Wesley rarely mentioned grace in these sermons, although it is assumed. His moral theology emphasizes the importance of law and beatitude. He concludes his thirteen discourses with a reference

---

114. Sermon 33, "Upon Our Lord's Sermon on the Mount, XIII," §1, *Works* 1:687.
115. Matt. 7:21; see also ibid., §2, *Works* 1:687.
116. Ibid., §§III.1-3, *Works* 1:694-95.

to the law. It comes as no surprise that these thirteen discourses are followed by three sermons on the law

THE LORD OUR RIGHTEOUSNESS: A CHRISTOLOGICAL LAW

In his third sermon on the law, John Wesley returns to the theme "the Lord Our Righteousness" and argues that to "preach Christ" fully requires preaching the law.[117] What is the law? In his first sermon on the law, "The Original, Nature, Properties, and Use of the Law," Wesley discusses the law's origin. He understands it according to the biblical narrative. The law was that liberty God originally gave Adam and Eve to discern good from evil. This original law was "wellnigh effaced" from the human heart by human sin.[118] Given that Wesley claimed the doctrine of total depravity, it is unclear what he means by "wellnigh effaced." However, he does not argue for a moral sense that residually works in the human heart. One cannot find in Wesley a doctrine of the "natural law" as a moral sense or consciousness that is innate to the human being itself. We have seen that he vigorously attacked such a doctrine in his critique of Frances Hutcheson, calling it a species of atheism. Wesley argues instead that the work of the Second Person of the Trinity "in some measure reinscribed" the original moral law that enabled our first parents to discern good from evil. God did this act *prior to* the Incarnation, for Christ is the "light which enlightens every man that cometh into the world."[119] Once again we see Wesley's Augustinian-Malebranchian doctrine of illumination. The moral law is not known separate from Christ, even if someone does not know Christ. Christ is the Law, for as the Wisdom of God he alone distinguishes good from evil. We do not know it if we do not know him.

This can easily, albeit falsely, lead Methodist interpreters to read in Wesley something similar to some interpretations of Rahner's "supernatural existential" where to affirm the transcendental nature of one's own being is to affirm grace irrespective of its categorical status and historic mediation.[120] Wesley's "prevenient grace" can be, and often is, construed in a similar fashion. But Wesley does not play the transcendental against

---

117. Sermon 36, "The Law Established through Faith, II," §I.6, *Works* 2:37-38.
118. Sermon 34, "The Original, Nature, Properties, and Use of the Law," §I.4, *Works* 2:7.
119. Ibid., §§I.4-5, *Works* 2:7.
120. Perhaps I should say "Rahnerian" rather than Rahner. Those interpreters of Rahner who find in his work primacy for a "transcendental" rather than a "categorical" revelation may not be the best interpreters of his work.

the categorical in his interpretation of the moral law. The "light" that enlightens does not function without the historic mediation that comes through "a peculiar people." Wesley writes,

> But notwithstanding this light, all flesh had in process of time "corrupted their way before him"; till he chose out of mankind a peculiar people, to whom he gave a more perfect knowledge of his law. And the heads of this, because they were slow of understanding, he wrote on two tablets of stone; which he commanded the fathers to teach their children through all succeeding generations.
> And thus it is that the law of God is now made known to them that know not God.[121]

The moral law is found in the Ten Commandments, mediated through time. It is not found in some secure interiority of human consciousness or existential relation.

Wesley began his moral theology with Christology. He then discussed the Sermon on the Mount and explained the gifts, Beatitudes, and theological virtues. In these three sermons on the law, he reads the Decalogue backward from Jesus' Sermon on the Mount. The "ten words" make best sense for Wesley when they are understood within the context of Jesus' teaching on the Mount. It is as if to see the moral life properly we have to see it in terms of a palimpsest where the original image is the Second Person of the Trinity, whose face can too easily be effaced by the ten words written on stone. This is why after Wesley explains the original of the law as the gift of the Ten to Moses that reinscribes the natural law, he then explains its nature in startling christological terms. "Now this law is an incorruptible picture of the high and holy One that inhabiteth eternity. . . . It is the face of God unveiled. . . . Yea, in some sense we may apply to this law what the Apostle says of his Son—it is 'the streaming forth' or out-beaming 'of his glory, the express image of his person.'"[122] And Wesley relates it directly to the virtue tradition.

> The law of God is all virtues in one, in such a shape as to be beheld with open face by all those whose eyes God hath enlightened. What is the law but divine virtue and wisdom assuming a visible form? What is it but the original ideas of truth and good, which were lodged in the uncreated mind from eternity, now drawn forth and clothed with such a vehicle as to appear even to human understanding.[123]

Of course, if it were not for the language of the Incarnation—"in such a shape as to be beheld with open face, . . . assuming a visible form, . . .

---

121. Sermon 34, "The Original, Nature, Properties, and Use of the Law," §§I.5-6, *Works* 2:7-8.
122. Ibid., §II.3, *Works* 2:9.
123. Ibid., §II.4, *Works* 2:9-10.

clothed with such a vehicle as to appear even to human understanding"—this would be pure Platonism. But this is such a significant conversion of Platonic thinking that it undoes it precisely as it affirms it. The ideas in the uncreated mind (God) are not discovered by overcoming the prison of the body and releasing the soul, especially through death as Socrates seems to suggest in the *Phaedo*. Instead, the ideas are discovered only as they can be seen in the shape, visible form, and clothed vehicles through which God presents them. The Torah and flesh of Jesus merge in Wesley's thinking. So he writes, "The law of God (speaking after the manner of men) is a copy of the eternal mind, a transcript of the divine nature; yea, it is the fairest offspring of the everlasting Father, the brightest efflux of his essential wisdom, the visible beauty of the Most High."[124] This is why its properties are holy, just, and good. And why it has three uses, which differ significantly from Calvin precisely in their christological determination. The first use of the law is "to convince the world of sin." The second use is "to bring him unto life, unto Christ, that he may live." And the third use is "to keep us alive." It does this because it is "the grand means whereby the blessed Spirit prepares the believer for larger communications of the life of God."[125] The law functions like a sacrament in Wesley's moral theology.

To understand this well we have to remember that part of the function of the moral law is precisely to observe the sacraments. This sermon does not make sense without recalling that Methodism was a movement where persons joined together to observe the General Rules. They are the moral law. Through these concrete, material practices we receive as a gift the infused virtue of faith that will issue forth in love and hope. For this reason, Wesley's last two sermons on the Law are both entitled "The Law Established through Faith," and return to themes he has consistently developed throughout these sermons beginning with "The Lord Our Righteousness." They are discourses on the infused theological virtue of faith and its relationship to law.

In "The Law Established through Faith" duo, Wesley exegetes Saint Paul's statement in Romans 3:31, "Do we then make void the law through faith? God forbid: yea, we establish the law." The first discourse examines how we make the law void, the second how we establish it. The law is made void when it is not preached or when we teach that faith supersedes the law such that holiness no longer matters. Wesley recognizes that this produces a false form of liberty. "Indeed the using the term *liberty* in such a manner for 'liberty from obedience or holiness' shows at once that their judgment is perverted, and that they are guilty of what they imagined to

---

124. Ibid., §II.6, *Works* 2:10.
125. Ibid., §§IV.1-3, *Works* 2:15-16.

be far from them; namely, of 'making void the law through faith,' by supposing faith to supersede holiness."[126] Would this correct Wesley's earlier affirmation of the liberty of indifference? As we have seen, that teaching did little to no work for Wesley. Of course, the liberty of indifference does not entail disobedience, but it does assume the will remains aloof from the chain of practical reasoning involved in human action. Nothing Wesley has set forth in his moral theology suggests that the liberty of indifference has any bearing on his account of human action.

Finally, the law is made void *in fact*. Wesley returns to many of the same themes found in his discourses on the Sermon on the Mount where he noted hindrances to the religion of the heart.[127] He appeals to the "evangelical principles of action" as more, but not less, than legal to counter, making the law void. This evangelical principle of action is *legal* in that it requires certain activities to be accomplished. Many of those activities are identical with the actions the Mosaic law required. However this evangelical law is not legal in the sense that the performance of the law is the condition for acceptance with God. It is instead a gift. "And he now performs (which while 'under the law' he could not do) a willing and universal obedience. He obeys, not from the motive of slavish fear, but on a nobler principle, namely, the grace of God ruling in his heart, and causing all his works to be wrought in love."[128] Grace here is not an existential orientation; it is a shorthand way of expressing the religion of the heart, the sum of all true religion. Wesley is drawing on a very Catholic and biblical theme: grace is "the new law of the gospel."

Having warned of the hindrances that make the law void, Wesley's final discourse on the law sets forth how it is established through faith. The theological virtue of faith establishes the law. How does faith establish the law? "We 'establish the law,' first, by our doctrine: by endeavouring to preach it in its whole extent, to explain and enforce every part of it in the same manner as our great Teacher did while upon earth."[129] Where does this occur in Wesley if not in his Sermons on the Mount? The law is to be set forth in both its literal and spiritual sense. The literal sense is the external prohibitions and permissions that the law entails—do good, avoid evil, attend the ordinances of God. The spiritual sense is the internal disposition of faith in Jesus as the law's true end. The second establishment of the law through faith is as it produces "all manner of holiness, negative and positive, of the heart and of the life."[130] This occurs only through an obedient love. The infused virtue of faith, by which we are

---

126. Sermon 35, "The Law Established through Faith, I," §II.2, *Works* 2:26-27.
127. Ibid., §III, *Works* 2:29-32.
128. Ibid., §III.3, *Works* 2:29-30.
129. Sermon 36, "The Law Established through Faith, II," §I.1, *Works* 2:34.
130. Ibid., §II.1, *Works* 2:38.

justified, will immediately result in the infused virtue of love by which we can be obedient. As Wesley put it, "faith then was originally designed of God to re-establish the law of love."[131] He concludes this sermon—and it is a fitting conclusion to his moral theology—on what at first might appear as a truism. The third, and most important way of establishing the law is by "establishing it in our own hearts and lives."[132] This is a truism—establishing the law is through establishing the law—but it is not trivial. Even if we have all proper doctrine, rules, and mysteries of the kingdom and declare them openly to all persons, if these are not established in our hearts by faith, then in fact the law will not be established, and we will not be restored into the image of God, who is Jesus Christ.

Throughout his work, Wesley draws on an ancient and Catholic theme that faith presupposes more than mere intellectual knowledge of external realities. Faith is not mere intellectual assent, although it must assume intellectual assent. Augustine recognized this by speaking of faith in terms of *"credere Deo, credere Deum,* and *credere in Deum." Credere Deo* implies believing what God says. It assumes God can be trusted. *Credere Deum* believes that God is. It assumes that we know not only that God exists but also who God is; we know God's character. Neither of these is sufficient for true belief or faith, for the demons themselves can believe such things and tremble. The theological virtue of faith implies something more, it implies *credere in Deum.* Nicholas Lash explains this well: "God is the object of our faith as heart's desire, as goal towards which all our life and thought is set."[133] The virtue of faith cannot settle (or do without) the doctrine that God is, and who God is, and what God says can be trusted. However, for true faith, this disposition of the heart must be present.

Wesley's work assumes that the foundation of moral theology is faith. It begins with humility, which is where he claimed ancient pagan virtue could take you. Humility is no virtue, it is "a right judgment of ourselves."[134] It is Socrates' "know thyself." But humility is no end in itself; there is no philosophical fallibilism as a necessary epistemological feature of human being (as we will examine below). In having a proper judgment about ourselves, we will recognize that morality is not an achievement we accomplish on our own power. We have a disposition to receive a gift, the first of which is faith. Wesley writes, "The true, living, Christian faith, which whosoever hath is 'born of God,' is not only an assent, an act of the understanding, but a disposition which God hath wrought in his heart; 'a sure trust and confidence in God that through the merits of Christ his sins

---

131. Ibid., §II.6, *Works* 2:40.
132. Ibid., §III.1, *Works* 2:41.
133. See Nicholas Lash, *Believing Three Ways in One God* (Notre Dame, Ind.: University of Notre Dame Press, 1992), 20.
134. Cf. Sermon 17, "The Circumcision of the Heart," §I.2, *Works* 1:403.

are forgiven, and he reconciled to the favour of God."[135] Faith is not only intellectual assent; that would be *credere Deo* or *credere Deum*. If faith were only this, then theologians and clergy would have faith more so than the laity because of their scholarly training. But that seems to be falsifiable in nearly every generation of the Christian tradition.

Faith requires something more, not anything less, than intellectual assent. It is this disposition toward God in the heart. If faith is true it will of necessity receive also hope and love. Wesley recognizes the ancient virtue tradition, which opposed hope to presumption and despair. Hope opposes presumption because life requires something more than us in order for us to be happy and live as we should. Hope opposes despair for the same reason. Hope is the virtue that makes possible endurance, steadfastness, and constancy of character. "Indeed it is the same Spirit who works in them that clear and cheerful confidence that their heart is upright toward God; that good assurance that they now do, through his grace, the things which are acceptable in his sight; that they are now in the path which leadeth to life, and shall, by the mercy of God, endure therein to the end."[136] If faith and hope, then love. Love is not some internal disposition that no one has access to because it is private. Love is external and observable. Wesley states, "'Love is the fulfilling of the law,' 'the end of the commandment.' Very excellent things are spoken of love; it is the essence, the spirit, the life of all virtue."[137] These infused theological virtues are how we receive the precious and great promises of "becoming partakers of the divine nature." The life of virtue and the life of Jesus collapse into one in Wesley's moral theology. Ethics and doctrine, goodness and God cannot be finally divided. Jesus himself is "the new law of the Gospel." To understand Wesley on this point, we must understand not only the role Scripture plays in his work but also the tradition of moral theology he inherited and assumed.

---

135. Sermon 18, "The Marks of the New Birth," §I.3, *Works* 1:418-19.
136. Sermon 17, "The Circumcision of the Heart," §I.9, *Works* 1:406.
137. Ibid., §I.11, *Works* 1:407.

CHAPTER 5

WESLEY, AQUINAS, AND MORAL THEOLOGY

Throughout the first four chapters of this work, I related Wesley to a tradition of moral theology that used Thomas Aquinas as the examplar. In this chapter I will bring Wesley and Aquinas more directly into conversation with each other. Wesley's moral theology is a substantive, albeit limited, presentation of the Christian moral life. If his work is all that we have, then the ecclesial traditions that bear his name can only have a diminished theology. But Wesley never assumed we would depend solely on his work. Any fetishization of Wesley's work is both improper and unWesleyan. In his *Christian Library* Wesley pointed us to other sources. His "Address to the Clergymen" exhorted us to read Aquinas, Scotus, Clarke, Malebranche, and More. Without the context of these kinds of arguments, the Wesleyan tradition quickly becomes unintelligible. It needs a richer intellectual tradition than Wesley's work alone to bring out the best of his work. This is not a criticism of Wesley; it restates what he himself set forth.

My argument for reading Wesley in the context of Thomas Aquinas's moral theology is relatively simple and seemingly obvious. I am not arguing that Wesley was in any explicit sense a Thomist. Who could have been in the eighteenth century? Thomism would not reemerge as the heart of Catholic Christian thought until Pope Leo XIII's 1879 encyclical letter "On the Restoration of Christian Philosophy According to the Mind of St. Thomas Aquinas, the Angelic Doctor." The debates that encyclical engendered in the twentieth century made it possible for theologians to engage Thomism(s) in conversation with the best and worst of modernity. Wesley was neither a modern nor a Thomist, but he was first and foremost an Anglican. He inherited a rich Catholic tradition of practice and thought that gave him his orientation in everyday life. He loved the church, the sacraments, the Scriptures, and the patristic era, as well as critical engagement with philosophy. Unlike Luther, he did not fear pagan philosophy. These loves were such a part of his life that he did not need to raise them up as "sources" to be used to do theology, as if the doing of theology were something different from these sources. They were theology. To define them as sources already implies too much distance between Wesley and the immediate context in which he did theology: the Anglican Church, the sacraments, the Scriptures, and philosophy.

But the similarities between Aquinas and Wesley were more than intellectual inheritances. To state the obvious, the focal practices that made up Wesley's everyday life in the eighteenth century were more like those of Aquinas in the thirteenth century than those that came after Wesley in the nineteenth and twentieth centuries. Both Aquinas and Wesley rode horses for transportation. (Although that came as a shift in Aquinas's life in that for a time Dominicans were banned from riding horses.) They both sailed on ships propelled by wind. The thirteenth-century University of Paris was not identical with eighteenth-century Oxford, but surely they were more similar in their structuring of everyday life than what orders our life in the twenty-first century university. Cathedrals, the church year, and liturgy ordered time and space for them (including university life) providing a daily orientation that must have differed from ours. Both Wesley and Aquinas preached regularly, and their theology emerged from, and fed into, their preaching.

Everyday life for us is not oriented by the church year, cathedrals, or liturgical celebrations, apart from an intentional effort on our part. The default mode that orients us is technological; it is the superhighways and malls with their daily and seasonal patterns. These devices structure time and space for us and force us to be individuals whose primary role is to make free choices among competing options. When I enter a mall to make an exchange in one of its seasonal celebrations, such as the spring sale, my particularity on the whole does not matter. No explicit confession of faith or vows are asked, even though it is a credit transaction. The mall is an open, egalitarian space where persons are suppose to be individuals.[1] All that distinguishes individuals is their willingness (or ability) to exercise purchasing power. But when I enter a church during Holy Week services, it is not the same kind of space. The vows and confessions I have made should have an explicit connection to the kinds of exchanges I can make. Wesley and Aquinas inhabited a world where the latter rather than the

---

1. I realize that for a variety of reasons this ideal situation is not always honored.

former constituted everyday exchanges. Their notions of justice, the virtues, and a quest for holiness were more determined by those exchanges than ours could ever be. Neither of them had any moral qualms in emphasizing primary moral obligations to people who shared a common confessional life. Neither seemed troubled by the Christian teaching that God loves us because God first must love God's own self, for only God is worthy of such a love. Such thoughts have become difficult if not impossible for us.

Both Aquinas and Wesley were primarily interested in the formation of preachers. They wrote "practical divinity" intended for converts and preachers.[2] Their theology was done toward that end. If theology is contextual, then Aquinas and Wesley shared much more of a practical context within which theology was given shape than either one of them share with us. Their work has a certain alien quality to it precisely because of these different focal practices. Rather than seeing this as a liability to be overcome by making them relevant to our context, the irrelevance and alien character of their work may be what we need to help us see something other than the dogmatic certitudes of modernity. As those certainties come to an end, even if it is an end that can only be endlessly repeated, then other visions begin to emerge.

One of the dogmatic certainties that emerged after Wesley was that ethics is a larger and more universal category than theology or doctrine. "Ethics" arose from that modern (putatively) universal space where the focal practices of everyday life seem to be less evident and influential than they were for either Wesley or Aquinas. They lived on the other side of the "death of God." We live on this side of it. We cannot act as if it has not happened, even in our churches. Those of us who gather for the exchanges that take place in the Eucharist may be more influenced by the technological orientation that assumes the death of God than by the focal practices that assumed God's presence. Wesley and Aquinas may have been able to see some things that have become difficult for us to see. This is not to deny that we see some things more clearly than they did. Nor is it to be romantic about thirteenth-century Paris or eighteenth-century Oxford. It is to be unromantic toward twenty-first-century Evanston,

---

2. The prologue to Aquinas's *Summa Theologica* should not be forgotten. Aquinas wrote,

we purpose in this book to treat of whatever belongs to the Christian Religion, in such a way as may tend to the instruction of beginners. We have considered that students in this Science have not seldom been hampered by what they have found written by other authors, partly on account of the multiplication of useless question, articles, and arguments; partly also because those things that are needful for them to know are not taught according to the order of the subject-matter, but according as the plan of the book might require, or the occasion of the argument offer; partly, too, because frequent repetition brought weariness and confusion to the minds of the readers. (*Summa Theologica*, xix)

173

Illinois, and wonder why what they saw has become so problematic for us. What did they see?

They saw the Christian moral life primarily as the recovery of the image of God in the human creature, an image that has been effaced but which is restored in and through Jesus via the sacraments, laws, and, above all, the theological virtues of faith, hope, and love. Both Aquinas and Wesley situated the moral life in terms of Christian dogmatics. The doctrine of the Trinity, as well as the classical account of God's attributes, preserves the proper way of speaking about our renewal in the image of God, which is also our sanctification or deification. This renewal into the image of God takes place by the embodiment of a new law, which the Holy Spirit gives internally. This "new law" is a participation in Christ's human righteousness where the Spirit sanctifies the believer. But both Wesley and Aquinas set forth deification without blurring the ontological distinction between God and creation. Both also held to a kind of Augustinian doctrine of illumination along with a metaphysics of participation. As Alasdair MacIntyre has argued, Aquinas's great achievement was synthesizing Augustine with Aristotle. Wesley did not produce such a great theological achievement, but he assumed that of Aquinas. Finally, both Wesley and Aquinas understood the moral life primarily in terms of gifts, beatitudes, and virtues.

THE IMAGE OF GOD RENEWED

In his helpful book, *Politics in the Order of Salvation*, Theodore Weber states, "John Wesley set forth a concept of the *whole image of God* with three dimensions—*natural, political, moral*—and made the recovery of the whole image the focus of his evangelism and its supporting theology."[3] This is also true of his moral theology, which Weber notes concerned Wesley more so than the recovery of the "natural" or "political image." Wesley develops this doctrine of the image of God in his sermon, "The End of Christ's Coming." We will fail to understand what he meant by "the image of God" if we do not recognize that Christ is first and foremost this image. Jesus' human performance is the renewal of the image of God in creatures; this is the "end" of Christ's coming.

This sermon begins with a criticism of any ethics that eschews Christology. Wesley states, "Many eminent writers, heathen as well as Christian, both in earlier and later ages, have employed their utmost labour and art in painting the beauty of virtue."[4] Although such treatises

---

3. Theodore R. Weber, *Politics in the Order of Salvation: Transforming Wesleyan Political Ethics* (Nashville: Kingswood Books, 2001), 36.

4. Sermon 62, "The End of Christ's Coming," §1, *Works* 2:471.

have some validity for Wesley, they are limited in that they seek the source for the achievement of virtue and remedy of vice in humanity as it is. Virtue is not, for Wesley, the cultivation of a human potentiality intrinsic to human being. Virtue assumes that the intellect and will are ordered to something external to the human person. He states, "there is no virtue but where an intelligent being knows, loves, and chooses what is good."[5] The "good" which is to be known, loved, and chosen is the manifestation of God's own life in Jesus Christ. His work is the "restoration of man." This is "real religion"; which is "a restoration not only to the favour, but likewise to the image of God."[6] Wesley recognized that the Enlightenment challenged this traditional Christian understanding of the moral life as the renewal of the image of God. He does not state, nor express his awareness, that it was Thomas Aquinas who first and foremost developed moral theology in terms of the renewal of the image of God in the human creature.

For Wesley, Christ restores the human creature to the natural and moral image of God. The natural image of God is a healing of understanding, will, and liberty. The moral image of God is a recovery of our intended righteousness and holiness. This recovery takes place through Christ's manifestations. When we glimpse these manifestations they illumine our understanding and heal our broken will so that we can faithfully use our liberty. Wesley notes a series of these manifestations that begins with Jesus' existence as the only begotten Son of God, in glory equal with the Father before creation; leads through his appearance to Adam and Eve in the Garden; and culminates in his "grand manifestation" in the Incarnation, where he offered a full, perfect, and sufficient sacrifice for our sins, was raised from the dead, ascended into heaven, and poured out the Holy Ghost.[7]

These manifestations reveal God's glory and thereby open and enlighten "the eyes of our understanding."[8] This involves more than discursive reasoning, though it is mediated through historical and material means. It is also a "kind of intuition" because it is a participation in the logic of the Incarnation itself.[9] It is quite similar to the role Aquinas gave to *intellectus*. The renewal into the image of God does not follow without this original vision. As we saw in the previous chapter, that renewal is a participation in the human righteousness of Christ.

Wesley's moral theology assumes the dogmatic theological context of Christ's righteousness as our true end that renews us into the image of

---

5. Ibid., §I.6, *Works* 2:475.
6. Ibid., §III.5, *Works* 2:482.
7. Ibid., §§II.1-6, *Works* 2:478-80.
8. Ibid., §III.1, *Works* 2:481.
9. Ibid.

God. His moral theology was not based on a system of cases as was customary prior to Aquinas in someone like Raymond of Pennafort. Leonard Boyle suggests that Aquinas developed the *Summa Theologica* to offer something more than just a practical theology based on a system of cases. Aquinas was dissatisfied with the lack of any Christian dogmatic foundation for moral theology. It needed more *theology* and thus, "Thomas puts practical theology—the study of Christian life, its virtues and vices—in a full theological context. . . . To study human action is therefore to study the image of God and to operate on a theological plane."[10] This initiates a new theological tradition that Wesley clearly inherited, whether he knew its source or not. Likewise, A. N. Williams has brought out how central this doctrine of the renewal of the image of God is in Aquinas's *Summa Theologica*. It is the bridge between the moral teaching in the *secunda pars* and the dogmatic account of the Trinity in the *prima pars*.[11]

In the *prima pars*, Thomas Aquinas develops his doctrine of the Trinity in the first forty-three questions.[12] He can only develop his doctrine of creation after he has set forth his teaching on the Triune God because creation is a reflection of the Triune processions themselves. Aquinas notes that our relations with others are never univocal with that of the Triune processions, but we could only understand this after we first understand what the Triune processions are. In other words, once we have a proper language to identify the Triune God, we can see how we as created beings are both a reflection of and yet fundamentally different from the Triune Persons.

Thomas Weinandy captures this nicely when he tells us, "the act of creation mirrors, though imperfectly, the processions of the Trinity."[13] We are an *imperfect* mirroring because our relations are not subsistent relations, as are the Triune relations. As Weinandy notes, our relations are possible through "mediating words (words of kindness and love) and actions (hugs, kisses, sexual relations, etc.) which express only a partial giving of oneself even if one's intention is to give the whole of oneself. This is not

---

10. Leonard E. Boyle, "The Setting of the *Summa Theologiae* of St. Thomas—Revisited," in *The Ethics of Aquinas* (ed. Stephen J. Pope; Moral Traditions Series, ed. James F. Keenan; Washington, D.C.: Georgetown University Press, 2002), 5-7.

11. See A. N. Williams, *The Ground of Union: Deification in Aquinas and Palamas* (New York: Oxford University Press, 1999).

12. I recognize that Karl Rahner challenged this interpretation of Aquinas, suggesting he wrongly separated the first twenty-six questions on the unity of God from questions twenty-seven through forty-three on the Triune processions. But Fergus Kerr (building on the work of Victor Preller and David Burrell) has shown the strong connection that Aquinas actually made between God's unity and the Triune processions (Fergus Kerr, *After Aquinas: Versions of Thomism* [Oxford: Blackwell, 2002]). Williams's work also stresses these connections and adds additional insight into how the questions of God's unity, Trinity, and work in creation in the *prima pars* illumine all that occurs in the *secunda pars* of the *Summa*.

13. Thomas G. Weinandy, *Does God Suffer?* (Notre Dame, Ind.: University of Notre Dame Press, 2000), 142.

the case with the Trinity."[14] These relations are subsistent. When it comes to the Triune processions we can say with Aquinas and Gregory of Nazianzus that the Son is everything that the Father is, but the Son is not the Father. As a subsistent relation, the Son only is in relation to the Father in an immediate gift and reception that has no substance outside that gift and reception. To say the same of my relationship as father to my children, as husband to my wife, or of a friend to friend would be improper. We can clearly speak of subsistent relations (the *res significata*) even when the only language we have to speak of them is through relations that are not themselves subsistent but mere reflections of such relations (the *modus significandi*).

When Aquinas develops the heart of his doctrine of creation he does so by relating anthropology to the Triune processions. This occurs in question 93 of the *prima pars* where he writes, "Now it is manifest that in man there is some likeness to God, copied from God as from an exemplar; yet this likeness is not one of equality, for such an exemplar infinitely excels its copy."[15] Aquinas, like Wesley, uses the Platonic language of "copy" to explain creation. He also relates this to Christology. This image is a likeness from an exemplar; it is not a direct copy. Aquinas states, "The First-Born of creatures is the perfect Image of God, reflecting perfectly that of which He is the Image, and so He is said to be the *Image*, and never *to the image*."[16] Because our image as likeness is possible through The Image as copy, the likeness is also a likeness of the Triune Persons. "Moreover the Word of God is born of God by the knowledge of Himself; and Love proceeds from God according as He loves Himself."[17]

These processions of Wisdom and Love, the Son and the Spirit, are also the processions of Intellect and Will. The will must be rational appetite, and the intellect must be moved by love, precisely because these gifts are reflections of the Triune processions in us. They mirror the relationship between the Son and the Spirit, which are subsistent relations. It is these relations that allow Aquinas to use Augustine's psychology as the basis for an anthropology that is a likeness of the Triune processions. Aquinas quotes Augustine in order to explain the image of the Triune God in human creatures, "*the mind remembers itself, . . . and loves itself. If we perceive this, we perceive a trinity, not, indeed, God, but, nevertheless, rightly called the image of God.*"[18] Aquinas quickly adds "But this is due to the fact, not that the mind reflects on itself absolutely, but that thereby it can furthermore turn to God."[19] The human mind's ability to remember and love does not

---

14. Ibid., 116.
15. *Summa Theologica* I.93.1, resp.
16. Ibid., ad. 2.
17. *Summa Theologica* I.93.8, resp.
18. Ibid.
19. Ibid.

provide direct access to knowledge of God. It allows the human mind to be illumined by that which is outside of it and thus be oriented toward God. Thus the *imago Dei* is not a secure interior presence that gives us a supernatural existential orientation. Instead, as A. N. Williams notes, "The *imago Dei* theology tells us primarily what we will be, not what we are."[20]

The renewal of the image of God in human creatures, explaining how they proceed and return to God, unites the dogmatic theological context of the *prima pars* with the moral theology of the *secunda pars*. This occurs through the crucial question 93 of the *prima pars* where creation as made *into* the image of God is set forth. Williams finds this the essential link between the first two parts of the *Summa*. "If we read the *Secunda Pars* in light of Question 93, we come to understand that the treatise on habits and virtues is not, in the Thomistic scheme of things, a study of human endeavor—not even, in the first instance, graced human endeavor—but rather an extended meditation on the trinitarian processions."[21]

The analogy between creation and the Triune processions occurs because of a mind that speaks and, in speaking, knows and images perfectly what that mind is. Because the mind speaks perfectly it also loves what comes forth from it with a perfect love, even as this love is a gift between the mind and its word. These are the terms Aquinas uses to explain the Triune processions. The Son is the "Image" of the Father because the Son is "entirely alike" with the Father. The Son is the Word "to show that he is not begotten carnally." The Spirit is both "love" and "gift."[22] The Son as Word and Image has been identified with the essence of God in questions 14 through 17 of the *prima pars*, where this divine procession is related to God's knowledge, ideas, and truth. At question 18 Aquinas moves from a discussion of God's knowledge and intellect to examine God's life, will, and power. These operations of the divine life identify the Spirit, who is later named Gift and Love. Here we see how closely related Aquinas's discussion of God's unity and Trinity will be and how linked this is to salvation as our renewal in the image of God.

That the Son is the Image is essential for our sanctification. Aquinas establishes this at *prima pars* question 35: "man is not simply called the image, but *to the image*, whereby is expressed a certain movement of tendency to perfection. But it cannot be said that the Son of God is *to the image*, because He is the perfect Image of the Father."[23] Note that we are not *made* the image of God; it is not something we already possess, but we are made *to* the image of God as something that needs to be brought to

---

20. Williams, *Ground of Union*, 69.
21. Ibid., 71.
22. *Summa Theologica*, I.37–38.
23. *Summa Theologica* I.35.2, ad. 3.

completion. Williams notes that this renewal to the image of God is the work of grace. "Grace . . . may be appropriately described as re-creating the human person so that her essence participates in divine knowledge and love, both of which Thomas has, in differing ways, associated with divine essence."[24]

This provides the pattern for Aquinas to explain how we return to God through the three-step process of *nature-grace-glory*. Intellectual activity in humanity allows for a reflection of the Trinity, which allows us to know what we love and love what we know. We first have a natural aptitude for understanding and loving God. This is not complete but is a potentiality that must be actualized, which is done through grace. Thus, in the second step in our return, a person actually or habitually knows and loves God. This is grace. But it is not yet the perfect return. A third possibility exists where one knows and loves God perfectly. This is glory.[25] Nature, grace, and glory combine to renew us into the image of God. This is the basis for the moral teaching in the *secunda pars*. It was something of a revolution in moral theology, even as it recovered important patristic themes.

Aquinas began developing this new context for moral theology in his teaching at Santa Sabina. It was not one of the five official *studium generale* of the Dominican order, nor even a *studium provinciale*. The five official *studium generale* were at Paris, Bologna, Cologne, Montpellier, and Oxford. It is possible that the dissatisfaction Aquinas expresses about theology in the prologue to the *Summa* has to do with the lack of an integration of dogmatic and moral theology in the standard curriculum of the *studium generale*.[26] By incorporating moral theology into a dogmatic context beginning with the renewal of the image of God in humanity, Aquinas challenged and revised the standard Dominican curriculum.

Wesley's moral theology is a repetition of this pattern found in Aquinas where human action is discussed within the dogmatic theological context of renewal in the image of God. Wesley begins in the exact same place Aquinas began in the *prima secundae*. In the prologue that begins his "treatise on the last end," which sets the foundation for his discussion of the virtues, gifts, beatitudes, passions, laws, and so on, Aquinas writes,

> SINCE, as Damascene states, man is said to be made to God's image, in so far as the image implies *an intelligent being endowed with free-will and self-movement*: now that we have treated of the exemplar, *i.e.*, God, and of those things which came forth from the power of God in accordance with His will; it remains for us to treat of His image, *i.e.*, man, inasmuch as he too is the principle of his actions, as having free-will and control of his actions.[27]

---

24. Williams, *Ground of Union*, 85.
25. Ibid., 70. See also *Summa Theologica* I.93.4.
26. See Boyle, "The Setting of the *Summa Theologiae*," in Pope, *Ethics of Aquinas*, 9.
27. *Summa Theologica* I-II, prologue.

If we did not know what Aquinas had already written in questions 35 and 93 of the *prima pars*, the prologue to the *secunda pars* would not make sense. Everything that follows explains how knowledge and love move in the human creature in order for him or her to return perfectly to God.

The similarities between Wesley and Aquinas here are intriguing. Both begin their moral theology with an account of the renewal of the image of God. Both do so assuming that one must first understand and be able to identify the Triune God in whose image we are to be renewed. Both understand that this renewal requires a healing of the understanding and will. Both discuss this renewal under the category of the "last end," which is christologically determined. But Aquinas gives us a much richer account of human agency than did Wesley.

Aquinas begins his account of human agency by stating that all human action is on account of an end. As previously noted, Wesley assumed this same teleological account of human agency. Aquinas notes that such an account of human action seems surprising in that action would appear to be the result more of a cause that originates actions than an end that elicits them. If the will were simply the slave of the passions, then human action would be less for an end than the consequence of preceding passions. But for Aquinas, while the end is last in execution, it is first in intention. Without the end, even when we have not yet attained it, the will would not move. This means there would be no will, for it is nothing but rational appetite or deliberate movement. This movement of the will is not from necessity. Aquinas insists that our movement toward the end is not mere instinct or even inclination. This is why the will and reason must be linked in human agency in a way that is not in animal instinct. He writes,

> Now man differs from irrational animals in this, that he is master of his actions. Wherefore those actions alone are properly called human, of which man is master. Now man is master of his actions through his reason and will; whence, too, the free-will is defined as *the faculty and will of reason*. Therefore those actions are properly called human which proceed from a deliberate will.[28]

The will is not necessarily moved by the willed, even though voluntary human acts occur both through the will's power to command and to be elicited. The will commands through a deliberating movement toward an end. Willing is elicited in order for the will to move voluntarily toward that end. But the willing elicited is not the last end otherwise willing would be an end in itself. The willing occurs for some other reason than

---

28. *Summa Theologica* I-II.1.1, resp.

action alone; it is directed toward a "last end."[29] It is not just a will to power that does what it does for no other reason than it can.

The will is not an end in itself, and the mere act of willing does not constitute the will's freedom. But Aquinas does not posit some third faculty of the soul called "liberty" behind will and understanding in order to affirm the will's freedom. The will is free because of the relationship between the will and the intellect. The intellect moves the will of necessity, but the will need not be moved properly. It can resist by refusing to be turned toward the true and the good, but it cannot refuse all movement toward the end, which makes the movement of the will possible in the first place. This end is happiness. The will cannot will unhappiness, even though it is often confused about what constitutes true happiness. Happiness is both uncreated and created:

> our end is twofold. First, there is the thing itself which we desire to attain. . . . Secondly there is the attainment or possession, the use or enjoyment of the thing desired. . . . In the first sense, then, man's last end is the uncreated good, namely, God, Who alone by His infinite goodness can perfectly satisfy man's will. But in the second way, man's last end is something created, existing in him, and this is nothing else than the attainment or enjoyment of the last end.[30]

Happiness as cause or object of the will is uncreated. But "as to the very essence of happiness, then it is something created."[31] If it is to belong properly to creatures and the distinction between God and creation remain intact, then our happiness will be created. This is the role for the theological virtues. They are our *inherent* righteousness.

Aristotle also taught that all human action only occurred in the context of a quest for happiness, but he could not name happiness as well as Aquinas. As we shall see, Aquinas can make happiness or beatitude the end of human action because of Christ's teaching on the Sermon on the Mount. Beatitude is no longer a formal quest we seek to achieve, it comes as gift. This is not to say that Aquinas failed to recognize the moral life is a quest. It is because of the natural desire to know that this journey toward happiness begins. He writes,

> If therefore the human intellect, knowing the essence of some created effect, knows no more of God than *that He is*; the perfection of that intellect does not yet reach simply the First Cause, but there remains in it the natural desire to seek the cause. Wherefore it is not yet perfectly happy. Consequently, for perfect happiness the intellect needs to reach the very

29. Ibid., ad. 2.
30. *Summa Theologica* I-II.3.1, resp.
31. Ibid.

> Essence of the First Cause. And thus it will have its perfection through union with God as with that object, in which alone man's happiness consists.[32]

This natural desire for knowledge of God relates back to question 2 in the *prima pars* where Aquinas told us, "To know that God exists in a general and confused way is implanted in us by nature, inasmuch as God is man's beatitude."[33] We have a confused natural knowledge of God in that we all seek to be happy. But without divine illumination, this confused natural knowledge will not become through grace the true glory God intends. Nature here is a potentiality, an unfulfilled desire that sets us out on the return journey to God. This is a journey where intellect and will work together beginning with their natural potentiality, receiving grace, and becoming perfect.

The first thirteen questions of the *prima pars* in the *Summa* tell us what natural knowledge of God accomplishes. It is not much. As Aquinas puts it in his discussion of God's simplicity, "Now, because we cannot know what God is, but rather what He is not, we have no means for considering how God is, but rather how He is not."[34] The so-called attributes of God—simplicity, perfection, infinity, immutability, eternity, and unity—let us know that God is not a creature. But they do not provide beatitude. They should only incite a natural desire to know more. This natural desire to know more cannot rest until it knows the divine essence, which Aquinas has told us we cannot naturally know. We can know that God is, but not who God is. To know who God is we must know that God is Triune, and that cannot take place through natural reason. Aquinas states, "It is impossible to attain to the knowledge of the Trinity by natural reason. For, . . . man cannot obtain the knowledge of God by natural reason except from creatures. Now creatures lead us to the knowledge of God as effects do to their cause."[35] Knowledge by effects from causes is not finally the true knowledge of things. If we stop there we cannot attain perfect happiness.

Aquinas acknowledges limits to the knowledge of God presented in his first twenty-six questions. "By natural reason we can know of God that only which of necessity belongs to Him as the principle of all things."[36] More is needed than this to attain happiness. That more is the dogma of the Triune processions, which must be remembered to understand how human action unfolds in the context of the end of beatitude in the *secunda*

---

32. *Summa Theologica* I-II.3.8, resp. 1.
33. *Summa Theologica* I.2.1, ad. 1.
34. *Summa Theologica* I.3, prologue.
35. *Summa Theologica* I.32.1, resp.
36. Ibid.

pars. It is no surprise that Aquinas tells us, "If therefore the human intellect . . . knows no more of God than *that He is* . . . it is not yet perfectly happy. Consequently, for perfect happiness the intellect needs to reach the very Essence of the First Cause. And thus it will have its perfection through union with God as with that object, in which alone man's happiness consists."[37] This assumes all that he already taught us in the *prima pars*. In fact, he told us explicitly that knowledge of the Triune Persons is necessary for us to understand creation rightly. The Trinity helps us understand that God creates not out of need by some bare causal will to power, but solely from the procession of love.

> There are two reasons why the knowledge of the divine persons was necessary for us. It was necessary for the right idea of creation. The fact of saying that God made all things by His Word excludes the error of those who say that God produced things by necessity. When we say that in Him there is a procession of love, we show that God produced creatures not because He needed them, nor because of any other extrinsic reason, but on account of the love of His own goodness. So Moses, when he had said, *In the beginning God created heaven and earth*, subjoined, *God said, Let there be light*, to manifest the divine Word; and then said, *God saw the light that it was good*, to show the proof of the divine love. The same is also found in the other works of creation. In another way, and chiefly, that we may think rightly concerning the salvation of the human race, accomplished by the Incarnate Son, and by the gift of the Holy Ghost.[38]

This is the theological background for Aquinas's account of happiness as the last end that makes possible all human action. It proceeds from us freely from love of the good and not of necessity. Thus we can be made into the image of God.

This theological context is always assumed when Aquinas speaks of our happiness as existing in knowing God's essence. God's essence is the Triune Persons. Natural reason cannot give this to us, it can only come as a gift. But it is not beyond creatures, or we could not be happy. In fact, Aquinas told us long before beginning the discussion of happiness in the *prima secundae* that happiness is the vision of God through the "*operatio intellectus*."[39] The activity of the intellect illumines us so that we understand first principles. This illumination occurs through the intellect's participation in the Word that "expresses every creature." In language Malebranche, Norris, and Cudworth mediated to Wesley, Aquinas wrote, "as the Father speaks Himself and every creature by His begotten Word, inasmuch as the Word *begotten* adequately represents the Father and

---

37. *Summa Theologica* I-II.3.8, resp. 1.
38. *Summa Theologica* I.32.1, ad. 3.
39. *Summa Theologica* I.12.1.

every creature; so He loves Himself and every creature by the Holy Ghost, inasmuch as the Holy Ghost proceeds as the love of the primal goodness whereby the Father loves Himself and every creature."[40]

Aquinas begins his discussion of human action assuming that the reader already knows that the vision of the Triune God constitutes our happiness. He tells us, "Now it has been shown . . . that Happiness is a good surpassing created nature. Therefore it is impossible that it be bestowed through the action of any creature: but by God alone is man made happy,—if we speak of perfect Happiness."[41] This perfect happiness is uncreated, but for us to participate in it as creatures it must be created in us. This occurs through "merits." I think Wesley would object to Aquinas at this point, but if we understand how this works for Aquinas it is very similar to Wesley's own position, as the Calvinist James Hervey rightly recognized. Jesus Christ is the Image of God whose life is the meritorious cause. He enables us to exercise works of mercy and piety by which we too can actualize a natural potentiality we have for God. But we must actualize this operation for happiness; it cannot be merely forensic. If we are to be actually happy it must also be inherent. Aquinas writes, "Now since Happiness surpasses every created nature, no pure creature can becomingly gain Happiness, without the movement of operation, whereby it tends thereto."[42]

Here happiness and holiness are linked. Our happiness is always a gift, but it is a gift we must exercise by the proper movement of operation toward which it tends. The actualization of this natural potentiality can only occur through grace, but the grace of justification is not the movement toward the end itself. Such a movement requires human cooperation, even though such cooperation always assumes grace is the principle of movement. As Aquinas puts it "grace is not a term of movement, as Happiness is; rather is it the principle of the movement that tends towards Happiness."[43] Why is "Happiness" capitalized in this translation of Aquinas's *Summa*? Because the happiness or beatitude toward which the movement of human action should tend is Christ offering beatitude on the mountain.

In the *Summa Contra Gentiles*, Aquinas outlines the Sermon on the Mount and claims that it contains all moral teaching. As Servais Pinckaers notes,

> In the Beatitudes, Thomas sees Christ's answer to the question of happiness, which no philosopher had ever truly been able to resolve, not even

---

40. *Summa Theologica* I.37.2, ad. 3.
41. *Summa Theologica* I-II.5.6, resp.
42. *Summa Theologica* I-II.5.7.
43. Ibid., ad. 3.

Aristotle. . . . Thomas gives the beatitudes exactly the same position [in the *Summa contra gentiles*] as in the treatise on happiness in the *Summa*: they establish happiness as the end of human life.

. . . In writing the *Summa*, Thomas is aware that he is listening to the Lord teaching on the mountain, in the company of the fathers and the holy Doctors of the church, in the same fellowship with all those, philosophers and others, who, without having been able to hear this voice directly, had nonetheless known how to welcome, even if imperfectly, the light of truth shining at the summit of their souls.[44]

Aquinas does not invent this. He is not the first moral theologian to develop his teaching based on the Sermon on the Mount. He explicitly draws on Augustine's work. Aquinas writes,

As is evident from Augustine's words just quoted, the sermon, which Our Lord delivered on the mountain, contains the whole process of forming the life of a Christian. Therein man's interior movements are ordered. Because after declaring that his end is Beatitude; and after commending the authority of the apostles, through whom the teaching of the Gospel was to be promulgated, He orders man's interior movements, first in regard to man himself, secondly in regard to his neighbor.[45]

As was noted in the previous chapter, Wesley made an identical claim. The Christian life is formed through the new law of the gospel, a principle of action that moves us toward happiness through an obedient love of God and neighbor.

THE "NEW LAW" OF THE GOSPEL

Because both Wesley and Aquinas fundamentally think of the Christian moral life in terms of the relationship between Jesus' teaching of the Sermon on the Mount and Moses' reception of the Law on Sinai, both also think of the gospel in terms of law.[46] Aquinas defined the old law as judicial, ceremonial, and moral. Christ did away with the ceremonial and the judicial but fulfilled the moral law.[47] Wesley followed Aquinas in this interpretation of the Law. For Aquinas the Ten Commandments are the revelation to Israel of the natural law. That they are revealed lets us know

---

44. Servais-Théodore Pinckaers, "The Sources of the Ethics of St. Thomas Aquinas" (trans. Mary Thomas Noble) in Pope, *Ethics of Aquinas*, 24, 28.

45. *Summa Theologica* I-II.108.3.

46. For this in Aquinas, see Thomas F. O'Meara, "Interpreting Thomas Aquinas: Aspect of the Dominican School of Moral Theology in the Twentieth Century," in Pope, *Ethics of Aquinas*, 357.

47. Cf. *Summa Theologica* I-II.104.3.

that even though they are also natural, we need to be illumined to understand them in their natural state.

Like Aquinas, Wesley made the first precept of the natural law central to the Christian moral life. Aquinas stated that the first precept of the natural law was "*good is to be done and pursued, and evil is to be avoided.* All other precepts of the natural law are based upon this: so that whatever the practical reason naturally apprehends as man's good (or evil) belongs to the precepts of the natural law as something to be done or avoided."[48] This first precept of the natural law is known by practical reason. It plays a role as the speculative intellect in relating truth and being. Aquinas notes, "The precepts of the natural law are to the practical reason, what the first principles of demonstrations are to the speculative reason; because both are self-evident principles."[49] These precepts and the first principles of demonstration are self-evident principles intuited by the *intellectus*. They are not known through discursive reasoning; they are the a priori conditions that make discursive reasoning possible. Without these self-evident principles neither the good nor truth could be pursued. But *intellectus* never stands alone.

Because the will is rational appetite, the practical and intellectual virtues cannot be separated. Aquinas set forth five intellectual virtues, each of which relates the human knower to truth. The first is *intellectus*, which knows truth *per se notum* (known self-evidently). It is the kind of intuitive insight that illumination provides. It presents self-evident principles that cannot be denied. All the other virtues are not *per se notum*, but *notum ex alio* (known from something other). These virtues require judgment. The second intellectual virtue is *sapientia*, which makes "judgments on higher realities." The third, *scientia*, makes "judgments on lower realities." The fourth virtue is *prudentia*. It concerns contingent matters that can be other. Unlike the previous three, it requires "deliberation, choice, hope, fear, love." It is also necessary in helping us pursue the good; it is both an intellectual and a practical virtue. It occurs in us and not in things outside of us, which differentiates it from the fifth intellectual virtue of *techne* or "art."[50]

These five intellectual virtues, of which the fourth and fifth are also practical virtues, relate the will and intellect. They provide a schematic of human action. Wesley assumes a similar account of human action, but he never develops it with this kind of thoroughness. Clifford Kossel succinctly presents Aquinas's position in four steps.[51] First, prior to any act of

48. *Summa Theologica* I-II.94.2.
49. Ibid.
50. Cf. Gregory M. Reichberg, "The Intellectual Virtues (Ia IIae, qq. 57–58)," in Pope, *Ethics of Aquinas*, 135-36.
51. In Clifford G. Kossel, "Natural Law and Human Law (Ia IIae, qq. 90–97)," in Pope, *Ethics of Aquinas*, 174.

the will, which is a passive power, it must be formed (specified) by some object. Second, the intellect provides an object for specification. Third, this first specification is common Being and the True, which arouses the natural love of the will. We love what we know to be true, and we know to be true what we love. Finally, this natural love attracts and adds through the appetitive power in humans, giving the specification of the good as an end. Only now does the question arise, *what shall I do?* And what follows is the first precept of the practical reason: "do good and avoid evil." This is the natural necessity that binds practical reason and will; it is the first precept of the natural law. But the natural law, as revealed in the old law, is only a beginning point in Aquinas's moral theology. It is fulfilled in the new law, which requires us to ask the question, *how does the new law relate to the first precept of the natural law?*

Pamela Hall has explained the relationship between the old law (the Decalogue)[52] and the new law (the gospel) in Aquinas. "The Old Law at its core thus prepared the way for the New Law by its moral pedagogy: it helped the Jewish people to relearn the natural law."[53] The new law offers us a more substantive account of what it means to pursue good and avoid evil. The purpose of the Decalogue was to "promote full virtue."[54] The new law of the gospel does not contradict the Decalogue's purpose, but the "New Law makes possible . . . perfection of obedience [to the old law]."[55] The new law "presents the completion and fulfillment of the Law given on Mt. Sinai." Both remind us, "holiness is the point of Divine Law, Old and New."[56] The new law finally is grace. It is "the Holy Spirit given internally."[57] But this does not imply that one can separate internal and external; the Sermon on the Mount illumines but does not negate the teaching received by Moses on the Mountain. As Daniel Westberg makes clear in his discussion of Aquinas and human acts, "In assessing morality, the interior act of the will and the exterior deed compose a single act."[58]

We already saw this same sentiment in Wesley. It comes as no surprise then that grace is discussed in Aquinas only after he has taken us through the virtues, gifts, beatitudes, and the Law. The new law is grace, which is a life infused with theological virtues, gifts, and beatitudes. Aquinas writes,

---

52. Aquinas argued that "all the moral precepts of the Old Law . . . can be reduced to the decalogue." Pamela M. Hall, "The Old Law and the New Law (Ia IIae, qq. 98–108)," in Pope, *Ethics of Aquinas*, 197.

53. Ibid., 196; see *Summa Theologica* I-II.99.2–3.

54. Ibid., 197; see *Summa Theologica* I-II.100.9, ad. 2.

55. Ibid., 202; see *Summa Theologica* I-II.108, ad. 3.

56. Ibid., 203.

57. Kerr, *After Aquinas*, 6.

58. Daniel Westberg, "Good and Evil in Human Acts (Ia IIae, qq. 18–21)," in Pope, *Ethics of Aquinas*, 99.

the New Law consists chiefly in the grace of the Holy Ghost, which is shown forth by faith that worketh through love. Now men become receivers of this grace through God's Son made man, Whose humanity grace filled first, and thence flowed forth to us. . . . Consequently it was becoming that the grace which flows from the incarnate Word should be given to us by means of certain external sensible objects; and that from this inward grace, whereby the flesh is subjected to the Spirit, certain external works should ensue.[59]

Grace is "that divine motion by which the human will is directed toward the final end, perfect beatitude."[60] It "specifies" the will through the illumination of the intellect, providing the only true principle of action human creatures have that can order them toward their true end, Uncreated happiness. The result is that, like Wesley, the end of the Christian life is deification, which occurs when our lives are ordered by the Beatitudes.

DEIFICATION AS EMBODIMENT OF THEOLOGICAL VIRTUES: METAPHYSICS OF PARTICIPATION AND ILLUMINATION

What is "deification"? If it is understood as blurring the distinction between the Uncreated and the created, then neither Aquinas nor Wesley can be properly said to have put forth a doctrine of deification. But the doctrine of deification does not blur this distinction. As noted above in Wesley and Aquinas, our deification results from the Incarnation. We do not participate in a divine righteousness that would make us God, and therefore simple, perfect, immutable, infinite, and a unity of the fullness of being where our essence equals our existence. This can never be our righteousness, for this defines what is not creation. Creatures are not God. These terms that we attribute to God are reminders of this distinction. However, through Jesus' human righteousness, which through the hypostatic union is a type of his divine righteousness, a way is made for us to be "partakers of the divine nature" (2 Peter 1:4). Although this is a mystical reality, it is also human, social, and political. Deification is a life of beatitude lived out in common with others. Deification is "grace bestowed in the form of the theological virtues."[61]

---

59. *Summa Theologica* I-II.108.1. Aquinas goes on to relate the external acts and internal grace in a twofold manner. Internal grace flows from the external works of the sacraments. But it also issues forth in a faith that works through love keeping the law.

60. Theo Kobusch, "Grace (Ia IIae, qq. 109–114)" (trans. Grant Kaplan and Frederick G. Lawrence), in Pope, *Ethics of Aquinas*, 209. See also *Summa Theologica* I-II.109.5.

61. Williams, *Ground of Union*, 35.

Both Aquinas and Wesley draw on 2 Peter 1:4 for their doctrine of deification and for their explanation of the gift of the theological virtues. Aquinas writes, "Now the gift of grace surpasses every capability of created nature, since it is nothing short of a partaking of the Divine Nature, which exceeds every other nature. . . . For it is as necessary that God alone should deify, bestowing a partaking of the Divine Nature by a participated likeness."[62] As with Wesley this is christologically determined, linked to the Chalcedonian grammar of the Christian faith. Aquinas states, "Hence Christ's humanity does not cause grace by its own power, but by virtue of the Divine Nature joined to it, whereby the actions of Christ's humanity are saving actions."[63] Our participation in Jesus' blessedness is taken up into the life of God. Through this participation, we actually participate in the "forms" or "ideas" by which God creates the world. Such participation renews and deifies at the same time.

Williams notes that the distinctive feature of Thomistic epistemology is "knowledge as a form of participation."[64] This is a participation whereby the "intelligible species of an object," which is the object's form, actually "comes to exist in the intellective soul."[65] Our knowledge of the world is analogical to God's knowledge. What a thing is, is not known simply from its brute givenness. Its existence (*that* it is) is also a participation in its essence (*what* it is). That essence has a form from which its givenness in existence cannot be abstracted. Those forms are found in the mind of God. To see what anything is, is to see both its existence and the form of that existence at the same time. This form would be the intelligible species of the object that comes to rest in our own mind. But since those forms are finally only in the mind of God, any knowledge of those forms will require at the same time illumination, which is a participation in the mind of God. This Thomistic epistemology helps us understand Aquinas's doctrine of deification. Serge-Thomas Bonino puts this succinctly: "It is, in fact, absolutely impossible to separate the vision of Ideas of creatures in God from the beatifying vision of the divine essence."[66]

Aquinas draws on this vision of ideas of creatures in God both in the *prima pars* when he discusses God's knowledge and in the *secunda pars* when he explains the beatific vision. Aquinas discusses God's knowledge as one of two operations, the other being God's will. These two operations are identical with the Triune processions. He first raises the question of

---

62. *Summa Theologica* I-II.112.1.
63. Ibid., ad. 1.
64. Williams, *Ground of Union*, 45.
65. Scott MacDonald, "Theory of Knowledge," in *The Cambridge Companion to Aquinas* (ed. Norman Kretzmann and Eleonore Stump; Cambridge: Cambridge University Press, 1993), 161.
66. In Serge-Thomas Bonino, "Charisms, Forms, and States of Life (IIa IIae, qq. 171–189)" (trans. Mary Thomas Noble), in Pope, *Ethics of Aquinas*, 344.

whether there would be *scientia* (learning) in God. Recall that *scientia* differs from *intellectus*. The former comes from things outside of one's self, the latter from things that are self-evident. That God's knowledge has the virtue of *intellectus* makes sense, but that God's knowledge contains *scientia* would seem to contradict God's aseity. Yet Aquinas argues that God has *scientia* for God is perfect and must know all things, even things that are known through *scientia*, and *sapientia*, as well as *intellectus*.

But God knows them not as caused from outside of God or from some matter that exists other than God. For Aquinas, a thing's freedom from matter is the reason it is able to know. Plants have no knowledge for they cannot receive the "form" of sensible objects. But we can receive the likeness of things without matter. This is what allows us to have *scientia*. God also has *scientia* but in a way different from our *scientia*. As Aquinas reminds us, whenever a description taken from any perfection of a creature is attributed to God, we must eliminate from its meaning all that pertains to the imperfect way in which it is found in the creature. Therefore God has *scientia* but not as an accident of God's being or as a habit, which would imply a potentiality in God. God possesses *scientia* as "pure act."[67]

God's *scientia* makes possible knowledge of things other than God while at the same time preserving *creatio ex nihilo* and the real distinction between God and creation. If we say that God knows all things and that God's knowledge of all things does not change (that is to say, it is not that God through *scientia* learns from objects and causes outside of God), then how do we make sense of the fact of creation? It is not eternal. It began with time. It is other than God. But if it is other than God, how can God know it? Would this not imply that God's knowledge *increased* after creation? Of course, Aquinas must insist that God knows it and all things without implying any increase in the knowledge of God. How does God know it? Because God not only knows but comprehends himself, which means that God fully understands his own being. God is not a mystery to himself but is fully intelligible. This is what it means to say that God's essence is God's existence.[68] Because God comprehends God's self, God sees himself in himself. This is what allows God to have knowledge of all other things, things other than God. Aquinas states, "He sees other things not in themselves, but in Himself; inasmuch as His essence contains the similitude of things other than Himself."[69]

In knowing and loving himself, God knows and loves all things. This knowledge of things other than God, which God knows in comprehending

---

67. *Summa Theologica* I.14.1. Thus Aquinas writes that God's *scientia* is not a *qualitas vel habitus sed substantia et actus purus* ("Not a quality or habit but rather essential and pure act").
68. See *Summa Theologica* I.14.4.
69. *Summa Theologica* I.14.5.

God's own self, is not a vague or generic knowledge. It is a perfect knowledge. "We must therefore hold that God knows things other than Himself with a proper knowledge; not only in so far as being is common to them, but in so far as one is distinguished from the other. . . . All the perfection contained in the essence of any other being, and far more, God can know in himself all of them with proper knowledge."[70] The particular perfection of each thing that is, which is its true form, is found not in the thing itself, but in God. Perfection, or deification, is that process whereby a particular thing actualizes the potential it has to achieve its singular perfection, which is already contained in God.

Only when Aquinas has explained how God knows each particular thing in its true perfection can he then explain the divine ideas. He begins with a concern that these ideas will be understood too Platonically. Aquinas cites the objection of Dionysius that God cannot know things by ideas, for if God did, then their forms would not be in the divine mind but would be external to it. Aquinas insists that by "ideas" we do not mean eternal forms separate from God's self-knowledge. In something of a rather forced interpretation of Aristotle, Aquinas argues, "God does not understand things according to an idea existing outside Himself. Thus Aristotle rejects the opinion of Plato, who held that ideas existed of themselves, and not in the intellect."[71] Aquinas will insist that ideas do exist in God, but they are not external Platonic forms.

Why must ideas exist in God? Without them, neither perfection nor teleology is possible. If there are no ideas in God, there can be no true happiness. The moral life is at stake. Aquinas writes,

> It is necessary to suppose ideas in the divine mind. For the Greek word Ἰδέα is in Latin *Forma*. Hence by ideas are understood the forms of things, existing apart from the things themselves. Now the form of anything existing apart from the thing itself can be for one of two ends; either to be the type of that of which it is called the form, or to be the principle of the knowledge of that thing, inasmuch as the forms of things knowable are said to be in him who knows them. . . .
>
> In all things not generated by chance, the form must be the end of any generation whatsoever. But an agent does not act on account of the form, except in so far as the likeness of the form is in the agent. . . . As then the world was not made by chance, but by God acting by His intellect, . . . there must exist in the divine mind a form to the likeness of which the world was made.[72]

---

70. *Summa Theologica* I.14.6.
71. *Summa Theologica* I.15.1, ad. 1.
72. *Summa Theologica* I.15.1.

The ideas in God are the multiple forms of all things that are. Creation has a purpose, which is contained in God's own life. Our renewal into the image of God is our receiving and cooperating with that perfection, which is present in God's ideas. These ideas are also all contained within the Triune processions.

At this point it is important to pause and recall that question 15 in the *Summa* was central in Norris's *Reason and Religion*, which Wesley drew upon. Norris began his argument by quoting it: "For 'tis impossible that God should make a World with Counsel and Design, unless he make it according to something, and that can be nothing else but something existing within himself, something in this *Ideal* and *Archetypal* world." And he recognized that these ideas, like God's knowledge and Word, were the consequence of a trinitarian procession. Norris added, "And what if I should further say, that this Ideal World, this Essence of God consider'd as variously exhibitive and representative of things is no other than the Divine *[Logos]*, the Second Person in the ever Blessed Trinity."[73] Wesley's theology drew explicitly on this Thomistic doctrine of the ideas of God mediated through Norris. It is the best way to account for perfection, deification, and the correlation between happiness and holiness.

Aquinas's doctrine of deification through the beatific vision assumes the account of the divine ideas present in the *prima pars*. We have already seen this in question 15. But Aquinas returns to this when he explains the Son's procession from the Father as God's Word at question 34. He writes,

> Word implies relation to creatures. For God by knowing Himself, knows every creature. Now the word conceived in the mind is representative of everything that is actually understood. Hence there are in ourselves different words for the different things which we understand. But because God by one act understands Himself and all things, His one only Word is expressive not only of the Father, but of all creatures.
> . . . in the Word is implied the operative idea of what God makes.[74]

Notice how richer an account of language this assumes than we saw in Hobbes and Locke. For them, words are always tied to simple ideas. We go astray when we think words do more than mark single ideas. Thus they always set us out on a quest for definitional simplicity. If we just get our definitions straight, metaphysical complexity would disappear. But for Aquinas, words have a complexity to them such that a word can stand for both singulars and universals at the same time. In fact, the Word can stand for the generation of the Second Person of the Trinity and for the entirety of creation at the same time.

73. John Norris, *Reason and Religion: or, The Grounds and Measures of Devotion, Consider'd from the Nature of God, and the Nature of Man. In Several Contemplations*, 2nd ed. (London: Samuel Manship, 1693), 84-85.

74. *Summa Theologica* I.34.3.

Only when we understand this dogmatic theological context, can we understand Aquinas's doctrine of deification as indebted to both illumination and a metaphysics of participation. This allows us to actualize a potential to become what we were intended to be, which is contained in the divine life. This occurs without diminishing the necessary distinction between our creaturely being and God's Uncreated being. Aquinas's discussion of prophetic vision and how it differs from beatific vision explains this:

> Now it is not possible to see the types of creatures in the very essence of God without seeing It, both because the Divine essence is Itself the type of all things that are made,—the ideal type adding nothing to the Divine essence save only a relationship to the creature;—and because knowledge of a thing in itself,—and such is the knowledge of God as the object of heavenly bliss,—precedes knowledge of that thing in its relation to something else,—and such is the knowledge of God as containing the types of things. Consequently it is impossible for prophets to see God as containing the types of creatures, and yet not as the object of bliss. Therefore we must conclude that the prophetic vision is not the vision of the very essence of God, and that the prophets do not see in the Divine essence Itself the things they do see, but that they see them in certain images, according as they are enlightened by the Divine light.[75]

The prophetic vision is not the final blessed vision because the prophet only sees "images" whereas the blessed vision sees the types of all things in God and therefore sees God's essence itself. Nevertheless, as Theo Kobusch notes, the divine ideas imply that at some level to see anything rightly is to see God because "in everything known, being is co-known as the universal being of things, and because this being is not independent (that is, is not subsistent), it is understood as 'a participation and image of the subsistent, divine Being.' For this reason, Thomas can say that all knowers know God implicitly in each thing."[76]

All knowledge is, at some level, a participation in the life of God. However, Aquinas is concerned about the kind of participation in the life of God Christian theology sets forth because he seeks to maintain the distinction between creation and the Uncreated. This can be seen in his discussion of charity as the form of the virtues. He recognizes that our participation in the life of God is through charity, for it defines God's own being. He asks whether the Holy Spirit creates charity in us or if it is the actual movement of the Holy Spirit itself in us. If it is the latter then Aquinas fears sanctification will not be a human action, which he insists has a voluntary character to it. If we are merely possessed by the Holy

---

75. *Summa Theologica* II-II.173.1.
76. Kobusch, "Grace," in Pope, *Ethics of Aquinas*, 210.

Spirit independent of our will, then our actions would no longer be human actions. The distinction between creation and the Uncreated dissolves. Therefore he disagrees with Augustine, who held that charity is not something created in the soul but is the Holy Spirit dwelling in the mind. Aquinas writes,

> But if we consider the matter aright, this would be, on the contrary, detrimental to charity. For when the Holy Ghost moves the human mind the movement of charity does not proceed from this motion in such a way that the human mind be merely moved, without being the principle of this movement, as when a body is moved by some extrinsic motive power. For this is contrary to the nature of a voluntary act, whose principle needs to be in itself. . . .
>
> Likewise, neither can it be said that the Holy Ghost moves the will in such a way to the act of loving, as though the will were an instrument, for an instrument, though it be a principle of action, nevertheless has not the power to act or not to act, for then again the act would cease to be voluntary and meritorious. . . . Given that the will is moved by the Holy Ghost to the act of love, it is necessary that the will also should be the efficient cause of that act.[77]

Charity cannot simply be the movement of the Holy Spirit in us without it also being our act. In order for it to be the latter, it must be voluntary, something of which we are the master. But this poses a dilemma for us because the act of charity surpasses the nature of the power of the will.

Our dilemma is that our will must be the principle of charitable actions for us to become whom we are intended to be, yet for charity to be such a principle of action is beyond our nature. Aquinas resolves this dilemma by appealing to grace, which is infused virtue. "Therefore it is most necessary that, for us to perform the act of charity, there should be in us some habitual form superadded to the natural power, inclining that power to the act of charity, and causing it to act with ease and pleasure."[78] This superadded habitual form is infused virtue. It is not an "immediate participation" in God's goodness, wisdom, and charity.[79] In other words, God permits that which is not God to participate in God's being without God ceasing to be God or that which is not God from becoming anything other than it was naturally intended to be. This is the christological archetype of all things. Charity is both a divine gift and a uniquely human act. The infused virtue of charity, like all infused virtue, is "the imprinting of a form as dispositive to its acts, or of a created principle of action."[80] Charity

---

77. *Summa Theologica* II-II.23.2.
78. Ibid.
79. Ibid., ad. 1.
80. Eberhard Schockenhoff, "The Theological Virtue of Charity (IIa IIae, qq. 23–46)" (trans. Grant Kaplan and Frederick G. Lawrence), in Pope, *Ethics of Aquinas*, 250.

as a form provides the creature with a graced created principle of action that allows it to become what it naturally is to be. Grace and nature, like law and gospel, are not in opposition. No antagonism exists between them.

This has a political significance. As Eberhard Schockenhoff phrased it, "The last word spoken about human life does not speak of battle, struggle, and exertion, but instead of peace over all grasping, rest without boredom, and joy beyond measure."[81] The partial virtues that Aquinas associates with charity are nearly identical to the holy tempers that Wesley developed in his discourses on the Sermon on the Mount: joy, peace, mercy, beneficence, almsgiving, and fraternal correction. The vices that oppose charity are the very hindrances Wesley noted in those same discourses. They are hatred, boredom, envy, discord, contentiousness, schism, war, quarrel, riotousness, bothersomeness.[82] This similarity is not surprising; Aquinas defines charity in terms of the Beatitudes as well as the charisms of Isaiah 11:2.[83]

Aquinas will quote Augustine to argue that virtue without charity is imperfect, but he never goes as far as to call Roman virtues "splendid vices" or to say "love and do what you please."[84] Instead, as Schockenhoff puts it, "charity gathers the effective power for the good present already in the moral virtues to guide them to the ultimate end that transcends the natural tendency of the will."[85] The consequence is that Aquinas can appreciate and name the ancient virtues but can also see them as imperfect without the true end of charity ordering them toward God. Grace perfects as it transcends nature.

GIFTS, VIRTUES, BEATITUDES, LAW, GRACE

Aquinas's moral theology best fits that of Wesley for four reasons. First, at the heart of moral theology for both of them is a passage of Scripture (2 Peter 1:4) that discloses the Christian moral life as the perfection of the human person and community through participation in the life of God. Because virtue is the perfection of a power to achieve its end, we should not be surprised that virtue is used to express this doctrine of perfection. In fact, virtue (aretê) is appealed to in 2 Peter 1:5 to explain this perfection.

---

81. Ibid., 256.
82. See *Summa Theologica* II-II.34–43.
83. Schockenhoff, "Theological Virtue," in Pope, *Ethics of Aquinas*, 254.
84. *Summa Theologica* II-II.23.7.
85. Schockenhoff, "Theological Virtue," in Pope, *Ethics of Aquinas*, 251.

Because of the centrality of Scripture in his moral theology, Aquinas found Aristotle's use of virtue helpful in elucidating the Christian doctrine of perfection. However, Aquinas's theological development of virtue also led him to incorporate elements that Aristotle could not have used, such as the theological virtues, the gifts, the fruits of the Holy Spirit, and the Beatitudes. This is the second reason why Aquinas's model fits Wesley's moral theology. He also drew upon the gifts, the fruits, and the Beatitudes. In fact the Beatitudes are the core of his moral theology. For Aquinas, an appeal to the Beatitudes is also an appeal to virtue because the Beatitudes are the act of a habit; they are our movements toward an end for which we hope, which is then, to a certain extent, already possessed. To find ourselves involved in those actions that constitute the Beatitudes is to find ourselves already caught up in the movement of the Holy Spirit, ordering us to our proper end: beatitude in the vision of God. Such a movement implies virtue.[86] Wesley explicitly used Aristotle's definition of virtue as a mean between extremes when he set forth the Beatitudes.

The third commonality of Wesley and Aquinas is the way they use theological elements to render the Law intelligible and not vice versa. Thus neither of them should be read as preoccupied with an ethics of obligation based on rule-following or policy implementation.

Finally, both Wesley and Aquinas have a realist ontology, which is the basis for their moral theology. Moreover, that realist ontology is expressed in law, but law christologically determined. For Aquinas that law is the Eternal Law, and for Wesley it is Jesus as the Torah of God. All good and fitting moral action will be consistent, implicitly and explicitly, with this basic structure of things.

Second Peter 1:4 and the Theological Virtues

The moral theology of Wesley and Aquinas is comparable less because they shared commitments to Plato or Aristotle (although they did) and more because of their shared starting point in Scripture.[87] For both of them, Scripture functioned as the authoritative text for theological and moral considerations. In this sense, Wesley's method resembles that of Aquinas. It is not a critical method where truth is a function of a skeptical critical investigation but a method of authority where truth has a givenness to it

---

86. See *Summa Theologica* I-II.69.1.

87. Aquinas begins the *Summa* by arguing for the central role of Scripture because human creatures are directed to God as their true end, and this entails a knowledge beyond them that can only be found in divine revelation (*Summa Theologica* I.1). This is important for his development of the virtues, for they are the habits by which people are properly directed toward God as their supernatural end (*Summa Theologica* I-II.1).

that can be and has been known through the intellectual virtue, *intellectus*. We can assume that we are not the first persons to have this virtue. It was infused in some who have come before us, and we must listen to their witness. Neither Aquinas nor Wesley had a modern critical method where, for the sake of certainty, everything that has been thought until this moment must be held as fallible and subject to doubt so that we can prepare for a truth not yet received. Wesley and Aquinas were willing to grant a certain authority to Christian antiquity. But they shared a particular propensity in starting with Scripture in moral theology, particularly with 2 Peter 1:4-5 and the Sermon on the Mount.

Aquinas made 2 Peter 1:4 central in his turn to the theological virtues in question 62 of the *prima secundae*, where he explained the insufficiency of the natural virtues alone and the need for them to be infused with something more: the theological virtues. Our ultimate happiness is only found in our participation in God as disclosed in 2 Peter 1:4. To participate in the divine nature is the end for which all humanity aims. But this produces a severe limitation on natural virtue, for the attainment of such an end surpasses our natural capacities. Thus, to partake of God's nature requires that we must receive from God some additional principles whereby we may then be directed to supernatural happiness. And such a principle, Aquinas defined as a "theological virtue."[88]

In the case of Wesley, 2 Peter 1:4 was integral to his Aldersgate infusion of faith. At 5:00 A.M., on May 24, 1738, long before he went out to the evening meeting on Aldersgate Street to hear a reading from Luther's *Preface to the Epistle to the Romans* and had his heart-warming experience, Wesley was contemplating this passage.[89] In his reflections immediately after that evening, Wesley claimed the reality of the transformation promised by Peter: "then I was sometimes, if not often, conquered; now, I was always conqueror."[90] Drawing on this experience, when Wesley was later confronted by those who limited salvation to simply the imputation of Christ's righteousness, he insisted that believers recover a capacity of spiritual life, be reunited with God, and be "made partakers of the divine nature."[91] In other words, he refused to cast law in a polar relationship to grace. Grace provided a power to be the conqueror of disordered desires rather than being conquered by them (as Wesley was before Aldersgate). This power of the human soul to achieve perfection is what Aquinas called virtue.

---

88. *Summa Theologica* I-II.62.1.

89. *Journal* (May 24, 1738), §13, *Works* 18:249.

90. Ibid., §16, *Works* 18:250. Note also how Wesley appeals in this context (§15) to two of the beatitudes, mournfulness and persecution for righteousness' sake. He will develop these two beatitudes in his discourses on the Sermon on the Mount consistent with his use of them here.

91. *Minutes of Some Late Conversations* (June 25, 1744), q. 16, *Works* (Jackson) 8:277-78.

Wesley's Moral Theology: Gifts and Beatitudes

Wesley explained this power in his comments on 2 Peter 1:4 in his *Explanatory Notes upon the New Testament*, where he defined our participation in God's nature as "being renewed in the image of God, and having communion with him, so as to dwell in God, and God in you."[92] To be renewed in the image of God is to receive from God the gifts of God. But the reception of such gifts is not a passive endeavor; quite the contrary, we are to receive these gifts through our diligence. As Wesley put it in these comments, "Our diligence is to follow the gift of God, and is followed by an increase of all his gifts." Those gifts are then defined as courage, knowledge, temperance, patience, godliness, kindness, and love.[93] Wesley also warns that the one who lacks these gifts "cannot see God or His pardoning love. . . . He has lost sight of the precious promises." Since the end of humanity is the vision of God, the gifts are necessary for proper moral action.

However, such a *telos* cannot be achieved through the acquisition of the natural virtues alone. Only the theological virtues and their requisite gifts allow it to be fulfilled in us. But theological virtue is not a mere passive reception independent of the person's will and intellect. It requires an active striving, which nevertheless does not achieve its end through its own efforts but can only achieve its end when it receives gifts from God. Such gifts then become a power of the soul to perfect it to achieve its end. The sacraments, the Sermon on the Mount (particularly the Beatitudes and the petitions of the Lord's Prayer) and the Law interpreted in light of the Sermon on the Mount are the resources that allow us to pursue, and finally receive, these theological virtues.

A life of diligent seeking—we could call this the life of natural virtue—will ultimately end in frustration without the theological virtues. But once the theological virtues are received, this diligent activity issues forth in the addition of all the gifts and graces in a wonderfully harmonious dance. These are the terms Wesley used to define what Aquinas called gifts and virtues, which order us to our proper end. This can be found in Wesley's commentary on 2 Peter 1:5, "*For this very reason . . . giving all diligence . . . add to . . . your faith . . . courage [aretê].*" The comments in the *Explanatory Notes* read,

---

92. John Wesley, *Explanatory Notes upon the New Testament* (3rd ed.; New York: Daniel Hitt and Thomas Ware, 1812).

93. That is, Wesley is talking of the traditional "sevenfold gifts" of Isaiah 11:2, not the "gifts of the Spirit" in Galatians 5. These gifts are central to Aquinas's account of the moral life as well, as developed in *Summa Theologica* I-II.68 (for a good secondary summary, see Servais Pinckaer, *The Sources of Christian Ethics* [trans. Mary Thomas Noble; Washington, D.C.: Catholic University of America Press, 1995], 156-58).

Add to—And *in* all the other gifts of God. Superadd the latter, without losing the former. The Greek word properly means *lead up*, as in a dance, one of these after the other, in a beautiful order. *Your faith*, that evidence of things not seen, termed before *the knowledge of God and of Christ*—The root of all christian graces; *courage*—Whereby ye may conquer all enemies and difficulties, and execute whatever faith dictates. In this most beautiful connexion, each preceding grace leads to the following: each following, tempers and perfects the preceding.

Wesley has taken the admonition to add *aretê* to faith and has translated *aretê* as both "virtue" and "courage."[94] This shows how familiar Wesley was with the virtue tradition. As R. E. Houser explains it, the virtue tradition arises from the effort of the ancient Greeks to make sense of Achilles' *aretê*. Plato does this through his tripartite division of the soul. Reason, emotion, and desire related to the virtues of wisdom (prudence), courage, and temperance. When everything is in balance the result is justice. Achilles certainly had courage, but he lacked other virtues that would lead to a just life.[95]

We have seen that Wesley gave little to no attention to the virtue of courage when he developed his moral theology in his discourses on the Sermon on the Mount. He gave a great deal of attention to temperance and justice, seeing the latter culminating in the virtue of peacemaking. But courage is listed in 2 Peter 1:5 as something to be added to faith, and Wesley provides a place for it in his *Explanatory Notes*. Courage helps us stand against those hindrances to faith. Courage is as a power to execute what faith demands. This definition resembles quite closely the Thomistic definition of the theological virtues. As Reginald Garrigou-Lagrange defined it, "any act that is supernatural, and yet connatural, needs to emanate from a proportionate principle energizing within us a kind of second nature. Nothing but infused virtue can bring such a thing to pass."[96] The theological virtues are powers to execute what faith demands. And as Garrigou-Lagrange noted that this power becomes connatural to the human agent, so Wesley insisted that these "graces" are "really *in you*—Added to your faith, *and abounding*—increasing more and more."[97] Courage becomes an infused virtue, contributing to faith.

---

94. In *Explanatory Notes* Wesley translates the biblical text of 2 Peter 1:3, where the term first appears, as "virtue." Then, in his comments on this text he suggests that this "glorious power" of God whose end is eternal glory had as its means "christian *virtue*—Or fortitude." From then on he translated *aretê* as "courage."

95. See R. E. Houser, "The Virtue of Courage," in Pope, *Ethics of Aquinas*, 304-5.

96. Reginald Garrigou-Lagrange, *On Faith: A Commentary on St. Thomas' Theological Summa* (trans. Thomas a Kempis Reilly; vol. 1 of *The Theological Virtues*; St. Louis: B. Herder Book Co., 1965), 6. Then he goes on to state, "all Thomists hold most firmly that the formal object *quo* and *quod* of any theological virtue cannot be anything but God" (p. 7).

97. *Explanatory Notes*, 2 Peter 1:8.

Wesley also had an important place for the fourth cardinal virtue of prudence in his moral theology. In his sermon "The Reformation of Manners" he argued, as did Aquinas, for the primacy of the virtue of prudence to all other natural virtues.[98] Moreover, Wesley emphasized, as did Aquinas, its infused nature. He provided an excellent interpretation of prudence. "*Prudence*, properly so called" Wesley suggested is, "not that offspring of hell which 'the world' *calls* prudence, which is mere craft, cunning dissimulation; but . . . that 'wisdom from above' which our Lord peculiarly recommends to all who would promote his kingdom upon earth. . . . This wisdom will instruct you how to suit your words and whole behaviour to the persons with whom you have to do, to the time, place, and all other circumstances."[99] Wesley defined prudence itself as an infused virtue, as wisdom from above. Interestingly, Aquinas did something quite similar in his discussion of prudence. First he outlined the virtue consistent with Aristotle's discussion of it, but then he discussed the "gift of counsel" which corresponds to prudence. And he noted,

A lower principle of movement is helped chiefly, and is perfected through being moved by a higher principle of movement, as a body through being moved by a spirit. Now it is evident that the rectitude of human reason is compared to the Divine Reason, as a lower motive principle to a higher: for the Eternal Reason is the supreme rule of all human rectitude. Consequently prudence, which denotes rectitude of reason, is chiefly perfected and helped through being ruled and moved by the Holy Ghost, and this belongs to the gift of counsel. . . . Therefore the gift of counsel corresponds to prudence, as helping and perfecting it.[100]

Aquinas recognized that perfection to our supernatural end requires an infusion of not only the theological virtues but also the cardinal virtues as well.[101] Prudence needs the gift of counsel. This is significant because prudence, even more so than justice, is the virtue necessary for a good political life. As Romanus Cessario has pointed out, "Prudence [*phronêsis*], then, transforms knowledge of moral truth into specific virtuous actions which are not burdensome, that is, which do not include friction, internal strife, forcing oneself."[102] A prudence infused by divine counsel will be recognized in those persons who are capable of knowing not only what

---

98. In *The Moral Virtues and Theological Ethics* (Notre Dame, Ind.: University of Notre Dame Press, 1991), Romanus Cessario argues for the primacy of prudence in the Christian realist tradition of the virtues. He suggests that it is the virtue of prudence, rather than conscience per se, that "particularizes moral truth for application to concrete cases" (85). This is an extremely significant point because it calls into question the dominance of conscience within Catholic moral theology as a faculty that insures a person's autonomous actions.

99. Sermon 52, "The Reformation of Manners," §IV.4, *Works* 2:318.

100. *Summa Theologica* II-II.52.2.

101. *Summa Theologica* I-II.63.4.

102. Cessario, *Moral Virtues and Theological Ethics*, 80.

should be done or how we should live but also how such actions can be peacefully embodied in particular, contingent circumstances.

This emphasis on an infused natural virtue also shows the primary place given to the gifts and beatitudes in Aquinas's moral theology. In fact, as Servais Pinckaers has explained it, "the gifts of the Holy Spirit perfect the moral virtues themselves."[103] Thus, even though we can distinguish the philosophical level of Aristotelian ethics and the moral virtues from revealed Christian teaching on the theological virtues and gifts, this does not imply any separation or opposition between the two.[104]

Virtue as the Basis for Law

Once we recognize that Aquinas's virtue theory includes the gifts and beatitudes for the perfection of moral action, we can more easily read Wesley within the context of the virtue tradition than within the context of an ethics of obligation. The latter does not satisfy as an interpretation of Wesley because something more than obedience to the law is necessary. What does satisfy are the gifts and the Beatitudes. Laws, rules, commands, and precepts lack purpose without such gifts. The Law merely stands over and against us without directing us toward virtuous ends. Laws and rules will then produce a "formal" religion. Only God can make such a formal religion substantive by the beatitude of God's goodness, which gives the Law purpose.

This interpretation of rules and precepts also fits quite well with a moral life based on the virtues. For as Alasdair MacIntyre has argued, one must "attend to the virtues in the first place in order to understand the function and authority of rules."[105] In fact, MacIntyre sees the ethics of obligation found in modernity as troubling precisely because we still have rules and precepts but have lost the virtues that would give them direction. Thus the rules can only be perceived as arbitrary and capricious and incapable of rational justification resulting either in cynicism or directionless yet incessant protests.

As we have seen, the very order of Wesley's sermons from "The Great Privilege" through "The Lord Our Righteousness" followed by his discourses on the Sermon on the Mount and culminating in his three sermons on the Law, reveals how virtues, gifts, and beatitudes both fulfill the law and render it intelligible. This appropriateness of this order is suggested by the fact that Aquinas's *prima secundae* is composed of a similar

---

103. Pinckaers, *Sources of Christian Ethics*, 180.

104. Ibid., 181.

105. Alasdair MacIntyre, *After Virtue* (Notre Dame, Ind.: University of Notre Dame Press, 1984), 118.

threefold structure.[106] First is our true end, which is the beatitude prompted by the vision of God, then comes a treatise on the virtues, gifts, and beatitudes, and a treatise on the Law follows this.

Jesus as the Law of God, the eternal Wisdom upon which creation rests, is a consistent theme throughout Wesley's moral theology. It is a theme readily found in Cudworth, Malebranche, and Norris. It is also central in Aquinas's work, starting with the *prima pars* where the generation of the Word becomes the basis for the generation of all of creation. It is most prominent in his discussion of the law in the *secunda pars*; Christ is the archetype, the Eternal Law through whom, and in which, all things are. Our most visible manifestation of this Eternal Law is found in the Sermon on the Mount. Augustine and Aquinas stood in a long tradition of moral theologians who correlated the eight Beatitudes of the Sermon on the Mount with the seven gifts from Isaiah 11 and the seven petitions of the Lord's Prayer. Wesley's work shared in this tradition.

Wesley, like Aquinas, made the Sermon on the Mount the centerpiece of his moral theology. But in one respect he produced a marked advance over Aquinas: Wesley did not read the sermon in terms of the distinction between counsels for the religious and precepts for ordinary Christians. He avoided the "Catholic" tendency of interpreting the sermon as counsels for a religious elite and the Decalogue as commands for the masses.[107] Likewise he explicitly avoided reading the sermon in terms of a Protestant law-gospel dialectic. Wesley's discourses on the sermon are a creative recovery of the centrality of Jesus' teachings for the moral life of all Christians. The notion that counsels of perfection were only to be pursued by members of religious orders was not available to Wesley. In some sense all the Methodists were to pursue the counsels of perfection (celibacy excepted). This has an important social and political significance, which we will consider in the final chapter.

---

106. In *The Structure of Caroline Moral Theology* (London: Longmans, 1949), H. R. MacAdoo notes that "Our Caroline forbears read and used Aquinas and Calvin and studied the spiritual descendants of both" (1). Thus we should not be surprised that the structure of moral theology found in Wesley bears a resemblance to that of Aquinas. What is striking is that Wesley, like Aquinas and unlike Calvin, begins with gifts and beatitudes and discusses the Law in the light of that previous discussion. Calvin is preoccupied with law and only discusses virtue after he has articulated the central role of the law. Cf. Calvin, *Institutes*, bk. 2. For his discussion of virtue, see *Institutes*, bk. 3, ch. 14.

107. Wesley explicitly rejected the limitation of the sermon to some elite group in Sermon 21, "Sermon on the Mount, I," §5, *Works* 1:472. By contrast, Aquinas himself often uses the distinction between counsels and precepts to avoid some of the difficult teachings of Jesus for the laity. Present-day Catholic moral theologians have recognized the difficulty with such an interpretation of the Sermon (cf. Pinckaers, *Sources of Christian Ethics*, 136).

BUT IS THIS "SOCIAL ETHICS"?

As we move to the final chapter in this work, we must take up the question of whether Wesley's moral theology has any relevance to political and social ethics as it is done today. Someone might raise the objection that this language of theological virtues is fine as spirituality, but how is it ethics? I have argued that the emergence of "ethics" in the eighteenth century divorced from theology was a mistake. It policed God out of social and political matters and thus made moral theology difficult if not impossible. Perhaps it is only when we accept this policing that we feel compelled to ask how theology can contribute to social ethics. In the next chapter I hope to show how this question only perpetuates theology's marginalization from social and political reality. Nevertheless we should take into account criticism such as Philip Wogaman's on the language of virtue: "Some ethicists prefer to think of the moral life almost entirely in terms of the development of character, the cultivation of virtues, mature growth as a moral being. And who could deny the importance of that? But the moral life is also profoundly social."[108]

Perhaps we should turn that question around. Why does Wogaman think that a virtue ethic is about personal development while an ethic of obligation is concerned with social reality? How can his question make sense of the profound analysis of virtue in Aristotle's *Nicomachean Ethics* and *Politics* or Aquinas's *secunda secundae* of the *Summa Theologica*? Wogaman clearly recognizes that the medieval theologians spoke about social issues. He is quick to suggest that "medieval thought on justice in wages and prices offers comparatively little help today, based as it was on obsolete conceptions of money and hostile as it seemed to postfeudal economic development."[109] Thus, his concern is not that virtue theory lacked social import but that he no longer finds this social import relevant to the modern world defined by postfeudal economics. An ethics of obligation is more useful because public order is defined for us in terms primarily of process, that is, those laws, duties, principles, and public policies that will insure that the allocation of rights, property, and so on is as fair and equitable as possible, irrespective of any common conception of a (or *the*) good life. If this is what is meant by "social ethics" then Wesley's moral theology and its connection with Thomas Aquinas may be of historic interest, but it will have little to do with moral, social, or political life today.

But why does the virtue of justice as it relates to wages and prices no longer have political and social relevance? Is it because we must now

---

108. J. Philip Wogaman, *Economics and Ethics: A Christian Inquiry* (Philadelphia: Fortress, 1986), 7.
109. Ibid., 85.

accommodate morality to the liberal tradition where self-interest rules? Given the difficulties that tradition has produced for moral living, I would think that concern for the just wage is more relevant now than ever before. What philosophical account demonstrates that previous moral wisdom on justice, truth, goodness, beauty, faith, hope, and love is no longer relevant because of new economic arrangements? Is this not a capitulation to nihilism, where we must always recognize that the highest values devalue themselves? Who taught us this? Why must we still be bound by such dogmatic modern certitudes? Wesley's moral theology can instruct us to live by different dogmas.

Christ as the eternal Wisdom of God gives us the purpose for both creation and redemption. He gives us our *telos* within which the moral life can function without appearing as purely formal or even arbitrary because we are "plunging continually, backward, sideward, forward, in all directions where there is no up or down left, straying as through an infinite nothing, feeling the breath of empty space."[110] The moral life, along with its correlates in all forms of political and social life, is not directionless for Christian moral theology. We are returning to God, who meets us in Christ, and we invite the entire world to join us on the return journey. The virtues provide the power to be able to achieve that end. The church is the social community that mediates those virtues and reminds people that social life has an order; social life should not merely be a formal process whereby each individual is freed as far as possible from every other individual to pursue his or her own self-appointed good.

But the recovery of moral theology is not just a romantic, antiquarian hobby. It may help us avoid the ongoing violence of an ethic that knows no end other than its own will to power through the pursuit of self-appointed goods. While this world may appear tolerant and open, it may contain within it a hidden violence that erupts without cause, for it can only enforce laws that are arbitrary and capricious. I do not know how prophetic Nietzsche will finally be proved to be, but he recognized that he lived at "the end of Christianity—at the hands of its own morality . . . which turns against the Christian God."[111] Nietzsche embraced the end of Christianity by its own morality, but he also recognized that in its place was emerging nihilism. In 1887 he claimed to tell us the history of the next two centuries. He called it the advent of nihilism and suggested that "our whole European culture has been moving as toward a catastrophe, with a tortured tension that is growing from decade to decade: restlessly,

---

110. The words of Nietzsche's madman, who announces God's death and the greatness of the deed, which the crowd (including the moralists?) has not yet recognized. See *The Portable Nietzsche* (ed. Walter Kaufmann; New York: Viking, 1954), 95.

111. Friedrich Nietzsche, *The Will to Power* (ed. Walter Kaufmann; trans. Walter Kaufmann and R. J. Hollingdale; New York: Vintage, 1968), 7.

violently, headlong, like a river that wants to reach the end."[112] I am unsure how serious anyone should take Nietzsche, if it were not for the fact that he seems to have named well the first century that came after him. Has he named well the one we embark on at present? Is he correct to see it related to the "ethics" that Christianity produced in the modern era, which then turns against Christianity?

If law directs human actions to virtuous ends, then it assumes a virtuous life as the context for the law's intelligibility. Law without virtue is capricious; virtue without law lacks direction. Jesus presents to Christians the social and political life that directs our actions toward virtuous ends. He institutes the church to carry on that activity in time and space. No other social institution bears the immediacy of this gift. Thus, we should never expect the state to force persons to turn toward this end, for that would be a usurpation of the only political society that has been authorized to be ruled by Christ in all things, the church. Yet the church has no other "social ethic" than to hold forth Christ as the end and source of all fitting human action—moral, economic, social, and political—to remind the world of the laws that direct our actions toward that end; to use the means at its disposal—particularly the sacraments and the proclamation of the Word—and to offer to the world those more than natural means necessary to achieve the end of our common journey. We should not be surprised if we find resonances of the theological virtues outside the church, for the task of the church is to give its life to and for the world.[113] Neither should we be surprised if such theological virtues are met with resistance, for "He came to what was his own, and his own people did not accept him" (John 1:11 NRSV). Also, one of the Beatitudes is the persecution of the righteous, which requires the gift of courage.[114]

God is the beginning, the end, and the necessary means for this common journey. To put this in the language of the ancient virtue tradition, the formal object, both *quo* and *quod*, of the theological virtues is God. But this does not produce a two-tiered anthropology where the supernatural is merely added above the natural. This does not allow us to develop social ethics on the basis of a natural that is sufficient unto itself and

---

112. Ibid., 3. For an excellent discussion of the significance of this see David Toole, *Waiting for Godot in Sarajevo* (Boulder: Westview Press, 1998).

113. I find the way that Oliver O'Donovan puts this very helpful, "the Church must be prepared to welcome the homage of the kings when it is offered to the Lord of the martyrs" (*The Desire of the Nations: Rediscovering the Roots of Political Theology* [Cambridge: Cambridge University Press, 1996], 215). Of course this must be done with great caution because sometimes the homage of the kings is a pretext for the slaughter of the innocents.

114. In this regard, I find it interesting that Latin American liberation theologians have recovered the Sermon on the Mount as central to their social ethic, even though they have not sought any recovery of virtue. Surely the number of persons who "disappeared" in El Salvador show us the action of the virtue of courage whereby people are reordered to God, the action that is known as the beatitude of persecution for righteousness' sake.

makes possible a public space free from theology. Such interpretations of a pure nature sufficient for social and political life can certainly be found in Thomistic scholarship. Henri de Lubac charged Tommaso Cajetan's interpretation of Aquinas with precisely this bifurcated sense of human agency between the natural and supernatural because of Cajetan's doctrine of pure nature. If it were not for twentieth-century interpretations of Aquinas like that of de Lubac, we would not be able to see similarities between Aquinas and Wesley.

In his *Mystery of the Supernatural*, de Lubac spoke of a "natural aptitude" for the love of God in the human creature. And he viewed Aquinas as logically explaining this need for God and its implications for Greek virtue. Aquinas "was not satisfied with establishing his first point, that Greek man could, in the strictest sense, adapt himself to Christianity; he wanted to prove positively that 'Christianity was necessary for him' because 'only it could fully guarantee his ideal and let him fully realize it.'"[115] Thus, the theological virtues are not merely added on to some pure nature; they are its necessary fulfillment. Without them, the moral agent could only be frustrated, for she is directed toward an end which she cannot achieve.

> In short, for Christians created nature is no kind of divine seed. The "depths" of the spiritual soul, that "mirror" where the image of God is reflected secretly, is indeed . . . the "birthplace" of our supernatural being: but it is not its seed or embryo. . . . It is not even the promise of it, so long at least as the objective promise has not been heard there. The longing that surges from this "depth" of the soul is a longing "born of a lack," and not arising from "the beginnings of possession."
>
> . . . This work is completed by sanctifying grace, "gratia gratum faciens," of which St Thomas tells us that "disponit animam ad habendam divinam personam." And that natural "capacity," to which the natural "longing" corresponds, is not a "faculty"; it is no more than an "aptitudo passiva," and though the being who desires to see God is certainly "capax illius beatae cognitionis," it does not follow that his nature is of itself "efficax ad videndum Deum." The desire itself is by no means a "perfect appetite." It does not constitute as yet even the slightest positive "ordering" to the supernatural. Again, it is sanctifying grace, with its train of theological virtues, which must order the subject to his last end; at least, it alone can order him "sufficiently" or "perfectly," or "directly."[116]

The theological virtues, gifts, and beatitudes perfect nature in that they give nature a power it does not possess itself, but which it must possess if

---

115. Henri de Lubac, *The Mystery of the Supernatural* (trans. Rosemary Sheed; New York: Herder & Herder, 1967), 32.
116. Ibid., 111.

it is to achieve its true end: the beatitude that comes from the vision of God. Grace never perfects a nature sufficient in itself. Aquinas and Wesley agreed that ancient morality went wrong in assuming a self-sufficient human nature. Grace reorders nature toward its proper end. This reordering must be achieved through the theological virtues, gifts, and beatitudes. Thus the "natural virtues," which are the basis for political and social life, need completion through the theological virtues. This is why the church is a necessary social organization not only for itself but also for all political and social forms of life. The church bears the means by which the theological virtues are ordinarily infused.

CHAPTER 6
JOHN WESLEY AS PUBLIC THEOLOGIAN?

What is the social and political relevance of Wesley's and Aquinas's moral theology? What relevance does their moral theology have to ethics as it emerges from the modern era? I cannot answer that question if it assumes that we must do theological ethics within the confines of the modern era. I do not think Wesley and Aquinas offered us a private spirituality and that suffices. I find their moral theology to be more political and social than the tradition of social ethics that seeks to relate theology to politics, ethics, economics, and so on. Once we must relate "theology" to "society" and "ethics," it is a sign that we already assume their disconnect. This is the modern condition. They are disconnected for us in a way they were not for Wesley or Aquinas. Perhaps the best we can do is a social ethics that begins by recognizing that theology, the Social, and ethics are three distinct spheres that need to be brought together. But to recognize this and allow it to frame the question of the relevance of theology for ethics and society is to capitulate too readily to the changes occurring in the eighteenth century that Wesley opposed. I argued earlier that a significant shift occurred in this period that can somewhat simplistically be referred to as a shift from moral theology to ethics. This shift policed God out of questions of society, politics, and ethics by assuming that the good, or ethics, was a more universal category than God. Can we hear the witness of Wesley and Aquinas against this modern dogmatic inheritance bequeathed to us? And now that we are at the end of humanism, is it not incumbent upon us to rethink the relationship between God and goodness without those modern dogmatic certitudes? To accomplish this we will need to learn to ask new questions.

The question of "social ethics" is one Ernst Troeltsch bequeathed in his *Social Teachings of the Christian Church* published in 1911. He posed the question: "What role does theology have in the public realm?" Modern Christian social ethics and "public" theology is largely a response to this question, which is presented as a perennial question within Christian tradition that requires an answer if we are to be socially and politically responsible. This question holds theologians and church leaders captive. But to pose the question this way dangerously misleads us, for behind this question is the assumption that some discourse exists located in a social reality greater than that which, for Christians, is the only truly *catholic* reality, the church. Whether the assumed broader social reality is called "the public," "society," "civilization," or "the political," to ask the question of theology's relevance to such a grand social reality inevitably subordinates the church to it and consequently subordinates knowledge of God to some other discourse, usually to ethics, political philosophy, or to social sciences (including economics and marketing).[1] We lose a proper theological grammar for speaking about social reality.

Much as Saint Anselm gave us a grammar to speak well about God by reminding us that God is that than which nothing greater can be conceived, I would like to suggest that a proper theological grammar for social ethics should likewise assume that the church is that social reality than which nothing more universal or more public can be conceived. This is not to suggest that the church is the only social reality that exists or that morality outside the church is impossible. However, it does suggest this for Christians because the church is one of the three forms of Christ's body (the social form); it has a sociality rooted in the Triune life unlike any other social reality. This, however, is not a license for rule and tyranny by the church.

We cannot contain this social reality in our buildings and institutions. They, like the tomb of the risen Christ, are empty and thus are mere signs of that to which we witness. Christ's social body cannot become a fetishized object that we can control any more than we can now point to his risen body and say precisely what it is. His risen body, the empty tomb, and the expectation of his return should keep us from triumphalism. Nevertheless, no greater social reality exists than that of his social body. Both Aquinas's and Wesley's moral theology assumes this social body. They could not think the divine ideas or a metaphysics of participation without assuming that the church is the social reality than which

---

1. This is the compelling argument one finds in John Milbank, *Theology and Social Theory* (Oxford: Blackwell, 1990).

none greater can be conceived. Therefore, to ask Troeltsch's question—how do we relate theology to the social order—is itself a rejection of the tradition of moral theology.

Anselm's theological grammar preserved speaking about God in such a way that God's being is not subordinated to some larger category like "being" or "process" or even to some attribute that could be assumed to be greater than God, such as goodness, truth, or beauty. As Robert Sokolowski reminds us, the heart of Anselm's theological grammar is to help us think, speak, and pray well "God" within the grammar of faith where God plus creation is not thought or spoken such that it would constitute a greater reality than God alone.[2] Within this theological grammar, certain questions can arise while others cannot. For instance, we cannot ask the question, *what is the relationship between God and creation?* as if the latter two terms posited equivalent entities that needed to be brought together into a greater whole. Anselm's theological grammar serves to prevent us from speaking or thinking "God" grounded in a univocal relational concept both God and we share, such as *being* or *goodness*, that is greater than God alone. For if we think or speak "God" based on such a univocal concept, then that concept will inevitably be greater than God such that it mediates God to us irrespective of God's gracious gift of the Incarnation. Process, or being, or goodness (that is, metaphysics or ethics) rather than theology will mediate knowledge of God to us. Anselm's logic that God is that than which nothing greater can be conceived preserves the possibility that our knowledge of God will be spoken and thought of solely in terms of God's gift to us.

Anselm's theological grammar prevents the language of faith from losing the centrality of the Incarnation and replacing it with some other mediating language, such as metaphysics or ethics, whereby God of necessity is delivered into our hands to be contained and controlled by our actions. If we think God within this grammar, then certain problems simply cannot arise without becoming nonsensical, such as those that Alfred North Whitehead identified under the category "classical theism" or Plato raised in *Philebus* as to the relationship between God and goodness. Likewise, to think *social* ethics within this Anselmian theological grammar will dissolve some of the problems that have captivated the imagination of theologians, social ethicists, and church leaders. These problems disappear and more theologically substantive ones emerge. If we think within a theological grammar whereby we assume that we can conceive of no more universal or public social reality than the church, then our preoccupation with the question, *what role does theology have in the*

---

2. Robert Sokolowski, *The God of Faith and Reason: Foundations of Christian Theology* (Washington, D.C.: Catholic University Press of America, 1995), 8-10.

public realm? will become as nonsensical as the effort to draw a circle two by three inches in diameter.[3]

We can only ask the question of theology's relevance to the public realm when we find ourselves converted from the activity of an earlier Christian theological politics, which assumed the church was the greatest catholic social reality rendering public things intelligible *(res publica)* to a modernist politics where the state, the market, or a combination thereof is conceived as the greatest catholic social reality. Theologians as diverse as Tertullian, Augustine, and Aquinas assumed that the theological investigation of the *res publica* began with the question, *what role does the state (the state of the emperor, the state of the empire, the state of political or civil society) play within God's economy?* This assumed that because the church was the foretaste of the city of God, other social formations had to be given their intelligibility within the primary logic of the visible manifestation of God's city. Only the church's origin is divine, even though it is also human. Only the church, then, could be truly universal, truly public, *catholic.* To ask the question, *what role does theology have in the public realm?* is to forsake the primacy of God's city as the proper grammar of social ethics and replace it with the modern preoccupation that assumes something more universal—the political, society, civilization, or the public—to which the church must now be accountable. To ask this question is already to experience a fundamental conversion in our theology. It is to undo Augustine's political revolution. It is to dissolve the church into modern secular space.

Troeltsch related the social teachings of the Christian church to a notion of a "public" that was already known without any theological references. In other words, what constituted "the public" was defined before Troeltsch developed the church's "social" teachings. His question could not be asked without this assumption of an already stable and religiously neutral "public" space. This is a normative political claim behind his question, "What is the relationship between the Church's social teaching and modern social formations?" It assumes the inevitable rise of the autonomous nation-state, which is presented as the universal mediator among competing religious factions. But is this a politically neutral claim? William Cavanaugh argues that it is not. It is a peculiar narration of European history that speaks of the irrational "wars of religion" as the cause for the rise of the rational modern state. The story is told that the modern nation-state arose as a neutral entity in order to mediate among competing religious factions that would kill one another in the name of dogma.[4] In this myth, the nation-state is presented as a soteriology that saves us from a dogmatic church.

---

3. The example comes from Wittgenstein's *Tractatus.*
4. William Cavanaugh, "'A Fire Strong Enough to Consume the House': The Wars of Religion and the Rise of the State," *Modern Theology* 11 (1995): 397-419.

A second crucial antecedent is the theoretical distinction between a public political realm and a private confessional, theological realm where the only way for the latter to be political is to enter its claims through the register that the former constructs. This distinction is found in Hobbes's *Leviathan* and in Kant's famous essay "What Is Enlightenment?" It is repeated in Max Weber's influential essay "Politics as a Vocation," which Troeltsch, Rauschenbusch, and the Niebuhrs assume in their social ethics. Coupled with the political history of the rise of the modern nation-state, the theoretical distinction between a public political and a private theological realm insures the subordination of a *private* church to a *public* politics, unless theologians are willing to translate confessional particularities into a more putatively public discourse than the nation-state acknowledges. In other words, in the modern era only the nation-state and/or civil society render intelligible *res publica*. These political and intellectual conditions must be in place before Troeltsch's question can be asked. To continue to ask Troeltsch's question is to continue to make normative these political and intellectual conditions.

TROELTSCH'S QUESTION

The question, *what role does theology have in the public realm?* was given its most decisive articulation in Troeltsch's classic work *The Social Teaching of the Christian Churches*, which examined what he called "the social problem." This problem does not address the relationship between the church and the state so much as it does the relationship between the political community and other sociological phenomena such as market exchanges, family relationships, and everything that makes up the social, even though it is not regulated by the state per se. Troeltsch assesses the church's contribution to these sociological phenomena through the method of a social-scientific analysis, drawing heavily on Weber. He begins by defining state and civil society without reference to church. Only after the first two categories are established and their meaning firmly fixed can the role of the church's contribution to society be investigated.

In order to assess the church's contribution, Troeltsch adopted two seemingly neutral points of inquiry: first he investigates the "sociological idea of Christianity, its structure and organization" and then he addressed the question, "What is the relation between this sociological structure and the 'Social'?"[5] Note that the English translators of Troeltsch's text rightly

---

5. Ernst Troeltsch, *The Social Teaching of the Christian Churches* (trans. Olive Wyon; Chicago: University of Chicago Press, 1981) 1:34.

translated "the Social" with a capitalized S. For the latter is the invariable in Troeltsch's analysis. It is that social reality than which nothing greater can be conceived, and the church must be thought of in terms of its relationship to that greater social reality: "the Social."

"The Social" is the invariable grammar within which the church's teachings were to be rendered meaningful. This is explicitly stated in Troeltsch's introduction: "If we admit that the State and Society, together with innumerable other forces, are still the main formative powers of civilization, then the ultimate problem may be stated thus: How can the Church harmonize with these main forces in such a way that together they will form a unity of civilization?"[6]

Troeltsch assumed that a proper use of the term *society* was a combination of civil exchanges, family relationships, and religious and other voluntary associations. These along with the State make up civilization. It is the truly universal, public, or catholic formation. Therefore the ultimate problem that Christian social teaching confronts is what in its past can be usable to harmonize with state and society to form civilization. This question produced the tradition of Christian social ethics, which culminated in public theology and teaches us to ask the question, *what role does theology have in the public realm?*

Once this question captures our theological imagination, then the driving force in Christian social ethics is the effort to relate Christian social teaching to the benchmark of modern social formations. Rauschenbusch's *Christianizing the Social Order* perpetuated Troeltsch's question by recognizing that the vocation of the church was to mold "our public opinions and our institutions from the foundation up."[7] By "our" Rauschenbusch meant the American nation. It was the formative civilizing power such that the church's response to sociopolitical matters depended on its ability to mold the opinions of national institutions. The Methodist Episcopal Church adopted this same strategy by setting forth a Social Creed in 1908, beginning a tradition that has now become conservative and reactionary but goes under the title "progressive Christianity."

But why would this mainline protestant church find it compelling to qualify "creed" with "social"? This only makes sense against a tacit negative evaluative judgment that all previous creeds were somehow not social, and thus progressive Christianity was to address the new social reality with a new kind of creed. In so doing, they may have inadvertently adopted dogmatic certitudes of the modern era and gave them confessional status. By their actions, the Methodists assumed previous creeds were asocial. The United Methodists reaffirmed these tacit assumptions in

6. Ibid., 1:32.
7. Walter Rauschenbusch, *Christianizing the Social Order* (New York: Macmillan, 1912), 7.

1972 when they adopted the Social Principles. Once again, the adoption and promulgation of this confused document was a negative evaluation on the church's twenty-five articles. They were assumed to be *asocial*, so now they must be supplemented with social teachings. United Methodism stands firmly within the tradition of Troeltsch's assumptions and question, as does nearly every mainline Protestant denomination and most forms of "progressive" Christianity.

Rauschenbusch's witness was necessary and significant given the social conservatism of the church in his era. If the church had not already accommodated crucial modern notions such as that salvation was primarily an individual affair, then Rauschenbusch's work would not have been necessary. However, Rauschenbusch challenged this social conservatism with a neoliberalism that has now become quite conservative itself. He stated, "We are apt to think that progress is the natural thing. Progress is more than natural. It is divine."[8] And of course he argued, as has been endlessly repeated at least since David Strauss, that "we need a new foundation for Christian thought."[9] Oddly, the insistence on a new foundation in every generation of Christian theologians since the middle of the nineteenth century has not yet prevented us from adopting this conservative modern method and calling it "new."

Rauschenbusch's progressive Christianity had its downside, a downside that we saw present in the ethics of Knudson and Bowne. Because Rauschenbusch so valued progress and change he used it as a standard against which other races, nations, and cultures who did not value it were found wanting. So he also wrote, "There are nations and races that have not changed appreciably for ages."[10] Put that claim in the mouth of Anselm, Aquinas, or Wesley and it would be a positive affirmation of those races and nations. But for Rauschenbusch, it is a sign of moral infirmity—progress, development, and change are a priori signs of cultural superiority.

In many ways Rauschenbusch's social ethics set the questions that would be asked by Christian theologians in the twentieth century. These questions assume a priori that the kind of moral theology one finds in Aquinas and Wesley is fine as a private spirituality but has little to do with politics or *social* ethics. Social ethics deals with the technological question, *how can we create a blueprint to construct social institutions to run as justly and efficiently as possible?* Rauschenbusch's questions were a translation into the North American context of questions Troeltsch first set forth.

---

8. Ibid., 30.
9. Ibid., 42.
10. Ibid., 30.

Both of the Niebuhr brothers (even in Reinhold's opposition to Rauschenbusch) maintained Troeltsch's "ultimate problem" as the proper grammar if the church is to develop a "social" teaching. H. Richard's influential *Christ and Culture* is a version of Troeltsch's *Social Teaching*. It helped give rise to a new genre of theology: "public" theology. What tacit evaluative judgment is present in the positioning of the term "public" to theology? Whoever claimed to do nonpublic or private theology such that it now must be corrected by this new genre? *Public* theologians only make sense within the grammar of Troeltsch's question.

Troeltsch's question establishes the context for Christian social ethics both on the political left and the right. The differences between Niebuhr and Rauschenbusch, or public theologians and feminist or liberation theologians, represent a difference within a common grammar. The answers they provide for social questions may differ, but the underlying grammar, and the activity it assumes, is held in common. They all pose the question, *how can we make theology relevant to those main formative powers of civilization, the state and civil society?*

But why should this be our question? It has held us captive too long, and continues to do so in the mainline and evangelical churches. At the risk of being overly simplistic, I would suggest that organizations within my own United Methodist Church such as the Methodist Federation for Social Action, the Board of Church and Society, the Confessing Movement, and especially the Institute for Religion and Democracy all still assume that the term *social* or its contemporary equivalent *public* represents a universal or catholic whole to which the church must accommodate itself. What we see in these movements—as well as in strategies of evangelism such as the Igniting Ministry Campaign—is an assumption that the normative forces of society are the state and the market. If the church is to speak to the "real" world, then it must do so in terms that these social forms of exchange represent. We unwittingly accept and reproduce the notion that the "real social world" is defined by the kinds of natural exchanges and associations that occur in the privacy of the voting booth, in the marketplace, or in the sanctuary of the family. But why should these exchanges define the "real world"? To understand this, I think we need to return to a conversation only briefly alluded to in the first chapter of this work: the important influence of Reinhold Niebuhr on Wesleyan ethical thought.

THE NIEBUHRIAN CONSENSUS AND ITS DISSOLUTION: EITHER NIEBUHRIAN REALISM OR WESLEYAN PERFECTION

Reinhold Niebuhr was one of the most influential social ethicists in the twentieth century. He was one of only two theologians who made the cover of *Time* magazine in the twentieth century.[11] From the publication of his *Moral Man and Immoral Society* in 1932 until his death in 1971, he was, without a doubt, the most influential voice in protestant Christian social ethics. His influence was (and to a limited extent still is) so vast that it is downright confusing. Social pragmatists like Cornel West, market socialists and liberal Protestants like Philip Wogaman, and even Roman Catholic neoconservatives like Michael Novak all lay some claim to the Niebuhrian mantle. Evangelical Christians claim him as one of theirs, as do mainline Protestants. And his influence continues to be ever present in feminist and liberation theologians (even if implicit and primarily through Tillich) such as Rosemary Radford Ruether and James Cone. The vast and contested influence Niebuhr's work had, and continues to have, prompts the question, what work is his theology actually doing? How can groups that otherwise oppose each other politically and theologically find themselves so influenced—explicitly and implicitly—by his work?

Certainly Niebuhr's work has been so influential because of his insightful analysis of protestant Christianity and North American politics. Yet I think the connecting thread that makes his position attractive to such a diverse group is his commitment to fallibilism. Fallibilism is a philosophical position that asserts that claims to truth must always be held such that they are open to revision. This fallibilist position characterizes Niebuhr's realism and his insistence on the tragic. It is what attracts diverse constituencies to his position. For instance, Cornel West identifies the benefit he gained from Niebuhr as his "sense of the tragic, rejection of perfectionism, and sober historicist orientation."[12] Any Wesleyan moral theologian should take note what Niebuhr and West reject—perfectionism. Likewise, Novak and Wogaman find him useful because of his doctrine of sin; every action in history bears within it the inevitable limitations of finitude and thus tempts us to sin such that striving for perfection is more dangerous than acknowledging inevitable limits to all our social and political aspirations.[13]

---

11. The other theologian was John Courtney Murray, whose theology was very similar to that of Niebuhr. The "Methodist" theologian Stanley Hauerwas was named by *Time* "America's best theologian," but Hauerwas has a very tenuous relationship with the Methodists. Although his work may be as influential on my generation as Niebuhr's was on his, it has not yet infiltrated into churches in the Wesleyan tradition.

12. Cornel West, *Prophetic Fragments* (Grand Rapids, Mich.: Eerdmans, 1988), 152. I do not think any of the theologians I note as influenced by Niebuhr would disagree with what West affirms.

13. See Stephen Long, *Divine Economy: Theology and the Market* (New York: Routledge, 2000), 38, 64, for the details of this argument.

Robin Lovin explains that Niebuhr opposed Rauschenbusch because

> Rauschenbusch's writings shared with these sentimental pieties [such as, "a comprehensive and continuous reconstruction of social life in the name of God is within the bounds of human possibility"] one fundamental confusion: the moral vision of the New Testament is treated as a "simple possibility." It becomes a key point of Christian Realism that the ethics of Jesus cannot provide a social ethics.[14]

After Niebuhr, a moral theology such as one finds in Aquinas and Wesley, where it is assumed that the Sermon on the Mount is the social and political teaching revealed by divine law, is no longer possible. The key difference between Niebuhr and Wesley and Aquinas is the dogmatic context for the moral life. Niebuhr can only think Christian ethics in terms of an anthropology grounded in modern certitudes. He knows a priori that God cannot assume human flesh and work as one with it. Wesley and Aquinas can only make the claims they do because of the doctrine of the Trinity and Incarnation where Jesus Christ is the Eternal Law who is the pattern that renders all creation intelligible. They assume God incarnates human nature such that the two can cooperate as one without either losing its Uncreated or created nature. Niebuhr explicitly rejected the Chalcedonian grammar. He wrote,

> All definitions of Christ which affirm both his divinity and humanity in the sense that they ascribe both finite and historically conditioned and eternal and unconditioned qualities to his nature must verge on logical nonsense. It is possible for a character, event or fact of history to point symbolically beyond history and to become a source of disclosure of an eternal meaning, purpose and power which bears history. But it is not possible for any person to be both historical and unconditioned at the same time.[15]

One wonders how Niebuhr knows the a priori possibilities for what God can and cannot accomplish, for he presumes the infallible claim that God and humanity, the Unconditioned and conditioned, cannot be one in a harmonious relationship. And the presumption of this infallible claim leads to his insistence on fallibilism. It is self-refuting. For this reason Niebuhr will deny the political significance of the Incarnation and see it as an unfortunate "Hellenic" importation that still has too much hold on Roman Catholic and Anglican theologies. He rejects the church's teaching on the hypostatic union, and places the *paradox* of the atonement, where

---

14. Robin W. Lovin, *Reinhold Niebuhr and Christian Realism* (Cambridge: Cambridge University Press, 1995), 5.

15. Reinhold Niebuhr, *Human Destiny* (vol. 2 of *The Nature and Destiny of Man*; New York: Charles Scribner's Sons, 1943), 2:61.

the Unconditioned deity and conditioned humanity are in competition with each other, at the center of his theology.[16] One must give way for the other to be present. Niebuhrian realism must reject the Chalcedonian grammar of faith for the sake of a "realistic" ethical teaching that fits American pragmatism with its basis in fallibilism.

Niebuhr's realism takes as its dogmatic context the reality of sin, not only as a permanent factor in human history but also as an unintended consequence of even a saintly action. In fact, Niebuhr is credited with recovering the doctrine of sin against the liberal optimism of the Social Gospel movement. Such a recovery began with the 1932 publication of *Moral Man and Immoral Society* and was a continuous theme throughout his life. But this cure may have been worse than the disease. For Niebuhr's recovery of sin brought with it this commitment to fallibilism, a commitment which rejected the central dogmatic commitments of both Aquinas and Wesley, which made their moral theology possible.

Niebuhr's a priori commitment to fallibilism requires a dialectical approach to faith and reason that cannot render intelligible *fides quaerens intellectum*, for fallibilism is a performative contradiction. To suggest that every form of knowledge and every moral deed bears within it not only fallibility but even the perversity of evil, as Niebuhr does, is to claim what cannot be claimed. Such a claim assumes that Niebuhr himself inhabits some neutral space where he knows with certainty the limitations of others' knowledge. Thus, far from offering us a realist, soberly historical analysis, Niebuhr's fallibilism functions as a transcendental ideal. It is the a priori condition for the possibility of all knowledge and moral action that he must infallibly claim before any historical investigation of a teaching or deed performed in history. Niebuhr knows a priori that doctrine and morals cannot embody truth or goodness without error, including God's performance in the humanity of Jesus. Everything must now be thought of within the limits of this transcendental framework. The result is that the incarnation must be rejected. But how could we infallibly know the truth of fallibilism? The position is unstable.

Perhaps the ongoing influence of Niebuhrian realism results precisely from this instability. Like an all-purpose suit, Niebuhr's work fits nearly any context where the purpose of discursive reasoning is to offer a critical analysis of someone else's account of truth or goodness. It particularly suits a North American context where political and market exchanges flourish on such a critical analysis. But two theological contexts it cannot fit are Roman Catholicism and the Wesleyan holiness movement. Niebuhr was right to reject Catholic and Anglican theologies for the sake of his "realism." He also stated that Wesley "did not quite comprehend this

---

16. Ibid., 2:59.

mystery of evil in the redeemed man."[17] Likewise, these theologies must reject Niebuhrian realism if they are to be faithful to their own traditions.

Fallibilism

Fallibilism claims that a teaching or action is reasonable only insofar as one holds one's positions loosely. We must always be willing to look at our teachings with a cultivated ability of critique that often masquerades as humility. It is always to be willing to say, "but I might be wrong." While this appears tolerant and reasonable, it cannot account for how one might hold that one might be wrong in holding that one might be wrong. In other words, the one thing not subject to the cultivated critique fallibilism requires is the fallibilist position itself. This position makes humility rather than charity the form of all the virtues, and, as Wesley taught us, this is dangerous to do. Humility is not a virtue; it is at most an entrance into virtue. Humility is emptiness. To make it the form of the virtues would be to welcome nihilism as the heart of the moral life.

Niebuhr's realism is a version of fallibilism. He recognizes that political and metaphysical accounts of realism are not identical. He is a political realist and, whether he recognized it or not, a thoroughgoing metaphysical idealist because his fallibilism functions as a transcendental ideal that makes thought possible. "'Realism,'" he states, "denotes the disposition to take all factors in a social and political situation, which offer resistance to established norms, into account, particularly the factors of self-interest and power."[18] This requires a fallibilist account of knowledge because all our commitment to norms—whether of truth or goodness— bring with them unintended consequences whereby living consistent with an exceptionless norm of truth or goodness is more dangerous than holding all commitments loosely, subjecting them to possible revision, based on a practical, sober analysis of the real world and not the world as

---

17. Niebuhr's lectures on Wesley were recorded and transcribed at Duke University. Niebuhr discusses Wesley's perfectionism and notes that it assumes inherent rather than imputed righteousness. In opposition to Wesley, Niebuhr stated,

> The ultimate problem of human existence is whether the Reformation doctrine is right: *justus et peccator simul*, that the redeemed man is yet a sinner. Not because he consciously defies the Lord's law as he knows it, but because 'there is a law in his members which wars against the law that is in his mind' and because he is betrayed. Paul puts this in various ways, as you know. . . . This mystery of evil in the redeemed man, Wesley does not quite comprehend. This is the Augustinian in him.

Note that Niebuhr rightly recognizes the source of Wesley's Christian perfection in Augustine. The quotation comes from Reinhold Niebuhr, "Wesley; Church and Sect in America," tape 53, side A, of The Reinhold Niebuhr Audiotape Collection. Ⓟ 1979 by Union Theological Seminary in Virginia with the cooperation of Union Theological Seminary in New York. Original lecture date 1960.

18. Reinhold Niebuhr, *Christian Realism and Political Problems* (Fairfield, Conn.: Augustus M. Kelley, 1977), 119.

we wish it to be. As Lovin notes, "Christian Realism teaches us to do Christian theology in a modern intellectual world where critical consciousness makes us most suspicious of precisely those things we most strongly believe."[19] This is similar to the pragmatism put forth by Oliver Wendell Holmes, which was noted in the first chapter. But the questions that Wesleyan theologians must pose to such realism are, *must we do theology in such a world?* and *what must we sacrifice in order to do it?*

Niebuhr's fallibilism is predicated on his doctrine of unintended consequences, which often gets mistaken for a doctrine of original sin. Because self-interest and power are inextricably present in every exchange and self-interest is a priori understood as sinful (Niebuhr, like Hutcheson and Kant, assumes ethics must be disinterested), no true, good, and loving deed is possible. And to think that such a deed is possible is more dangerous than knowing with a priori certitude that it is not. For Niebuhr, to hold to the possibility of perfection or infallibility becomes dangerous, for it denies our most basic being—both individually and socially—and prevents analysis of the ineradicable element of self-interest and power by putting forth the possibility of an exchange where perversion is not always already present. For this reason, he found Catholicism in particular quite dangerous. "The Catholic doctrine of the Church," he wrote, "is, in fact, a constant temptation to demonic pretensions, since it claims for an institution, established in time and history, universal and absolute validity."[20] His critique of a catholic church is the same as his critique of the Incarnation. But notice how Niebuhr's fallibilist account of knowledge functions as a dogmatic a priori. We know, without argument, that any institution in history (and what other kinds are there?) that claims to be grounded in truth is a priori demonic.[21]

What would Niebuhr have said about a holiness movement that claimed it possible to be made perfect in love in this lifetime? He does say, "To understand life in its total dimension means contrition because every moral achievement stands under the criticism of a more essential goodness. If fully analyzed the moral achievement is not only convicted of

19. Lovin, *Niebuhr and Christian Realism*, 31.
20. Reinhold Niebuhr, *An Interpretation of Christian Ethics* (San Francisco: Harper & Row, 1963), 143.
21. That Niebuhr labels this "Augustinian realism" is of course quite ironic. After all, Augustine gave us this doctrine of the church. Niebuhr does recognize this, but also suggests that Augustine was inconsistent in describing the church as the perfect society. Niebuhr offers many reservations about Augustine's position; nevertheless, he calls it an error. In fact, Niebuhr identifies another error in Augustine even graver than his identification of the visible church as a perfect society. He writes,

> This error is probably related to his conception of grace which does not allow for the phenomenon, emphasized by the Reformation, that men may be redeemed in the sense that they consciously turn from self to Christ as their end, and yet they are not redeemed from the corruption of egotism which expresses itself, even in the lives of the saints. This insight is most succinctly expressed in Luther's phrase *"justus et peccator simul."* (*Christian Realism*, 137-38)

imperfection, but of sin. It is not only wanting in perfect goodness, but there is something of the perversity of evil in it."[22] No place for Wesley's doctrine of perfection is left after Niebuhr's dogmatic fallibility defines every speech and action. The Christian doctrine of perfection is not only utopian for Niebuhr; it is sinister. It too would participate in a demonic temptation. Why? It denies that every performance of a good action, every truthful speaking not only is insufficient in being good or true but also bears within it the perversity of evil. Christian realism, contra the Wesleyan holiness movement, dogmatically knows that perfection, deification, and a participation in God's goodness are impossible. There is only the will to power, and all we can do is minimize its inevitable evil consequences.

This makes Niebuhr's work not primarily a recovery of sin but a recovery of the Hellenistic or pagan tradition of tragedy. Moreover, this is not tragedy as used in a weak ordinary sense, which I think is quite proper in any Christian theology. Niebuhr's work depends on the strongest possible account of tragedy—an ontological account where we cannot have the good without evil, and we cannot have evil without good. The source of that strong ontological version of tragedy is precisely his metaphysical idealism. Niebuhr is a metaphysical idealist because the source of sin is discovered not in some fall or in the privation of the good but in the very structure of the "transcendent" self. We are always already betrayed by something other than our own doing.

Anthropology Begetting Tragedy

The only doctrine Niebuhr developed with care was anthropology. He began *The Nature and Destiny of Man* with the assertion: "Man has always been his own most vexing problem. How shall he think of himself?" The vexing problem is that if we think of ourselves entirely in terms of nature, we do not do justice to our rational faculties that transcend nature. If we think of ourselves in terms of those transcendent rational faculties, we do not do justice to our embeddedness in nature. This vexing problem—our location within both a transcendent realm of rationality and freedom and an immanent realm of nature, inclination, and instinct—generates all of Niebuhr's anthropology and makes tragedy necessary.[23]

This ontological structure—caught between nature and freedom, vitality and form, the natural fact of a particular body and the spiritual fact of

---

22. Niebuhr, *Interpretation of Christian Ethics*, 52.

23. This can be seen particularly in chapter 2 of *The Nature and Destiny of Man*, vol. 1, which is called "The Problem of Vitality and Form in Human Nature." *Vitality* refers to how "man" interprets himself with regard to nature and *form* refers to how "man" interprets himself with respect to reason.

self-transcendence—is irremediable. As he puts it, "No philosophy or religion can change the structure of human existence."[24] This unchanging structure is the source for the possibility of evil because it tempts us to misunderstand ourselves in two directions: idealism or naturalism. Both forfeit a proper interpretation of the human self, either by losing it to the universality of transcendent, rationality, and freedom or surrendering it to the immediacy of the particular, nature, and vitality. Only by providing an interpretation that gives unity to the relation of vitality and form can the temptation be avoided. This is what Niebuhr believes the Christian view of anthropology seeks to do. But all it can do is provide an interpretation that makes sense of the unity of the two; it cannot overcome the contradiction the two represent that tempts us toward evil.

Niebuhr's "Christian view" of the human person views him or her as *imago Dei* solely because of self-transcendence. The person is already made *imago Dei* but not made *into* the image of God. The unique human ability to transcend nature through reason and freedom constitutes our being made in the image of God. The temptation to sin is possible because this self-transcendence is ensconced in the natural vitality of space and time. Niebuhr does not claim that the embeddedness of the form of self-transcendence in the natural vitality of space and time necessitates sin. He holds out the possibility that a person could sacrifice all natural self-interest and overcome the limitations of being located in space and time, but no one except Jesus accomplished this. And he could only do it because he was willing to die on a cross, therefore sacrificing his conditioned, historical finitude to the good of the eternal that does not know space and time. The rest of us all sin precisely because we are unwilling to make this same sacrifice.

Sin, for Niebuhr, is the inordinate self-love that occurs—not necessarily but inevitably—as a result of the vexing problem where human nature participates in the eternal because of its potential for self-transcendence, freedom, and rationality, but it can only participate in it through natural and human finiteness. The freedom to transcend nature is the very source of possibility of good and evil. We sin—inevitably but not necessarily—because we make absolute our finite particularities. We refuse to sacrifice our partial historical materiality for the sake of the universal. That is why Niebuhr's fallibilism leads him to reproach Catholicism (and by implication Wesleyanism) as potentially demonic.

Theological Limitations

Niebuhr's anthropology places significant limitations on what he can accept as Christian doctrine. Incarnation, Resurrection, and eschatology

---

24. Ibid., 69.

are no longer crucially significant. Only the Crucifixion finally plays a substantive dogmatic role. Ecclesiology becomes a tertiary concern, thus its absence from Niebuhr's theology. It is his limitations on what is permissible within Christian dogmatics that allows the state and the market to preempt any role for the church within God's economy and thus allow his theology, unlike Roman Catholicism and the Wesleyan holiness movement, to be always relevant to Troeltsch's question.

Given that Niebuhr's anthropology generates the possibility for all other theological themes, we should not be surprised that he turned to Paul Tillich when pressed to explain more fully what his theology was. Tillich's theology fits well Niebuhr's anthropology. It too is dominated by the Crucifixion and has little place for theological themes such as incarnation, resurrection, eschatology, and ecclesiology. Redemption occurs in Tillich because Jesus sacrifices himself to the Christ of faith. As he put it, "Jesus of Nazareth is the medium of the final revelation because he sacrifices himself completely to Jesus as the Christ."[25] Niebuhr also identifies the essence of the cross as offering us a true performance of agape where "the self must sacrifice itself for the other."[26] Jesus' bodiliness is not redemptive; it is a threat to redemption. Only when it is sacrificed to that eternal, transcendent realm, which the term *Christ* symbolizes, can it be redemptive. Such a sacrifice includes sacrificing any resurrected body as well.

The traditional threefold form of the body of Christ is completely lost in Niebuhr's realism. That threefold form recognized that Christ is present to us first and foremost in the body of the historical Jesus of Nazareth. Only as God is incarnate in this body, without mixture or confusion, does that first form make sense. But that first form is still present to us today because that body is resurrected and now does not know the limitations of space and time. The first form of the body makes possible the second and third forms: the presence of Christ's body in the church and in the Eucharist. It is the ongoing presence of Christ's body in the church that gives us hope—even when we do not know what it means—that Christ will come again. Christian eschatology as well as the entirety of the Christian gospel only makes sense in light of this threefold form of Christ's body.

---

25. Paul Tillich, *Systematic Theology*, 3 vols. in 1 (Chicago: University of Chicago Press, 1967), 1:135.

26. Niebuhr, *Christian Realism and Political Problems*, 140. Like Niebuhr, for Tillich this means the inevitability of war. Just as the historical materiality of Jesus of Nazareth can only mediate salvation when that materiality is fully sacrificed to the transcendent Christ, so every possibility of higher unities in politics can only come about when we are prepared to recognize the "compulsory element of power" in history and are prepared to "answer in kind" (*Systematic Theology*, 3:388).

These themes are conspicuously absent in Niebuhr's theology, but the reason why is quite clear. If our vexing problem is to explain ourselves in terms of the form and vitality Niebuhr described, then little room exists for the threefold form of the body of Christ in theology. Christ's material, historical body presents a problem to be overcome, not a source of our redemption. Others have noted this in Niebuhr's work. As Henry B. Clark noted, "Niebuhr was sufficiently honest to know that orthodox ecclesiastical dogma was not intellectually acceptable."[27] Christian doctrines had to be understood as mythopoetic symbols that pointed to the essence of Christian faith: love thy neighbor. And Richard Fox notes the difference between Reinhold and his brother H. Richard precisely on the doctrine of the Incarnation.

> For Reinhold, God was outside history and history itself was "no more than tragedy." For Helmut, God "is always in history." . . . Helmut pointed out what Reinhold's other critics had not yet seen. Despite his fulminations against sentimental liberalism, against complacent faith in the redemptive character of human goodwill, Reinhold remained a thoroughgoing liberal. His God did not act in history.[28]

Fox recognizes the functional theologic in Niebuhr's work: God cannot be found in human flesh. No hypostatic union is possible. We do not discover God in the flesh; we discover God by abstracting from it—even negating it. This theology is grounded in his fallibilist account of knowledge and his tragic ontology. Theologically this rules out Roman Catholic and Wesleyan teaching. Socially and politically it fits well within the market and nation-state in the modern era.

THE SOCIAL AND POLITICAL SIGNIFICANCE OF DIFFERENT DOGMATIC CONTEXTS

Niebuhr's theology works well both as a legitimation for modern political arrangements and as a means for critiquing them, which is how they are legitimated, for they themselves are based on a principle like fallibilism. These political arrangements are grounded not in any substantive notion of truth or goodness but in critique and freedom. Although a federalist republic like the United States of America was forged against an original predominant and excessive zeal for liberty that worried the framers of the Constitution, it was still dependent solely on fallibilist

---

27. Henry B. Clark, *Serenity, Courage & Wisdom: The Enduring Legacy of Reinhold Niebuhr* (Cleveland: Pilgrim, 1994), 74-75.
28. Richard Wightman Fox, *Reinhold Niebuhr: A Biography* (New York: Pantheon, 1985), 134.

principles.[29] As Alexander Hamilton wrote in *The Federalist Papers*, "Is it not time to awake from the deceitful dream of a golden age and to adopt as a practical maxim for the direction of our political conduct that we, as well as the other inhabitants of the globe, are yet remote from the happy empire of perfect wisdom and perfect virtue?"[30] The common fear that one group might aggrandize itself against the others in its efforts to be that "happy empire of . . . perfect virtue" prompts both the necessity and the possibility of a more perfect union. It is forged not out of truth but out of common weakness. Niebuhr's theology safeguards this insight. As he wrote in *Children of Light and Children of Darkness*, "Man's capacity for justice makes democracy possible; but man's inclination to injustice makes democracy necessary."[31] All of life—political, social, theological—is a balance of power, a calculation of interests dominated by self-interest and power dynamics that make any exchange possible. The best we can do is counteract one self-interest with another so that none becomes absolute and destroys us all.

Nearly every theologian who defends some version of capitalist business practices draws on Niebuhr's fallibilism as the theological grounds for the justification of capitalism. The crucial doctrine they develop is the doctrine of original sin. The argument is that a socialist economics would not be possible, for it would require persons who are not tainted by sinful self-interest. The fact that we know sinful self-interest taints all our actions demonstrates that socialism is not possible. Because capitalism recognizes that our actions have unintended consequences, it is the form of economic exchange that fits best a sober Christian realism.

This common use of Niebuhrian realism to defend capitalism may come as something of a surprise to Niebuhr himself. After all, in 1932 he wrote, "it is a fact that Marxian socialism is a true enough interpretation of what the industrial worker feels about society and history, to have become the accepted social and political philosophy of all self-conscious and politically intelligent industrial workers."[32] But his much vaunted early defense of Marxism did not differ significantly from later interpreters' use of his work as an apology for capitalism. Both share the assumption that conflict, contending interests, and an ineradicable self-interest dominate every exchange. But as a putative doctrine of sin, Niebuhr's fallibilist presupposition falls short. His doctrine of unintended

29. James Madison, Alexander Hamilton, and John Jay, *The Federalist Papers* (ed. Isaac Kramnick; London: Penguin Books, 1987), 196.

30. Ibid., 108.

31. Reinhold Niebuhr, *The Children of Light and the Children of Darkness: A Vindication of Democracy and a Critique of Its Traditional Defence* (New York: Charles Scribner's Sons, 1960), xiii.

32. Niebuhr, *Moral Man and Immoral Society* (New York: Charles Scribner's Sons, 1960), 144.

consequences has little to no basis in Saint Augustine or Saint Paul. Its most immediate ancestor is Adam Smith, whose stoic philosophy informed his free market economics.[33]

A doctrine of unintended consequences forms the dogmatic basis for Adam Smith's free market economics. Persons act self-interestedly either virtuously or viciously recognizing that their actions are in competition with others. This competition of self-interests does not produce chaos but harmony and cooperation. How does this work? Only if Smith's stoic theology of providence is true can this work. As previously noted, Smith argued that a person "pursuing his own interest . . . frequently promotes that of the society more effectually than when he really intends to promote it."[34] Neither Smith's nor Niebuhr's fallibilism argued that individuals should be vicious because it results in virtuous ends. Yet both argued that the source for harmonious social and political cooperation did not come by directly intending the good—that led to the unintended consequences of social and political devastation. The source for social and political harmony is located in the unintended consequences of the permanent factor of self-interest that taints all our actions. Moral perfectionism was at least as dangerous, if not more so, than the pursuit of private vices.

Wesley's and Aquinas's dogmatic context is not one of fallibilism or the doctrine of unintended consequences. Wesley assumed the possibility of a perfect good that can be received and achieved because of Christ's human righteousness. It can become inherent in us. Aquinas assumed that truth can be infallibly known through the virtue of *intellectus*. Both of these claims occurred against the eschatological blessedness Jesus pronounced in history. This dogmatic context would allow for the possibility of a common life grounded in truth and goodness, which is primarily to be embodied in the life of the church. What do we lose when Troeltsch's work sets the question of a social ethics? We lose the insight of both Wesley and Aquinas that the church itself is the mission. Barry Harvey puts this well. He notes that first-century Christians developed an "ecclesial eschatology" where the making of a new community is the mission. Why? Because what they believed and practiced is true.[35] This alone can account for the risk that Christian discipleship finally requires. But such a statement is impermissible given the dogmatic certitudes of modern fallibilism. Wesley clearly presented this eschatologically renewed community as his "social ethic." Although Wesley could treat the Roman Catholic doctrine of infallibility sarcastically, he also questioned the Methodists:

---

33. See Adam Smith, *Theory of Moral Sentiments* (Indianapolis: Liberty Fund, 1976), 36.

34. Adam Smith, *The Wealth of Nations* (ed. Edwin Cannan; New York: Modern Library, 1994), 423.

35. See Barry Harvey, *Another City: An Ecclesiological Primer for a Post-Christian World* (Harrisburg, Pa.: Trinity Press, 1999), 25-31.

"Hath not the whole word of God been delivered to you, and without any mixture of error?"[36]

As previously noted, Wesley concluded his second discourse on the Sermon on the Mount with a call to be the "first-fruits" of the eschatological city Christ blessed on the Mountain. He wrote, "Surely all these things shall come to an end, and the inhabitants of the earth shall learn righteousness. 'Nation shall not lift up sword against nation, neither shall they know war any more.' . . . They shall all be without spot or blemish, loving one another, even as Christ hath loved us. *Be thou part of the first-fruits, if the harvest is not yet.*"[37] Here is a clear statement of the "ecclesial eschatology" Harvey notes as central to the "other city." Aquinas may have not put it quite so clearly, but even he had to assume it in that Christ's eschatological blessedness on the Mountain is the heart of the Christian moral life.

WESLEYANS AND THOMISTS MUST SAY NO TO FALLIBILISM

To ask Troeltsch's question is to move from Wesley's and Aquinas's moral theology with its dogmatic context of an eschatological blessedness to the modern dogmatic context of fallibilism. It assumes that the modern nation-state and the global market are the true driving forces of history, grounded as they are in the reality of a historicism that privileges power over goodness and truth. The result is that will is separated from truth and goodness, for only will forges the bonds of communal life. Notice how Troeltsch interprets Aquinas's moral theology.

Aquinas, wrote Troeltsch, reveals "the logical result of the sociological idea of a religious community based upon absolute truths and life-values."[38] The logical sociological result is either the rejection of the state or its necessary subordination to the church (and hence theocracy). This produced the "horrors" that were the Middle Ages, for Aquinas inherited an either-or approach to religion and natural sociological associations such

---

36. Sermon 107, "On God's Vineyard," §V.5, *Works* 3:516. For a sarcastic use of speaking *"ex cathedra* infallible," see Sermon 58, "On Predestination" (§3, *Works* 2:416) where he chides Calvinists for sounding like Roman Catholics when they set forth the doctrine of predestination. Wesley understood that all acts of human speech imply truthfulness. In Sermon 39, "Catholic Spirit" (§I.4, *Works* 2:83) he wrote, "every man necessarily believes that every particular opinion which he holds is true (for to believe any opinion is not true is the same thing as not to hold it) yet can no man be assured that all his own opinions taken together are true."

37. Sermon 22, "Sermon on the Mount, II," §III.18, *Works* 1:509, emphasis mine.

38. Troeltsch, *Social Teaching*, 1:230.

that if the former were held as absolute truth, then the latter were not given their proper independence. Troeltsch argued that if the "religious life" formed itself upon the basis of worship rather than the "natural forms of association" that the family, race, city, and Empire represented, then the religious life (that is, the church) would "regard itself as the superior authority." However, these "natural forms of association" will inevitably require to be taken into consideration. The church, at first, rejected the natural forms and viewed "itself as the superior authority," but when it took them into account, it could only do so by seeking to "penetrate and dominate" them. This is how Troeltsch understood the Middle Ages. He wrote, "The theocracy of the central period of the Middle Ages came to this conclusion with the full consciousness of its inner necessity, and upheld it by its terrible ecclesiastical methods of domination, which even today call forth the horror of the reader."[39]

This "spiritual domination" occurred through the sacrament of penance and was based on the doctrine of the incarnation and the concomitant threefold form of the body of Christ.[40] It taught that Jesus is truly God and truly human, and this Divine/human reality is represented in history, in the sacraments, and in the church.[41] Such an absolute truth claim lodged in human history will distort social reality by reading it in terms of such truth claims.

As long as this system was in place, the "social problem," as Troeltsch identified it, could not emerge. But for Troeltsch this system was deconstructed by nominalist theology, which "undoubtedly rendered a real service by its penetrating criticism of this [Thomistic] system of reconciliation, and by overthrowing this system it is manifest that the secular realm of life was allowed more scope."[42] The sociological result of nominalism's deconstruction was the development of the "religious idea, pure and simple."[43] This led to a separation of church and "the Social" where the latter began to develop based on its own natural forms of association.

Nominalist deconstruction of the Thomist synthesis coupled with the principles of the Reformation led to the consequent social form of the "Church-type."[44] This was a new sociological form unlike the medieval form of a unity of ecclesiastical civilization. Once this new social form is in place, then "the steady development of an ethic which accepts the life of the world" can finally begin.[45] Only at this point in Troeltsch's

---

39. Ibid., 1:230-31.
40. "This sacrament became the great support of the spiritual domination of the world" (ibid., 1:233).
41. Ibid., 1:234.
42. Ibid., 1:278.
43. Ibid., 2:466.
44. Ibid., 2:477.
45. Ibid., 2:494.

narrative can the "social problem" emerge. Only now can we begin to ask, *what role does theology have in the public realm?* The question assumes that church and theology are either subordinate to or, at best, partners with those natural forms of association that constitute the true "Social." They are designated as the "life of the world" and are known independently of any ecclesial or theological knowledge of them. They are no longer intelligible in terms of the presentation of the social body found in the church's traditional doctrine of the threefold body of Christ.

Neither the historical body of Jesus, nor its repetition in the sacraments or the church are necessary to know the "Social." For Troeltsch, the "Social" emerges only when this other social body is first marginalized. The social body presented to us by Aquinas was a dominating, diseased body that must first be deconstructed before the true "social problem" emerges. To ask the question, *what is the role of theology in the public realm?* deconstructs that ecclesial body. This very question repeats this story and its assumptions about social bodies.

A WESLEYAN ALTERNATIVE?

Once political and economic exchanges are based on the principles of fallibilism, it should come as no surprise that Niebuhrian realism has such vast influence. If the purpose of theology is to respond to questions a culture asks in an effort to be relevant to that culture, then Niebuhrian realism correlates well to twentieth-century culture. It is a relevant theological response to a culture trained to ask how we can speak of God when we know a priori all our utterances and actions bear the perversity of evil such that they cannot know the good or the true. In such a culture, the so-called Protestant Principle will become the background principle that defines theological possibilities.[46] It will dominate to such an extent that other forms of theological expression, such as Catholic infallibilism or Wesleyan perfectionism, could easily become unintelligible. Perhaps the pervasiveness of Niebuhrian realism among Catholic and Wesleyan theologians is a sign that infallibilism and perfectionism are irreparably broken.

Fallibilism has a powerful appeal, it seems intuitively correct. Both secular and religious institutions empirically demonstrate again and again

---

46. Tillich defines the Protestant principle as "Protestant theology protests in the name of the Protestant principle . . . against the identification of our ultimate concern with any creation of the church, including the biblical writings in so far as their witness to what is really ultimate concern is also a conditioned expression of their own spirituality" (*Systematic Theology*, 1:37). See also 1:227; 2:147; 3:177, 208.

that they are fallible. It would be easy to accept fallibilism as a theological replacement for infallibilism or perfectionism if not for two reasons. First, it is intellectually defective. Second, it is theologically limiting. As already noted, fallibilism is not reasonable. It can only be held as the true source of knowledge and action when one is willing to live with the performative contradiction it requires. That means institutions that claim a fallibilist grounding put themselves beyond critique. While fallibilism is intended to make critique possible, it actually prevents it. It provides a sure form of critique against all institutions except those who claim themselves to be grounded in fallibilism. Second, fallibilism will always work against the Christian doctrine of the Incarnation and the threefold form of the body of Christ. Fallibilism knows a priori—and not as a sober historical judgment—that the true and the good cannot be found in history without the taint of sin. But this only works because of a distorted notion of sin. Niebuhrian fallibilism wrongly identifies sin as self-interest and power. Only a purely disinterested action would be an action without sin. This lingering Kantianism in Niebuhrian fallibilism requires a sacrificial economy where the only way to be holy is at the same time to be free from all exchanges—socially, politically, and theologically. For only someone who had no intercourse with any other human being or even with God could possibly satisfy this condition of disinterest. To identify sin with self-interest is inevitably gnostic, for human beings cannot be without self-interest. If "sin" is to be concerned with one's self, then to be redeemed can only be to embrace the death of one's self. No wonder it is the cross at the expense of the Incarnation and the Resurrection that becomes the focus of Niebuhr's theology.

Wesleyan perfectionism is more reasonable than Niebuhrian fallibilism, for it does not produce a performative contradiction. Wesley rejected the very stoic disinterestedness he saw emerging in eighteenth-century British moral theology. This stoic disinterestedness is the basis for Niebuhr's theology. Wesley's perfectionism does not begin with a priori limitations on good actions and truthful utterances in space and time. It is not so thoroughly policed by modern epistemological assumptions. It suggests that because of the all-sufficiency of Christ's life, death, and Resurrection, we do not know a priori the limits in which the good and true cannot be performed. It must be possible to perform them without some element of the perversity of evil. In fact, Wesleyan perfectionism would be more like Roman Catholic infallibilism. Just as Wesleyans claim the possibility of perfection in this lifetime, the Catholic tradition has always held forth that the church can teach and live without error. This has to be asserted because the church is the body of Christ. It is a statement first and foremost about God's sanctifying work in Jesus, and only secondarily about us. Any good Wesleyan account of moral, social, and political life should take this into account.

Manfred Marquardt, Ronald Stone, and Theodore Weber have all offered us significant accounts of Wesley's social ethics, moral philosophy, and political ethics. In his *John Wesley's Social Ethics*, Marquardt rightly notes that Troeltsch did not narrate Wesley and the Methodist movement well. Wesley's opposition to the humanism of the Enlightenment did not entail that his movement was radically sectarian with respect to "the whole spirit of modern science and civilization" as Troeltsch stated.[47] Instead Wesley's social ethics was a life program where he sought to establish a movement in imitation of the first Christians.[48] This movement did not oppose faith to reason or call for a sectarian withdrawal, it was precisely an engagement with social reality through the movement itself. Marquardt nicely sets forth Wesley's moral theology, but he too seems to wonder if it is finally "social." He returns to Troeltsch's question by asking,

> Did Wesley consider it sufficient to renew society from below, that is, through the transformation of individuals, or did he include the transformation of social structures and of governmental institutions in the process of renewal that he perceived in comprehensive terms? In other words, did social ethics extend beyond the social environment of individuals and groups and lead to preparatory analysis and instructions including the possibility of transforming foundational social orders? Or did social ethics merely remain an individual ethic extended to include broader social connections that emerged from time to time?[49]

This question seems to return Marquardt's very persuasive reading of Wesley back to Troeltsch's question, for what does Marquardt mean by "foundational social orders"? He seems to mean institutions such as the nation-state and its governing apparatus as well as market exchanges. This raises a number of questions. Does he suggest that if we are to have a social ethics we must have some kind of blueprint to establish and run such orders? If so, where is the blueprint? Who has it, and what does it look like? Should Wesley be critiqued for not having such a blueprint? If the church does present such a blueprint to the world, who would take it seriously in our post-Christendom context? Finally, what role does the church itself have as a—or possibly *the*—foundational social order?

Ronald Stone offers a very different reading of Wesley than I offer here. He finds that Wesley's ethics bear little to no relationship to the Aristotelian-

---

47. Troeltsch, *Social Teaching*, 2:721.
48. Manfred Marquardt, *John Wesley's Social Ethics: Praxis and Principles* (trans. John E. Steely and W. Stephen Gunter; Nashville: Abingdon, 1992), 115.
49. Ibid., 123.

Thomistic framework. He writes, "Very little here [in Wesley] is reminiscent of an Aristotelian ethic other than a few terms used by both Aristotle and Wesley in different systems of ethical discourse."[50] Instead of this Aristotelian-Thomistic framework, he finds in Wesley a trajectory for key essential ethical themes that were later developed by Niebuhr and Tillich—love, liberty, and sin. For Stone, this constitutes a trajectory that Wesley did not always fully embody. His rigid Protestant discipline prevented him from making the transition completely to love and grace after his conversion experience. Stone writes, "It is Luther's interpretation of Paul in a Moravian context that permits Wesley to relax a little and to accept acceptance. Still, Wesley is too formed by his previous Protestant discipline to just relax in the love of Christ."[51]

Stone reads Wesley as an empiricist and a pragmatist.[52] He finds the compelling nature of Wesley's ethics to be its lack of any dogmatic theological context; it is more similar to natural law arguments where particular theological commitments are eschewed for the sake of universal accessibility. He points to Wesley's ethic in his "Thoughts upon Slavery" and states that it, "could be appreciated by a wide variety of readers because it did not depend on any particular christological distinctiveness or any particular Methodist arguments."[53] Stone finds in Wesley's ethic a method of Christian ethical analysis that is similar to modern ethics grounded in social science. He suggests that Wesley's ethics is best understood as "a natural law argument . . . on the grounds of natural rights."[54] But this is only one of seven emphases Stone finds in Wesley's ethics: (1) the priority of human liberty, (2) a life of love, (3) realism, (4) freedom rooted in natural law drawing on the fledgling social science of his day more so than Scripture or theological argument, (5) the normativity of Scripture, (6) the early church patterns in Acts, and (7) experience.[55] Stone notes that these seven emphases, especially Wesley's "passion for understanding Christian life as a *life of love,*" made it difficult for him to defend his teaching on Christian perfection.[56] I do not find this argument persuasive. It is unclear to me that Wesley found it difficult to defend Christian perfection or found it in tension with a life of love. Stone pits Wesley's ethic against his doctrine of perfection, and I am confused as to why he does that if not for an a priori commitment to Niebuhrian fallibilism that he then reads back into Wesley.

---

50. Ronald H. Stone, *John Wesley's Life and Ethics* (Nashville: Abingdon, 2001), 137.
51. Ibid., 78.
52. See ibid., 98, 165-66.
53. Ibid., 190.
54. Ibid., 192-94.
55. Ibid., 208-9.
56. Ibid., 208.

Stone finds Wesley's theology to be basically a rule or command-oriented ethic that is most similar to Paul Tillich's and Reinhold Niebuhr's work. He writes,

> Tillich shows how love becomes a command ethic because of the estranged nature of humanity. Wesley made the point two hundred years earlier than Tillich. A final word about the contemporary relevance of this presentation of Wesley's ethic of love is that in its claims for the absoluteness of love and the presupposition of social realism, Wesley's ethic prefigures Reinhold Niebuhr's great chapter on justice in the *Nature and Destiny of Man*.[57]

Stone recognizes that there are elements of end ethics or teleological ethics in the eschatological and personal hope of love being fulfilled, but he suggests that for Wesley these elements are not dominant.[58] And he suggests that "authors who try to impose theological formulas on Wesley's ethics often do it without many supportive quotations from Wesley."[59] Although there are some wonderful discussions in Stone's development of Wesley's ethics in terms of his opposition to slavery and his economic practices, he reads Wesley in terms of the very tradition of ethics that I think loses the heart of Wesley's moral theology. His Wesleyan ethics takes us deeper into the modern question Troeltsch posed.

While Stone's work seeks to understand Wesley's moral philosophy, Theodore Weber offers us a Wesleyan political ethic or political theology of which the purpose is to fill a gap in our Wesleyan theological tradition. Weber writes, "Wesleyans have no common symbols of discourse deriving from their own theological tradition with which to think and speak as *Wesleyans* about the meaning of political reality and responsibility."[60] This is not to say that Wesley did not have a political language; he did. "But," suggests Weber, "after the middle of the nineteenth century it disappeared into the sand. Even if it had continued, its conservative and repressive character was such that I could not give it such weight of authority."[61] Wesley was an "organic constitutionalist," where the people obey rather than authorize those set in authority over them. In order to speak to political orders today, this stance must be reformulated, and it can be in a way consistent with Methodism because of its "pragmatic" character.[62]

---

57. Ibid., 214-15.
58. Ibid., 214.
59. Ibid., 216.
60. Theodore R. Weber, *Politics in the Order of Salvation: Transforming Wesleyan Political Ethics* (Nashville: Kingswood Books, 2001), 17.
61. Ibid., 19-20.
62. Ibid., 30, 32-33.

Weber's reformulation of Wesley's political ethics is refreshing precisely because he does not fetishize Wesley as if he resolves all our problems. Nor does Weber turn Wesley into an Enlightenment thinker who is easily relevant to the modern era. He does not give us "John Wesley's relevance for today." He challenges any easy interpretation of Wesley that gives "primacy to an alleged transition from divine right to liberal thinking."[63] And he notes that "political authority as the right to exercise power over a political society is the central problem in John Wesley's political thought."[64] Wesley's political ethics is not the solution but the problem to be overcome. It is a problem because Wesley did not ground political authority in the people, rather he grounded it solely in God. But Weber never tells us exactly why this is a problem. He seems to assume that a theocratic politics is so obviously wrong that it does not need to be argued against. Yet other contemporary theological ethicists such as Allen Verhey and Oliver O'Donovan have defended the significance of a theocratic politics precisely because it is an inescapable feature of the biblical witness, and it provides a critique of potentially fascist modern forms of politics grounded in human sovereignty.[65]

Theocratic regimes should elicit deep concern and reservations when they use force and coercion to compel obedience. No one should seek to live in Margaret Atwood's Gilead in *The Handmaid's Tale*.[66] However, political societies fashioned "by the people for the people" have their own ability to foster terror and could use a necessary critique from something outside their own will to power. As Oliver O'Donovan notes, "The doctrine that we set up political authority as a device to secure our own essentially private, local, and unpolitical purposes has left the Western democracies in a state of pervasive moral debilitation, which, from time to time, inevitably throws up idolatrous and authoritarian reactions."[67] Theology offers a challenge to these Western democracies by reminding them that God is finally the true ruler who alone constitutes authority.

> Once we seriously believe in God as agent and author in the realm of politics, we shall always be conscious of the critical question: is this particular instance of human rule that we, he, or she exercises the kind of rule that God has authorized and blessed? or must it confront God as its judge and destroyer? The most timid and conservative of thinkers in

---

63. Ibid., 68.
64. Ibid., 157.
65. See Allen Verhey, *Remembering Jesus: Christian Community, Scripture, and the Moral Life* (Grand Rapids, Mich.: Eerdmans, 2002), 333-487.
66. See Verhey's excellent discussion of this in ibid., 157-212.
67. Oliver O'Donovan, "Response to Respondents: Behold, the Lamb!" *Studies in Christian Ethics*, 11.2 (1998): 101.

> Christendom never forgot that question, which hung like a sword of Damocles over the head of every ruler, however *christianissimus*. If, on the other hand, we don't believe that there is any other solidarity to be had than what we put together for ourselves, no serious challenge to human authority can ever arise.[68]

The very fact that Western democracies have been so prone to authoritarian and fascist regimes seems to suggest that O'Donovan's fear might need to be taken more seriously than Weber has taken it in his effort to reconstruct Wesley's ethics in terms of modern, democratic regimes where authority arises primarily from the people. We do need to ask whether Weber begins with what politics should be (some form of Western democracy) and then reformulates Wesley's theology to fit it. He can certainly answer Troeltsch's question in a way that I cannot. However, it must also be noted that Weber does not argue that sovereignty comes from a human will to power alone. His reformulated Wesleyan political ethic is a recovery of the "political image" where this is understood as "the governance of the world given by God to humankind as God's agent"; political authority emerges "from God through the people."[69]

Weber offers a convincing critique of the effort to turn Wesley into an Enlightenment liberal who advocates liberty and natural right as a precursor to what we would now call "human rights." He states, "Wesley clearly rejected the relevance of natural rights to political authority and participation."[70] He recognizes that Wesley's political ethics would be more Burkeian in that "one does not grasp the meaning of rights and liberties for Wesley without perceiving that he views them in the mesh of institutions and traditions."[71] Fitting with a premodern tradition, for Wesley, rights are inseparable from duties. After Weber's convincing analysis of Wesley's understanding of rights and liberties, it will be difficult to see how anyone can read him as a protomodern.

However, Weber does not necessarily see the political significance of Wesley's moral theology in itself. He thinks a reformulated Wesleyan political ethic needs to take into account more substantively than it has the role of governance through the means of the nation-state. He notes an interesting ambiguity in Wesley: he accepts the "erastian establishment," but he also writes about the "Constantinian settlement" in much the same terms as an Anabaptist.[72] Weber resolves this tension by bringing politics into the "order of salvation," which seems closer to the erastian than the Anabaptist element in Wesley's thought.

---

68. Ibid.
69. Weber, *Politics in the Order of Salvation*, 230-31.
70. Ibid., 304.
71. Ibid., 305.
72. Ibid., 191-92.

What exactly does it mean to bring politics into the order of salvation? Does it mean that the modern nation-state with its governing apparatus is part of God's salvific plan for creation? Do voting and citizenship become sacramental? Does this collapse the sacred and secular into the secular baptizing modern forms of government as that which brings us salvation? Weber explains this.

> Recovering the political image for Wesleyan theology draws politics [nation-state, government] into the order of salvation, thereby ending the exclusion of the people from the political process, and unifying the God of politics and the God of the *ordo salutis* as the Holy Trinity whose governing of a fallen world provides context and guidance for the political vocation of humankind.[73]

But is the nation-state and government what Wesley meant when he made his cryptic comment that we were made into the political as well as the natural and moral image of God? Wesley never developed what he meant by the "political image" of God; none of us knows what he meant by it.[74] I find it worrisome that we would develop it such that we would lose altogether the time of the secular and make the nation-state and government part of the order of salvation, especially when, for Weber, the church seems to play little or no role.

Perhaps Weber is correct that Wesley's political ethic lends itself to welcoming the nation-state and its governing apparatus as a constitutive feature of the order of salvation. This may be a residual feature of Wesley's support for Christianity during the reign of Henry VIII and his concern for English liberties as a superior form of life to French Catholicism.[75] I fear that Wesley's English Christianity was on occasion more English than Christian. If this is true, then I think we should exercise a certain amount of suspicion as to Wesley's use of liberty, tolerance, and catholicity (or inclusivity). Stanley Fish has made this point quite nicely on John Milton's use of English liberties. Fish notes how Milton extolled English liberties such as the virtues of toleration and unregulated publication but then catches himself up short and says: "I mean not tolerated Popery, and open superstition, which as it extirpats all religions and civill supremacies, so it self should be extirpat."[76] Fish notes that this is not an exception to the

---

73. Ibid., 392.
74. See Randy L. Maddox, *Responsible Grace: John Wesley's Practical Theology* (Nashville: Kingswood Books, 1994), 68, where he recognized that Wesley "occasionally mentioned three dimensions of the Image of God in humanity: the natural image, the political image, and the moral image. More often, he distinguished between only the natural and moral images."
75. See Sermon 68, "The Wisdom of God's Counsels," §11, *Works* 2:557.
76. John Milton, "Areopagitica," in *The Prose of John Milton* (ed. J. Max Patrick; Garden City, N.Y.: Anchor Books, 1967), 330.

rule of tolerance; it is intrinsic to the very core values that Milton affirms. Indeed, Fish concludes, "I want to say that all affirmations of freedom of expression are like Milton's, dependent for their force on an exception that literally carves out the space in which expression can then emerge."[77]

In other words, these English liberties have more to do with what it means to be English than what it has to do with being tolerant, inclusive, or free. They help construct an identity and every identity assumes some form of exclusion that allows it to differentiate itself from others. An "inclusive" identity does not exist, it simply hides the exclusionary principle upon which it is based. Thus when we read about English liberties it might be worthwhile to read them not so much as affirming something as excluding something. What does it mean to speak of "civil and religious tolerance"? It means to say we are not like the French; we are not like the Catholics; we cannot tolerate their intolerant way of life, and that is why we extol the virtue of tolerance. While that is obvious in Milton's work, I think it may also be present in Wesley's.

We see this in Wesley's so-called catholic spirit, which is, in truth, a claim for the superiority of Protestantism and the Reformation to Roman Catholicism. So Wesley writes, "No man can choose for or prescribe to another. But everyone must follow the dictates of his own conscience in simplicity and godly sincerity."[78] This could easily sound like James Madison in his "Memorial and Remonstrance against Religious Assessments" when he wrote, "The Religion then of every man must be left to the conviction and conscience of every man; and it is the right of every man to exercise it as these may dictate."[79]

Wesley and Madison seem to offer a similar notion of religious liberty. But before we celebrate this we must ask why. Why does Wesley extol this liberty of choice? Here he begins to sound like Milton. It allows, writes Wesley, a "Reformation from popery," which "entirely destroys the right of private judgment on which that whole Reformation stands."[80] Wesley will not impose a mode of worship on another because that is what the Catholics do, but he will impose "English liberties."

This might help make sense of a rather interesting contradiction in Wesley to which Weber draws our attention. He writes, "Wesley's commitment to liberties of various sorts does not fit well with the repressive implications of his assignment of moral and religious functions to

---

77. Stanley Fish, *There's No Such Thing as Free Speech: And It's a Good Thing, Too* (New York: Oxford University Press, 1994), 103.

78. Sermon 39, "Catholic Spirit," §I.9, *Works* 2:85.

79. James Madison, "Memorial and Remonstrance against Religious Assessments," in *Church and State in the Modern Age: A Documentary History* (ed. J. F. Maclear; New York: Oxford University Press, 1995), 60.

80. Sermon 39, "Catholic Spirit," §I.10, *Works* 2:86.

government."[81] But if we understand the function of English liberties in terms of the context of the superiority of the English/Anglican government to the French/Catholic, then this contradiction does make sense. It is because Wesley extolled these virtues that he wrote, "I insist upon it that no Government not Roman Catholic ought to tolerate men of the Roman Catholic persuasion."[82]

But here I would disagree with Weber's resolution of this contradiction in terms of inclusivity. He writes, "Wesley's basic social sentiments are comprehensive and inclusive. They are manifest, among other ways, in that he was ecumenical and neither doctrinally nor confessionally exclusive in religious practice, and welcomed Quakers, Baptists, Catholics, Presbyterians, and others into Methodist meetings without requiring any change in religious affiliation."[83] Wesley's affirmation of English liberties, including toleration, could very well be for the sake of excluding Catholics not so much from the Wesleyan movement but from English governance. If Fish is correct that tolerance and inclusivity are terms that carve out an exclusionary space that allows us to know who is in and who is out, then they easily lead to the false posture of modern fallibilism. Wesley's doctrine of perfection cannot be sustained through such a posture. It may only be able to be sustained by something more like the Catholic dogma of infallibility, for if the good is able to be performed in this life—something Catholics only seem to set forth for the religious— then the truth will have to be so also. Doctrine and ethics fit together. Otherwise, the will cannot be rational appetite.

When the Catholic commission of theologians issued the Syllabus of Errors in 1864, it recognized one of the errors to be that "the Roman Pontiff can and ought to reconcile and harmonize himself with progress, with liberalism and with modern civilization."[84] Had the commission recognized how central fallibilism was to modern civilization it could easily have viewed it as an error as well. The Vatican Council's promulgation of the dogma of infallibility in 1870 can only rightly be understood against this background of modern errors. Ecclesial infallibility was not a new doctrine, it had a lengthy history in the church's tradition. But it had never been precisely defined, nor had the Roman Catholic Church set in place a specific procedure for when it was exercised. In opposition to the modern error that "error" is now secured by right and "truth" by democratic consensus, the Vatican Council promulgated papal infallibility. Here we do find a specific procedure for determining with a certain amount of precision when the good and the true are performed without error.

---

81. Weber, *Politics in the Order of Salvation*, 269.
82. Quoted in ibid., 330-31.
83. Ibid., 270.
84. Pius IX, "Syllabus of Errors," in Maclear, *Church and State*, 167.

> We teach and define that it is a divinely revealed dogma: that the Roman
> Pontiff, when he speaks *ex Cathedrâ*, that is, when in discharge of his
> office of Pastor and Doctor of all Christians, he defines, in virtue of his
> supreme Apostolic authority, a docrine of faith or morals to be held by
> the Universal Church, is endowed by the divine assistance promised to
> him in Blessed Peter, with that infallibility with which our divine
> Redeemer will that the Church should be furnished in defining doctrine
> of faith or morals; and, therefore, that such definitions of the Roman
> Pontiff are irreformable of themselves and not in virtue of the consent of
> the Church.[85]

But as George Lindbeck has noted, even Vatican I "defined only some
of the necessary, rather than the sufficient conditions for the exercise or
recognition of infallible teaching."[86] Protestants should not dismiss too
quickly the similarities between Reformed and Catholic teaching on infallibility or its increasing importance at the end of Christendom. In fact,
Lindbeck predicts that "chastened infallibilists" in both Protestant and
Catholic communions may find they have more in common with each
other at the end of "accommodationist Christianity" than the "papalists,
anti-papalists and relativizing fallibilists in their own communions."[87]
Geoffrey Wainwright has traced the similarities between the Wesleyan
teachings on assurance and entire sanctification and the Catholic teaching
on infallibility. His work demonstrates that Wesleyans cannot dismiss
infallibility without abdicating their own charism, which is to fulfill Jesus'
high priestly prayer "sanctify them in the truth." Wesleyans have something to offer in their affirmation of the important task of "maintenance in
the truth."[88]

There is much in this dogma that Wesleyans should be able to affirm,
such as: (1) truth in doctrine and goodness in morals can be infallibly and,
therefore, perfectly performed in time and space, and (2) truthful speech
and good actions do not depend on any consensus of human wills for
their performance; they are a feature of divine illumination. Nevertheless,
this definition bears the marks of a kind of proceduralism that mimics the
fallible proceduralism that defines the very modern movements the
dogma opposed. Although the true and the good must be able to be perfectly performed after the example of Jesus, we cannot guarantee this by
institutional procedures. Instead, we are to look to the lives of holy persons to find examples, for the performance of truth and good is not

---

85. Pius IX, "The Vatican Council and Its Aftermath," in Maclear, *Church and State*, 172.

86. George Lindbeck, *The Church in a Postliberal Age* (ed. James J. Buckley; Grand Rapids, Mich.: Eerdmans, 2002), 128.

87. Ibid., 142.

88. Geoffrey Wainwright, *Methodists in Dialog* (Nashville: Kingswood Books, 1995), 64.

secured by a proper procedure; it is secured by returning to God what God has already given us.

For Wesley, perfection is not procedural and sin is not an ineradicable form of self-interest. While Niebuhr's fallibilism leaves us bound to the power of sin, Wesley's understanding of sanctification argues that, in Christ, God takes away the power of sin. Central to his understanding is 1 John 3:9, "Whosoever is born of God doth not commit sin." For Wesley, being born of God creates the possibility of a vast inward change, but, even more, "we live in quite another manner than we did before; we are, as it were, in another world."[89] What is this new world within which we now live? Wesley argued that we always subsist in God—even before the new birth.[90] In this sense, he recognized that our lives are enhypostatic; that is to say, our hypostasis is not securely found within us but solely in God. We are not autonomous agents secure in ourselves. We are sustained only by subsisting in God. This is true of our creation just as it is our redemption. The new world is not then a relation other than this subsistent one we already possess. How is the world new? For Wesley the change was aesthetic. A new sensibility is present that changes the manner of existence, such that the believer's "whole soul is now sensible of God."[91] Spiritual senses are awakened that allow believers to see a different world than the one they saw before, and it is this different sensibility that allows us to make sense of Wesley's claim that a believer "doth not commit sin."

The spiritual sensorium the believer now has is nothing but a participation in God's own life. The believer receives life from God, the gracious influence of his Spirit, and then continually renders it back. As Wesley put it, the "one who thus believes and loves, who by faith perceives the continual actings of God upon his spirit, and by a kind of spiritual re-action returns the grace he receives in unceasing love, and praise, and prayer; not only 'doth not commit sin' while he thus 'keepeth himself,' but so long as this 'seed remaineth in him he cannot sin,' because he is born of God."[92]

Wesley's doctrine of sanctification need not posit some mystical individual change in the ontological structure of a human being. The change is the gift and cultivation of an aesthetic sensibility to perceive God and thus see a different world. It is to recognize one's life enfolded into the very life of the Triune God such that we return to God what God is. Far from understanding sin as negating all sinful self-interest, Wesley's doctrine of sanctification is grounded in the reciprocity of gifts whereby what

---

89. Sermon 19, "The Great Privilege of Those that are Born of God," §I.1, *Works* 1:432.
90. See ibid., §§I.3-6, *Works* 1:432-33.
91. Ibid., §I.8, *Works* 1:434.
92. Ibid., §II.1, *Works* 1:435-36.

God gives us can be given back to God perfectly—without error—only because the reciprocity or reaction of the gift was the original gift of God.

Such reciprocity can be lost. A perfect infallible exchange is not guaranteed, and neither ecclesial authority nor national institution insures it. But it is possible, for it is God who gives, receives, and gives in return. Such reciprocity does not come to an end; it takes us ever more deeply into the life of God. It is a reaction that need not come to an end, nor negate in order to receive. It is a life of holiness. Those found who embody it have a privileged place in the social and political witness of the church. We know what such a life looks like because Jesus blessed it, and his blessings make it possible.

Niebuhr's fallibilism has no place for such a possibility. If we are looking for a theology that will fit modern theories of political and economic exchange—if they constitute the real world within which we live—then Niebuhr's fallibilism will always be tempting, for it will always be relevant. Wesley's perfectionism assumes that a different kind of exchange is possible—one that does not take as its measure of reality contending forces of self-interest that lead to the best possible balance of power as did Niebuhr's. Wesley's perfectionism only makes sense if the exchange that takes place between God and us in the Eucharist is the real world within which we live. It is a reciprocal exchange where our gifts can be true and good solely because they live out of God's own giving. We give back to God what God first gave us. God takes it and in turn gives it back to us making us ever more obligated to God such that we must give yet again. This reciprocal exchange continues throughout eternity. It cannot come to an end. Unlike the contractual obligations of the current market and national political system, these reciprocal exchanges seek not to protect us from each other but to draw us closer into each other's lives. They make us holy as God is holy, which necessitates perfectionism. And for this reason Wesleyans must finally not only reject Niebuhrian fallibilism but also sit uncomfortably with any political and economic exchange that flourishes on a doctrine of sin rather than one that bears witness to the exchange God makes with us in Jesus. We are obligated by the duty of a constant communion, an obligation that gains its intelligibility from faith, hope, and love.

Appendix A
Wesleyan Themes in Malebranche

Malebranche's affirmation of prevenient grace (which he refers to as "prevenient delight") is shown in *Search after Truth* (ed. Thomas M. Lennon and Paul J. Olscamp; Cambridge: Cambridge University Press, 1980), 22. His emphasis on the "circumcision of the heart" is evident on the next page. Like Wesley, Malebranche drew on Augustine's doctrine of divine illumination to explain how it is we can know "sensible" reality (see *Search*, 233; and *Dialogues on Metaphysics and on Religion* [ed. Nicholas Jolley; trans. David Scott; Cambridge: Cambridge University Press, 1997], 16). Wesley's notion of "spiritual reaction," where God acts directly on the soul and our response is to "react," seems nearly identical to Malebranche's law of the "union of the soul and the body," which John Clayton referred to in his letter to Wesley on August 1, 1732. Malebranche stated, "He who alone can act on minds has established certain laws, through the efficacy of which the soul and body reciprocally act and react" (*Dialogues*, 58).

Malebranche also insisted that "the happiness of the blessed . . . consists only in perfect virtue, that is, in knowledge and love of God, and in a delicate pleasure that always attends them" (*Search*, 77). This relates the end of the Christian life as happiness and holiness to the knowledge and love of God with an emphasis on perfection, like Wesley. However, Malebranche was more reticent than Wesley in proposing the possibility of perfection in this life (*Search*, 179). The heart of Malebranche's soteriology, like that of Wesley, was salvation as renewal of the defaced image of God. But *image* here had a specific connotation. It was a vision that we lost because of our preoccupation with the sensuality of the bodily. The original image of God in us is our participation in the ideas in God's mind, which allows us to see things as they are because they *are* only in God. "It is through this dependence, this relation, this union of our mind with the Word of God, and of our will with His love, that we are made in the image and likeness of God. . . . We shall be like God if we are like the God-man" (*Search*, 235). This original vision is compromised by the fall because a gaze toward the sensual and material now captures us. It captures our attention so that we cannot see in God as we should. We look at objects in the world and think we know them as they are but refuse to see them in God.

Wesley's listing of God's perfections as essential for Christian unity in his sermon "Catholic Spirit" is nearly identical to that developed by Malebranche in his *Dialogues*, particularly Malebranche's peculiar development of "immensity." He also gave the divine perfections a significant place in the spiritual life. "Never is the human mind better disposed than when in an enforced silence it worships the divine perfections" (*Dialogues*, 192). This could help explain why the divine perfections were so essential to Wesley for Christian unity. Malebranche allowed for something similar to the notion of a spiritual sensorium when he stated that "no one has any knowledge of his soul except through thought, or through the inner sensation of all that takes place in his mind, I am convinced as well that if someone wishes to consider the nature of the soul, he need only consult this inner sensation, which continually represents to him what he is" (*Search*, 202). See also his discussion of "grace" as "interior delight" (*Search*, 213). For his rejection of innate ideas in favor of a metaphysics of participation see *Search*, 226-29. Malebranche stresses sanctification as an essential part of Christ's work in *Dialogues*, 154. He opposes nominalism in *Dialogues*, 169. In the *Dialogues*, Malebranche also develops the doctrine that grace perfects nature as a way to explain the necessity of a christological reading of nature (p. 213).

Many of these themes in Malebranche and Wesley are not unique to them. They are a return to patristic sources, especially the doctrine of divine illumination. Malebranche stated, consistent with Wesley, that "in matters of theology we should love antiquity, because we should love the truth and the truth is found in antiquity" (*Search*, 146). However, both also thought Descartes had revived some of these ancient themes. It would be false to see Malebranche as an orthodox Cartesian as his rejection of innate ideas clearly shows. I must also add that although Wesley draws on many themes in Malebranche, he does not adopt his occasionalism.

APPENDIX B

WESLEY'S HOLY TEMPERS: THE THEOLOGICAL VIRTUES

Wesley consistently used his theological understanding of Christ's human righteousness with the attributes listed in his sermon "The Lord Our Righteousness" to explain "the religion of the heart," both before and after he published this sermon. For Wesley, the Sermon on the Mount was the quintessential articulation of these "heavenly and holy tempers." But he offered a number of different listings of them.

The most basic account of Wesley's use of the theological virtues for the Christian moral life is found in his 1733 sermon "The Circumcision of the Heart." He writes "To be more particular, circumcision of the heart implies humility, faith, hope, and charity" (§I.2, *Works* 1:403). Humility is never set forth as a virtue for Wesley. It is all that pagan morality can truly accomplish. We learn to "know ourselves" and realize that doing good and avoiding evil cannot be accomplished through human will or intellect alone. Humility is a posture that allows us to receive what matters most, the theological virtues of faith, hope, and charity.

In "Scriptural Christianity" (1744) Wesley stated that we were to have

> "the mind which was in Christ," those holy "fruits of the Spirit" which whosoever hath not "is none of his"; to fill them with "love, joy, peace, long-suffering, gentleness, goodness"; to endue them with "faith" (perhaps it might be rendered "fidelity"), with "meekness and temperance"; to enable them to "crucify the flesh with its affections and lusts," its passions and desires; and, in consequence of that *inward change*, to fulfill all *outward* righteousness, "to walk as Christ also walked," in the "work of faith, the patience of hope, the labour of love." (§4, *Works* 1:160-61)

245

Here we see that the inward virtues of love, joy, peace, long-suffering, gentleness, goodness, faith, meekness, and temperance will of necessity issue forth in external obedience characterized by the infused theological virtues of faith, hope, and love.

In his sermon "Justification by Faith" (1746) Wesley drew on article 12 of the Thirty-nine Articles of Religion to explain this relationship between the internal and external holy tempers. "All truly 'good works' (to use the words of our Church) 'follow after justification,' and they are therefore 'good and acceptable to God in Christ,' because they 'spring out of a true and living faith" (§III.5). There are no virtues without there first being justification.

> Whatsoever virtues (so called) a man may have—I speak of those unto whom the gospel is preached; "for what have I to do to judge them that are without?"—whatsoever good works (so accounted) he may do, it profiteth not: he is still a "child of wrath," still under the curse, till he believes in Jesus [§IV.4].
> . . . Plead thou no works, no righteousness of thine own; no humility, contrition, sincerity! (§IV.9, *Works* 1:192-99)

Here the internal theological virtue of faith issues forth in virtues that will entail good works. This seems to contradict what he wrote in 1744 where the internal and external were reversed. It may also show the complex relationship between internal and external in Wesley's work.

In "The Way to the Kingdom" (1746) Wesley asked,

> Dost thou now believe? Then "the love of God is" now "shed abroad in thy heart." Thou lovest him, because he first loved us. And because thou lovest God, thou lovest thy brother also. And being filled with "love, peace, joy," thou art also filled with "long-suffering, gentleness, fidelity, goodness, meekness, temperance," and all the other fruits of the same Spirit—in a word, with whatever dispositions are holy, are heavenly or divine." (§II.12, *Works* 1:231)

Drawing on Galatians 5:22-23, Wesley sees the virtues or "holy dispositions" as emanating from the infused virtue of love.

In "The First-Fruits of the Spirit" (1746) he uses the basic list from Galatians 5:22-23 again to explain the holy tempers. They are "'love, joy, peace, long-suffering, gentleness, goodness, fidelity, meekness, temperance,' and whatsoever else is lovely or praiseworthy" (§I.6, *Works* 1:237).

"God's Love to Fallen Man" (1782) notes "patience, meekness, gentleness, long-suffering" as the virtues needed to resist evil (§I.8, *Works* 2:429-30). Wesley consistently explores these virtues in terms of their relationship to the heart of the moral life, which he understands in classical fashion as doing good and avoiding evil—the first practical principle of the natural law.

In his sermon "On Patience" (1784) Wesley defines holiness as patience, meekness, resignation, peace, and love (§§2-8, *Works* 3:171-73).

"Of the Church" (1785) offers another example of the consistent use of both Galatians 5:22-23 and the Beatitudes of the Sermon on the Mount as the heart of the Christian moral life. Here it is correlated, as it is in Wesley's discourses on the Sermon on the Mount, to the importance of a common life. He urges the Methodists "'to keep the unity of the Spirit in the bond of peace'; to preserve inviolate the same spirit of lowliness and meekness, of long-suffering, mutual forbearance and love, and all these cemented and knit together by that sacred tie, the peace of God filling the heart" (§27, *Works* 3:55).

In "The Important Question" (1775) Wesley asks, "What is religion?" He answers that it is more than doing no harm or observing the sacraments. "This love, ruling the whole life, animating all our tempers and passions, directing all our thoughts, words, and actions, is 'pure religion and undefiled'" (§III.2, *Works* 3:189).

"An Israelite Indeed" (1785) correlates truth and love, which would also be a correlation between doctrine and morality. Wesley writes, "This then is real, genuine, solid virtue. Not truth alone, nor conformity to truth. This is a property of real virtue, not the essence of it. Not love alone, though this comes nearer the mark; for 'love' in one sense 'is the fulfilling of the law.' No: truth and love united together are the essence of virtue or holiness" (§II.11, *Works* 3:289).

The same list of virtues, this time from 1 Peter 3:8 is used to describe our duty to our neighbors in "On Pleasing All Men" (1787). "If you would please your neighbour," writes Wesley, then be "*lowly* in heart" (humility), "meek," "courteous," "pitiful" (tenderly compassionate), and a person of "veracity" (§II.2-7, *Works* 3:423-25).

Wesley returns to the theme of the new birth in "On God's Vineyard" (1787) correlating it again to the righteousness of Christ. He states again that the new birth is an "inward change, from all unholy to all holy tempers, from pride to humility, from passionateness to meekness, from peevishness and discontent to patience and resignation—in a word, from an earthly, sensual, devilish mind to the mind that was in Christ Jesus" (§I.6, *Works* 3:506).

In one of his last published sermons, "Walking by Sight and Walking by Faith" (1788), Wesley still uses the exact same terms he used to describe Christ's righteousness to explain how we walk by faith. We do so through "lowliness, meekness, and resignation" (§18, *Works* 4:57-58).

ABBREVIATIONS

AT Author's Translation.

Institutes John T. McNeill, ed. *Calvin: Institutes of the Christian Religion.* Translated by Ford Lewis Battles. Vol. 20 of *The Library of Christian Classics,* edited by John Baillie, John T. McNeill, and Henry P. Van Dusen. Philadelphia: Westminster, 1960.

Summa Theologica Saint Thomas Aquinas. *Summa Theologica.* Translated by Fathers of the English Dominican Province. 5 vols. New York: Benziger Brothers, 1948. Reprint, Allen, Tex.: Christian Classics, 1981.

Works *The Works of John Wesley.* Begun as *The Oxford Edition of The Works of John Wesley.* Oxford: Clarendon Press, 1975–1983. Continued as *The Bicentennial Edition of The Works of John Wesley.* Nashville: Abingdon Press, 1984–.

Works (Jackson) Thomas Jackson, ed. *The Works of John Wesley.* 14 vols. London, 1872.

NAME INDEX

Anselm, 67, 210-11, 215
Aquinas, Thomas, xix, 10-13, 33, 38-72,
    83-88, 92, 97-98, 111-14, 126-29,
    132-33, 136, 143-46, 149, 163, 171-
    212, 215, 218-19, 227-30
Aristotle, 13, 30, 45-52, 63, 65, 67, 81,
    126, 144, 146, 174, 181, 185, 191,
    196, 200, 203
Augustine, 10, 67, 83, 88, 121, 126-27,
    134, 143, 165, 169, 174, 177, 185,
    194-95, 202, 212, 220, 221, 227, 243
Ayer, A. J., 79

Bauman, Zygmunt, xvii, 1
Bonino, Serge-Thomas, 127, 189
Borgmann, Albert, xvi, 16, 30
Bowne, Borden Parker, 23, 27-28, 33,
    215
Boyle, Leonard, 176, 179
Brantley, Richard E., xiv, 79, 80
Brightman, Edgar Sheffield, 25-33, 69
Burrell, David, 176n12

Cajetan, Tommaso, 206
Calvin, John, 21, 143, 145
Carnap, Rudolf, xiv, xv, xvi, 86
Cavanaugh, William, 212
Cell, George Croft, 79
Cessario, Romanus, 200
Clark, Henry B., 225
Clarke, Adam, 39, 43, 45, 49, 57-60, 70,
    95, 108, 171

Clayton, John, 112, 243
Coakley, Sarah, 134n15
Critchley, Simon, xv, xvi, 16
Cudworth, Ralph, xviii, 11-13, 26, 39,
    42, 49-50, 54, 62, 70, 73-74, 83, 86,
    90, 95, 103, 108, 114-18, 120-22,
    130, 183, 202
Cushman, Robert, 37

Day, Dorothy, 161
Derrida, Jacques, xvii
Descartes, Rene, 11, 50, 57, 61, 78-80,
    108
Dionysius, 191

Eustachius, xix, 46

Fiering, Norman, 6n9, 38, 52
Fish, Stanley, 237-39
Foucault, Michel, xvii, 125
Fox, Richard Wightman, 225

Gallagher, Raphael, 136n17
Garrigou-Lagrange, Réginald, 199
Gregory of Nazianzus, 177

Hall, Pamela, 187
Hamilton, Alexander, 226
Harkness, Georgia, 28
Hart, David, 134n15
Harvey, Barry, 227-28

251

SUBJECT INDEX

Printed in the United States
122406LV00004B/25/A